.THE DURER AFFAIR

Alex Chisholm

I0505527

SAIR FECHT BOOKS

To my family with love and a cheery wave

Nuremberg, Germany, 1504

Chapter 1

The Feast of Saint Michael, September, 1504

The face staring back at Albrecht Durer on the morning of Michaelmas in the year of our Lord 1504 pleased him well enough despite some unevenness in the surface of the glass and darkling glow of a flint-grey morning in Nuremberg. And thus satisfied that he had lost none of his prettiness overnight, Albrecht Durer, a man in his thirty-third year, lingered to admire the intelligent pale eyes staring back at him then drawing a red-blotched Venetian tortoiseshell comb through his locks permitted himself a self-satisfied sigh of approval. Abandoning the glass, Durer, or Albi as he was known to those closest to him, picked up a black wool mantle from the counterpane finely stitched with exotic and colourful birds draped over his unmade bed, paused to admire the coat, his best, before carefully arranging it across his shoulders. This would be the cloak's second outing of the season for the air was growing cooler with autumn's approach and in any case the young Nuremberg painter knew it set off his tumbling honey-blond curls most dramatically which was the reason he had chosen to wear it two days earlier when appearing before Nuremberg's Burghers, sitting to consider his application to execute a pair of oil portraits to be hung in the city treasury. Today, as then, Durer embellished his outfit with the addition of a dead fox; disembowelled and cured and precisely arranged over the mantle. The leggings which artfully defined the firm contours of his long shapely limbs were woven from fine Lille yarn dyed Egyptian blue and almost invisibly darned by Susanna, a servant in the Durer house and confidante of his wife Agnes. Finally, Durer slipped his feet into the soft black cowhide ankle boots he had been unable to resist on a recent visit to Venice and bought with money left to him by his late father.

Albrecht Durer unlatched a second window in his chamber and pushed back the shutters to admit more light before turning his pale eyes to a sky veiled with thin cloud breached in part by javelins of dilute sunlight raining down on Nuremberg's handsome towers. He decided against wearing the feathered hat he had sported the previous Friday as being too formal for a day such as this, devoted to pleasure. Turning from the window Durer stepped up to an upright wooden chest made by his grandfather and brought to Bavaria from his native Hungary. There on top resting on a linen square sewn by his mother, Barbara, was a small copper-green glass amphora. Durer drew out its stopper and tipped a very few drops of sweet oil onto the palm of his hand, rubbed both his hands together and ran them down the pretty ringlets that tumbled sensually around his long elegant neck and the fox pelt then replaced the stopper in the bottle. Almost as an afterthought he pulled open a drawer in the chest fishing out a rosary of the deepest red carnelian beads which he lifted over his head and settled about his throat. Lingering for a moment Durer savoured the smoothness of the tiny beads against the sensitive skin of his fingertips.

The city's bells were ringing. It was Michaelmas and Nuremberg's citizens were gathering to pay their respects to Saint Michael through prayer and attendance at the Saint's procession. The city's main streets had been cleared of their stinking festering waste, washed by a small force of men armed with water butts and brooms and scattered with sand to prevent them becoming a quagmire from the impact of thousands of pairs of feet, horses' hooves and wooden wheels. Nuremberg's boisterous citizens excitedly anticipated the annual Michaelmas pageant; Albrecht Durer among them picked his way through the Hauptmarkt packed with people. Bells from the city's main churches had been tolling near incessantly since daybreak and sporadic cannon fire added to the cacophony making conversation difficult so Albrecht Durer simply waved to his neighbour, Hans, a little way off. Hans, dressed in his overlarge coat, was carrying a large wooden bucket for he was an Abtrittanbieter ready to assist anyone caught short in the street requiring the concealment provided by his coat as they passed water in exchange for a stiver. The two men nodded and smiled and went their separate ways.

Crippled Josef was in his usual spot in the Hauptmarkt; his elderly brown bear swaying from side to side as if entertaining himself; his dark chestnut dots of eyes gazing out blankly having long given up hope of finding whatever it was they sought. Josef prodded the beast at intervals entreating him to roar in the hope a coin or two might come his way and the bear would be urged to dance like he did as a cub making the heavy chain attached to his pronged iron collar clank pathetically; but any desire to please his master had long ago deserted the ageing attraction.

Many in Nuremberg were taking advantage of the holy day to escape their daily routine, but for a handful of shrewd merchants Michaelmas was an opportunity to earn extra money. People would still become hungry so early in the morning huge iron pots were man-handled off wagons and sledges. Fires were lit and straddled by iron tripods strung with chains and the cauldrons hooked onto them. Into them went water and once boiling were pitched sheep and pig carcases; cleaved and sliced into knuckles of mutton and pork. They collided and bobbed in those great steaming vats attended by small boys who fed the flames with bits of dry timber stored on hand carts.

Lined up along the north side of the square were barrels of brined herring which calloused fingers fished out and served on thick slices of good cracked bread. The market's usual pedlars of apples and pears, fattened hens, ducks and pigeon, chestnuts and acorns, spicy ginger and cinnamon bark, plaits of onions and garlic and bunches of rosemary and thyme were nowhere to be seen unless among the sea of laughing and singing souls, gossiping and generally making merry.

The crowd numbers grew quickly, among them Albrecht Durer made his way in among spectators composed mainly of women and children keenly awaiting a glimpse of their men folk. Durer was hoping to see his friends Willy Pirkheimer and Otto Beck.

Amidst the cacophony the thunder of drums and squealing of pipes grew louder. Someone shouted, "Here they come," at the first sight of the procession coiling its way down from the Kaiserburg where the Imperial family had watched it go by from the comfort of red velvet-draped benches. A whisper went through the crowd that Prince Ernest had to be physically held back from joining in by two burly footmen - for the Prince was a man of enthusiasms which had, on occasions, to be restrained. People snorted and winked; they knew his strange ways. Whenever Emperor Maximilian was absent from the city, as he was at this time, the Prince would spread his wings.

Every head was turned and every hand clapped; lean and stout, short and long, old and young swayed as one in time to the music and even the sun grew less churlish and sneaked out from behind sulking clouds to see what all the fuss was about.

Cheers rang out as St Sebaldus's clergy, resplendent in their milk white linen albs, waists girdled with white tasselled cinctures, strode along - proud and magnificent at the head of the procession led by a lanky bearded prelate carrying a golden crucifix high over his head. Falling in behind were men holding panels bearing images of Jesus, the Virgin Mary and the Archangel Michael, in whose honour they were gathered. Immediately behind with cheeks expanding like pig bladders a group of exuberant pipers struggled to hold their shrill notes while skipping along. They were accompanied by a contingent of drummers whose rhythmic beat set the pace for the marchers' feet and the crowd's eager hands. Falling in behind a trio of men wielding pole-candlesticks glittering in the sunshine and a body of Frankish trumpeters, their long

4

instruments screeching like trapped animals. On their heels came city tradesmen; Nuremberg's proud workforce of smiths of every kind: gold, silver, tin, copper, iron – every one of the metal crafts represented. Durer's thoughts drifted away to his father, one of Nuremberg's finest goldsmiths and two years in his cold grave who buried his disappointment in his son's rejection of the family's craft in favour of painting which, as was occasionally drawn to Herr Durer's notice, was not a trade worthy of guild status.

The bugling and shouting and drumming prompted the city's dogs to set up their own canine chorus and the fearful din all but defeated the most determined of conversations during the grand procession's now laggardly progress through the Hauptmarkt towards the River Pegnitz.

Albrecht Durer grinned on spotting his friend, the schlosser Otto Beck, among a group of around forty fellow-locksmiths walking behind a splendid painted linen banner, its golden fringes and tassels quivering while hoist aloft by Peter Henlein and Georg Glaser. Each man was turned out in his locksmith livery with ceremonial leather aprons pressed into service for the day, pristine and free from cuts and grease marks they were worn over tunics of moss-green and earth-brown. Durer called to Beck but his words were drowned out by the deafening din around him.

Otto Beck learned the art of metal turning from his locksmith father who was also responsible for his son's appearance. Beck could never be mistaken for any but a Bavarian; as round as he was tall with skin as fair as a lizard's belly and straw yellow hair shorn close to his skull. He was clean shaven to the extent of being obsessively so but that was as far as Beck fussed over his appearance and in that he was strikingly different from his good friend, Albrecht Durer; meticulous both in appearance and dress. The trace of facial hair on the pretty face was always well tended and in keeping with the tastes of the time. It was doubted there was another man in the whole of Franconia who devoted so much time rolling and waxing a moustache as the artist Albrecht Durer who could never have been mistaken for any coarse peasant.

Behind the smiths were St Sebaldus' priests showing off its precious ornaments; gold basins, ewers and even taller candlesticks – their magnificence met with gasps of wonder from citizens and strangers alike. In the wake of this ecclesiastical glitter and opulence came a mixed party of tradesmen including bee farmers who supplied the wax that went into the candlestick moulds. They formed a colourful assembly in their short blue tunics drawn around their middles and tied off with bows, burgundy fringed collars, long yellow caps with peaks and slung over one shoulder a crossbow and the other a quiver of arrows.

Some on parade were not entirely sober. This state of affairs appeared most common among the ranks of lesser trades although it was obvious each had gone to great lengths with their attire: tunics, caps, aprons and hose all well-presented so as not to bring shame on their craft; horologists were especially resplendent in reds and blues; leather men presented the day's best painted banners featuring their trade tools along with a fine portrait of a smith's cat – indispensable in the smithy to deal with mice with a taste for leather. Among the shoemakers was diminutive cobbler, Axel Marx, striding out with great purpose behind his rotund belly and accompanied by his faithful golden hound, Ulf, trotting obediently at his heels. Axel acknowledged the cheers of his many friends. Behind the cobblers in an explosion of hues - reds, blues, greens, golds and blacks were tailors and bakers, brewers, grain merchants and grain dealers, wheelwrights and carpenters. They strolled and skipped under magnificent illustrated banners, waving to loved ones and familiar faces in the crowd of onlookers.

The noise in the streets was deafening: musicians; shouts and laughter; barking hounds. By the time Nuremberg's civic representatives appeared, imperious in their robes and cloaks emblazoned with their badges of office, cheers intermingled with jeers. Deaf to criticism the Councillors nodded good-naturedly. In their midst, a good head taller than the majority, was the impressive figure of Willy Pirkheimer in a long black woollen coat and wide fur collar, a large broad-brimmed felted hat pulled down over his large intelligent head. Noticing Albrecht Durer in the crowd he appeared to call out to him but even his bellowing voice was drowned out by the ensuing racket so the two merely exchanged hearty waves.

Some onlookers weary of the time it took the parade to pass drifted away to purchase a cured herring or serving of boiled flesh while children countered boredom by creating their own amusements by skipping and chasing one another or tormenting excitable yapping dogs but at the sound of hunting horns signalling the approach of hunters and marksmen in their distinctive short smocks, hose and feathered caps and armed with bows and arrows (and a few hand guns) those same children hurriedly squeezed in between skirts and legs to reclaim the best viewpoints at the front of the crowd.

Then it was the turn of some thirty representatives of religious orders head-to-toe in white linen closely followed by widows; mistresses of their family's trades in their own right - also in salt-white garb. Men of the town's militia led out a group of devout prophets ahead of yet more pipers, clergy and scholars that had been joined by costumed players acting out scenes from the testaments; among them St Sigismund and Charlemagne representing Nuremberg's piety.

As the spectacle drew to its close a magnificent assortment of wagons decorated as ships pulled by small ponies and adorned with feathers and long grasses created a virtual-flotilla that amazed onlookers whose desire to get close to these clever illusions brought the procession to a temporary stop. Glad of the opportunity to rest a cheery set of men dressed as Old Testament prophets turned this way and that clapping their hands in time to a tattoo from a contingent of drummers surrounding the Archangel Michael who fluttered his mechanical wings and jigged a little dance hand in hand with two children to the amusement of everyone. Once the holy body moved off again the Virgin Mary had to run to catch up, having lingered to greet her son and daughter on the way. She was hurried along by one of the three Magi whose free hand held sprigs of what should have been myrrh but looked suspiciously like prickly hawthorn.

Latching onto these stragglers were around sixty small capering children, occasionally breaking ranks to chase friends in and out of the crowds. By the time the music was out of earshot Albrecht Durer was well on his way to Johannes Brauer's inn where he had arranged to meet Willy Pirkheimer and Otto Beck.

Chapter 2

Johannes Brauer's inn was tucked into a corner in the Am Ölberg district of Nuremberg. Herr Brauer was long dead but his popular beerhouse endured in the capable hands of his widow, Ana. Ana Brauer had a reputation for managing rowdy patrons who over-indulged on what was arguably the finest beer brewed in Nuremberg. Frau Brauer's success was also due in part to her excellent table of dishes such as boiled hock stuck with cloves served with peas and baked onions in a rich aromatic broth, eisbein - salted leg of pork and roast hare with honey-baked plums. Today, however, being Michaelmas, there was roasted goose for those with a taste for it and for others with small appetites Ana's tasty hechtsuppe made from pike fished out of the River Pegnitz. Ana Brauer was assisted in running the inn by her sister, Klara, and together they looked after Ana's grandson, Kläuschen, an orphan whose mother died while giving birth to him soon after his father was taken by the plague.

Albrecht Durer and his companions, the magistrate Willy Pirkheimer and master schlosser Otto Beck, could be found at Brauer's most afternoons after work and this being a holy day meant there was even longer to enjoy Ana's beer and food. But plans have a tendency to be torn asunder and so it was that Michaelmas in the year of our Lord 1504.

***

Albrecht Durer belched and drummed his fingers on the table; he knew he had drunk more beer than was wise. For the umpteenth time he turned towards the door but neither Beck nor Pirkheimer appeared. Durer had long since grown bored of his own company in an unaccustomedly deserted inn with many of its patrons delayed by the day's festivities. He bit his lip and considered returning home but with his wife Agnes abroad the welcome there would be no cheerier. Durer then considered calling in on his mother before realising she, too, was gone from home - visiting his brother, Hans. In any case she would only scold him for his drinking and attempt to impose herself on him for the duration of Agnes' absence. So Durer continued to drum his fingers and curse Willy and Otto for their tardiness.

Portly Axel Marx stopped by his table to say his hallos. Axel was also one of Ana's regular customers and usually the first to show his face each dinner time but today the grain merchant, Herr Müller, had beaten him to it and was well advanced devouring a veritable mountain of steaming flesh by the time Axel turned up. Müller sat in the chair he always occupied next to the inn's door. He liked to observe all who entered and the goings-on in Ana's inn despite appearing to be wholly preoccupied with his food; a short dagger clutched in one hand severed flesh from bone and a spoon in the other scooped up Ana's luscious gravy.

Not everyone who ate in the inn possessed a spoon so were obliged to use ones chained to the tables or else drain their dishes by raising them to their mouths like cups. Müller had inherited his spoon from his father, along with the dagger he used to spear and slice his meat; both spoon and knife bore his father's initials which happened to be the same as his own. The grain merchant relished spooning liquid from his plate, greedily, and with such little care it often ran, like now, in rivulets of warm fat down his considerable chin. He mumbled inaudibly for his mouth was filled with partly-chewed hock. Axel Marx acknowledged him with a cheery wave then picked up his faithful hound Ulf's paw and motioned it back and fore in the direction of the grain merchant. Müller snorted and tossed a piece of gristle across the floor towards the dog who devoured it then looked up expectantly for more.

Umberto Müller ignored the hound. He grinned across the inn towards Durer with lips drawn back to reveal a mouthful of mottled teeth worn down to stumps and a source of fascination for the painter who longed to capture their frightful likeness but was loathe to share the grain merchant's company for the time it would take to draw them. Müller wiped at strings of saliva drooling down his chin with the cuff of his jerkin and gazed into his bierkrug.

"Where's Herr Pirkheimer and Otto today, Albrecht?" Ana Brauer asked Durer while feeding the fire with logs.

"I wish I knew, Ana," Durer sighed.

Ana Brauer made sympathetic noises and wiped her hands down her apron. She picked up the beer pitcher from Durer's table and emptied its contents into his bierkrug.

By the time Durer drained his krug he had given up all hope of being joined by his friends. He stood up, swaying a little. The inn was filling up and the hum of conversations that he was not party to was irritating him. On his way out he noticed Herr Müller had already left.

This was no way to spend a holy day he told himself as the inn door closed behind him. Outside and away from Brauer's cheery fire the air felt chilly; summer was past and winter approached. Albrecht Durer fastened his woollen mantle against the stiff breeze that tugged at it.

Durer had not reached home but he was overtaken with a desire to pass water. He quickened his pace and nearly caught up with Müller also the worse for drink if his gait was any proof. Despite his discomfort Durer hung back for he had little wish to find himself in the company of the grain merchant yet his need to relieve himself was becoming urgent. At the Säubrücke he slipped down the embankment, but losing his footing he fell on his face. Recovering himself he took a path alongside the River Pegnitz. Here was a place popular with common fornicators and Durer recognised several townsmen as he did his business. After rearranging his clothing he turned again for home passing a group of young boys throwing stones at a line of birds perched on fishing skiffs tied up along the riverbank. A little way farther on an old fisherman emerged from a wooden shack shaking a fist at two laughing youths attempting to release his boat from its moorings.

In the town centre close to the Lorenzkirche Durer's dishevelled and muddied appearance attracted disapproving glances and so he quickened his pace. As he crossed the Hauptmarkt he heard the sonorous repetitive beat of a drum. Thinking it came from festive dawdlers Durer paid it no attention for he was close to home and longed to lay down to sleep off Ana's beer. But the drumming grew louder and he turned to see who was behind it for there was something arresting about its joyless rhythmic cadence. He stopped and listened and discerned not only drumming but voices chanting choruses and from the opposite end of the Hauptmarkt came a steady migration of poor-looking souls. Forgetting his weariness Durer advanced on the group and collided with an anxious-looking woman dragging a crying child along by the hand.

"Flagellants are come!" she cried, gasping, her face contorted in despair.

Other curious citizens were drawn to the approaching noise. Faces pressed up against windows: the interested, the shocked and the excited - eyes straining to catch a glimpse of the advancing horror while a few shutters were drawn to and bolted as a protection against it. There were some trapped by the growing frenzy of bodies pushing onto the streets. Several turned their heads away or shielded their faces with shawls and arms so as not to witness the loathsome spectacle making an unwelcome intrusion into their lives; on this of all days, the feast of Saint Michael.

Albrecht Durer gaped transfixed as three or four abreast shuffled a serpent of men, women and children. To his eye they had not the appearance of flagellants whose antics were the subject of stories of his childhood - pathetic and miserable specimens who lashed their near naked bodies or prostrated themselves in all manner of humiliation. These were mystics, he suspected, but whatever they called themselves they presented a queer apparition, poor but respectably dressed, as they pressed on towards the centre of Nuremberg. Leading this small pious army was a tall handsome figure in a snow-white tunic that hung loose without a waist girdle and fell three-quarters down his legs — a little above a pair of unfashionable black laced leather shoes.

Durer then noticed most carried birch switches which he thought had convinced the fleeing mother they were flagellants but there was no thrashing of flesh from these pilgrims. A few elderly and crippled among them struggled to keep up with the leading body but their voices rang out in spirited delivery of holy incantations. If any lagged too far behind a helping finger belonging to one of the younger men prodded them forward. Meanwhile their leader supported himself on a plain staff which he leaned on from time to time not from need it would appear but as a badge of his station. As the serpent of people drew close its principal's keen charcoal eyes caught Durer watching him.

Albrecht Durer gave a start. He turned at the pressure of a hand on his shoulder and looked up into the red-cheeked, good natured face of Willy Pirkheimer.

"My dear Willy, honourable and wise friend, you almost stole the life from me," he began. "These rascals," Durer gestured behind him, "distracted me on my way back from Brauer's. I waited for you but you abandoned me to my own miserable company and I quickly wearied of it."

"I am not surprised, my dear Albi, for I have often tired of it myself. But what is it poor Albi for you appear out of sorts? Is your conscience pricking you? As to my lateness the blame lies with these fellows for the Council had to debate long and hard over allowing them free passage but in the spirit of Saint Michael it was decided to be lenient and offer them hospitality."

"Are they mystics?" Durer asked.

Pirkheimer nodded and shrugged at the same time. "Something of the kind ... I believe they have some association with a body called the Teutonic Order whose doctrine was first promulgated at Frankfurt and whose ideas are gaining popularity. Somewhere in my library there is a tract I purchased three or four years ago called *Deutsche Theologie* which appears identical to a paper taken from the leader of this gory assembly. Its contents may be worthy of a discussion between us one day, Albi, but tell me is Otto not with you?"

"He is as poor a companion as you, dear Willy. I have seen nothing of him since the procession," Durer replied.

"And what has happened to you?" Pirkheimer asked brushing dried mud from Durer's fine coat, "Your face is grazed and you are unsteady on your feet."

Durer dismissed Pirkheimer's concern. "It is of no matter. As to my feet I blame their condition on Ana's beer. But what of them?" he pointed towards the sect "what is there business here? You must know since you allowed them entry to the town," he asked.

Pirkheimer's plump face took on a look of mock outrage. A man of considerable reputation and influence among Nuremberg society Willibald Pirkheimer was a member of the select body of men who ran the city, a military leader with a formidable intellect - a scholar with broad tastes for it was said of him he resided in his brain. The Pirkheimer and Durer families were closely linked and Willy and Albrecht friends from childhood. Slightly older than Durer, Willy Pirkheimer became the young artist's mentor encouraging him to pursue his interests in the natural world, philosophy and all matters affecting the heavens, mathematics and women.

"I mean to make up for my absence by buying you supper, dear friend, and in the meantime we should keep an eye on these strangers and pay attention to their utterances in case they persuade our fellow-citizens of their fanatical beliefs and have us all worshipping in the Hauptmarkt in our shifts." Pirkheimer extended a sausage-like finger towards the column of spiritualists. "Otto will be kicking himself for missing such theatre."

Otto Beck was at that moment at work in his craft premises under the Rathaus having returned following the Michaelmas procession meaning only to change out of his locksmith finery but then becoming absorbed in tackling a difficulty he was having with a mechanism. Beck lacked the bookish brains of Durer and Pirkheimer but he was a capable manipulator of metals, though not as proficient as his father, the locksmith Beck the elder. Otto's failings came, it was said, from a lack of patience; a tardiness of thinking and his inability to focus for prolonged lengths of time on any single matter preferring to flit from one interest to another. He was, nevertheless, an able locksmith and clockmaker who turned his hand to all manner of mechanical devices and he considered himself an inventor.

The workshop Beck kept at the city hall was one of two he used. A second was situated outside the city wall where much metal firing was carried out; at a safe distance from the town's houses in case of an outbreak of fire. The city hall workshop had been his father's and was a useful window for advertising wares as much as an ideal hideaway when Beck sought privacy to work on his experiments.

Today, however, the locksmith was disturbed by a rat-tat-tat against his window and on investigating he discovered Durer and Pirkheimer frantically signalling to him. With not a little annoyance the schlosser gathered up the pieces of metal scattered across his bench and deposited them in a drawer for safe-keeping before taking down his heavy brown woollen coat from its peg at the back of the door. Buttoning up his mantle Beck noticed one of its brass buttons hung loose on a single thread so he tugged it off and popped it into his leather purse before locking his workshop door and dropping the large iron key into a satchel slung over his shoulder.

"What's up?" he demanded testily, "that couldn't wait. How was your meeting with the Council, Albi?" Beck asked without waiting for a reply to his first enquiry.

"Albi has no rival and his reputation grows fast," Willy Pirkheimer quipped as he landed a hefty slap on Durer's shoulder. Pirkheimer omitted to add that the committee overseeing the portrait commission had been less impressed by Durer's self-confidence which some regarded as conceit and it had taken Pirkheimer's intervention to convince them here was an artist that merited having his work hung in the august offices of the city treasury.

"Heigho" Durer declared with studied casualness as he fingered his carnelian rosary. "We must serve when called upon by our civic masters. Oil panels of Sigismund and Charlemagne for the Schopper House do not inspire me if I am being honest but then I ought to be diligent for the spiritual and secular life of the city must be preserved and I am willing to sacrifice myself for the service of my community."

Beck rolled his eyes. He knew little about the painting assignment for the Schopper House but was acquainted with Durer's pretence of modesty.

Pirkheimer smirked. "And we're willing to pay you sixty florins for the privilege."

"And they're paying a measly sixty florins for them," Durer sniffed.

"For half a week's work, that's not bad," Beck remarked as he dug his short fingers into his head stubble and scratched.

Pirkheimer's eyes twinkled as he squinted towards Durer.

"Hardly that, Otto, can't see Albi taking more than one afternoon for each panel and let's say one fourth of that for Günter to prepare the boards. If only I could add painting to my many talents what a rich fellow I could become."

"Each will occupy eight days priming and planing then mounting ..." Durer hesitated, realising he was having his leg pulled. "I might get Günter to make them up," he yawned as if bored by being the centre of attention.

Beck stopped dead in his tracks.

"Are we not heading over to Brauer's."

"No ... listen..." Pirkheimer pulled at Beck's elbow and tilted his large head to catch a sound.

"What's that racket?" Beck asked spinning around.

"The reason we dragged you out," Pirkheimer said, "come little man, the day's entertainment is not yet done."

The three headed off in the direction of the Frauenkirche.

"Günter impressed with his piece for the apprentice boys' competition, Otto,' Durer was saying, adding, "only just losing out to Wolgemut's lad, Joachim, for the top prize."

"Poor Günter, he's a likeable lad but a short runt like myself and as I know to my cost short runts always lose out to bigger, fine honed boys like Joachim every time," Beck said, a show of mock resignation in his furrowed brow.

"A fine figure of a young man indeed," Pirkheimer said with a sigh, "Joachim not Günter, but a rascal."

Albrecht Durer nodded in agreement. The three approached the Hauptmarkt where a large crowd had assembled for the second time that day.

"Ah well there's no more to be said, Albi, you're going to have to accept your workshop has something to prove, not only in the calibre of your apprentice but in looks too," Beck said.

Pirkheimer chuckled.

"Young Günter's not so bad and let me hear you admit, Albi, the city has done you an honour by selecting you out of all Franconia's many master painters to decorate the Schopper House" he cried. "If I'd known you were going to be so sniffy about the idea, I wouldn't have wasted my time putting in a word for you."

"I know, Willy, your dutiful servant is most grateful it's just I'm not keen on commissions that's all. But I will do it."

"We could have chosen Wolgemut," Pirkheimer persisted.

"Willy, I'm happy to take it on."

"He's been in the business longer than you." Pirkheimer winked at Beck.

"And his apprentice is better-looking," Beck added.

"I've said I'm happy." Durer self-consciously turned back the cuff of his woollen coat.

"You've only to say," Pirkheimer began.

"Willy!" Durer turned to his friend, caught his eye and they both laughed.

Chapter 3

People were running in all directions; some to escape the menace in their midst and others out of curiosity.

"What is this?" Beck asked.

"We knew you'd have complained if you'd missed it," Pirkheimer said.

Folk were pushing and shoving to gain a better view of the spectacle that imposed itself on the good city of Nuremberg. A ring of spectators had formed, several still in their fine livery from the Michaelmas procession, and within the circle were twenty or so pilgrims waiting for the drummer to stop. The crowd pressed forward; many were mute and open-mouthed but a few like a squad of barrowmen blithely uninhibited after downing liberal quantities of beer jeered and cat-called the town's outlandish interlopers. Among their number was Joachim, apprentice to Franconian master painter and printer, Michael Wolgemut, and winner of the annual artist apprentice prize.

The drumming ceased and the group's bearded leader let his dark eyes sweep the sea of curious faces and engaged briefly with a few. Once again he captured Albrecht Durer's pale eyes for a few moments. Then raising his arms high over his head he demanded silence. When the crowd obeyed he slipped a hand inside his tunic and drew forth a folded paper; the whole time his gaze remained on that part of the crowd occupied by Durer and his companions. People waited - fascinated. What did he have there in his hand, they wondered?

Out of the side of his mouth the cult leader spoke to a young girl next to him. She picked up the staff abandoned by his feet and handed it to him. The leader let the staff take his weight, little though that was for he appeared a scrawny, ill-fed fellow.

"People of Nuremberg, there are those who are eager to lead you astray. They claim they are intercessors between God Almighty and your humble selves. I have witnessed a priest hold up a paper such as this to claim it was received from the

Holy Father in Rome who in turn received it directly from the hand of an Angel of Heaven." The leader's voice was powerful, belying his slender build.

Willy Pirkheimer's eyebrow shot up and he nudged Durer in the ribs with his elbow. He would listen attentively to what the pilgrim had to say for as a city Councillor it was his duty to monitor opinions designed to exert influence over Nuremberg's citizens especially from men such as this, strangers from outwith the region. At first the unfamiliarity of the man's manner of speech confused the crowd with many struggling to catch the preacher's meaning but attentiveness trained the townsfolk's ears to hear better.

"Do not be deceived. No man should come between you and the Divine Being," the agitator shouted. "Promises of sins being easily washed away are false and meant to trick you friends, made by men who care only for their own glory. Look inside their churches, at the riches housed in them. Their clerics stagger under the weight of treasures – the rich flaunt their excesses; gold and precious stones are found in the holiest of shrines that might be used to feed the hungry and clothe the naked, where is the virtue in that? And they mystify God Almighty's message to his people by reciting sermons in Latin that you cannot understand."

One or two heads nodded in agreement for the preacher's words rang true – had they not just seen with their own eye a fortune in gold, silver and precious jewels proudly displayed by the priests of St Sebaldus at the Michaelmas procession? Others listened with impatience at the interloper's condemnation of their great and holy church - and on this most auspicious of holy days. For them their discomfort turned to resentment as their piety was questioned and the church with its priests who had always carried out their duties as a channel to all that was good and righteous. The pilgrim's audience grew restless.

The mystic dipped his head and waited for the murmuring to subdue a little then slowly he began to sway first to the right and then to the left, like a pendulum, while around him his followers stood quite still. At first the crowd hushed a little but then the appeal of the white-clad leader lost its authority and the muttering and tutting grew in volume till at last the mystic's patience wore out and he bellowed at the top of his voice above their commotion. He urged townspeople to find God and live a Godly life for he insisted therein lay the path to everlasting goodness and mercy. But the good church-going folk of Nuremberg could not separate God from church and so they continued to grumble. A flash of anger passed over the preacher's jet eyes and his voice grew shrill.

"And I looked, and behold a pale horse and his name that sat on him was Death and Hell followed with him. And power was given unto them over the fourth part of the earth, to kill with sword, and with hunger, and with death, and with wild beasts."

"It's as well our Nuremberg stallions are as black as the night," Durer whispered to Pirkheimer who grunted in agreement.

"Our church teaches us we can be forgiven our sins so I'll mention this one coming up next time I call in on the priest," shouted out a cheeky young barrowman weighing a stone in his hand. Egged on by his fellows he then hurled the missile which caused the mystic to hop niftily aside to avoid being struck. The crowd laughed out of relief as much as amusement with a few voices heard scolding the youth for dishonouring God's words for whomsoever delivered them the most pious citizens of Nuremberg had no desire to mock any part of the holy message, for fear God was watching and listening.

The mystic tried to engage the young barrowman's eye but the youth would not look again at him.

"God and man can be one if we take the path of perfection shown by Christ when he was on earth but we must renounce all sin and selfishness for only then can God's will live within us. Through living a sinful existence," the mystic continued more quietly now, "man wilfully turns his back on the godly life. Those who sin by following vain glories and worldly pleasures will be made to suffer greatly."

20

His audience winced in unison.

"Man should no more regard himself than if he did not exist for all creatures on earth are but nothing compared with God but we must live as if we are as pure as God and so will be blessed for eternity. Only this one thing, God, must be loved."

"I think he has you in mind, Albi," Otto Beck said," the way he keeps looking in this direction. Word must have got round that you're in particular need of salvation." With that he laughed.

The mystics widened their circle and their leader preached a short sermon damning priests for their sins. The strange inflection to his words was becoming more familiar to his Nuremberg audience but for any whose ears resisted the unfamiliar sounds from the stranger's mouth printed tracts were distributed spelling out the mystic's message for any able to read. To the citizens of Nuremberg it mattered not whether the word of God was interpreted by priests, sinful or not, or in Latin or German or written by the hand of an angel or man.

"I am but a poor soul, subject to every weakness of body and spirit, as you are. I thought I had faith but I found it was a false faith. I was spiritually weak and a sinner, like many of you. The more I sinned the greater I presented myself as pious. I searched within my being until I found God and came to know that God alone spoke directly to me and thus I found a way to forsake all sin."

Without taking his eyes off the speaker Willy Pirkheimer leaned over and whispered into Durer's ear. "He has a bold and petulant tongue and I wonder if he lives under a delusion or has been led astray by the Evil One."

An emboldened member of the crowd demanded, "Who let them in?"

Another cried, "Who are they to question St Sebaldus?"

But it was a cry of "burn them" which drew a collective gasp of horror and buzz of assent in equal measure in the square that day. The tall figure of the prison superintendent, Jodocus Franke the Löchwirt, observed events with interest.

"Is the child baptised?" called out a woman.

21

Her question found favour in the crowd for it was repeated and repeated until the mystic grabbed hold of the young girl's hand and answered that she was not as his people were against the practice of infant baptism for no babe could know its mind and only those with knowledge and conscience could submit to God. His words were met with collective gasps of horror and concern for the child. Durer heard another woman near him groan and when he looked round he saw it was Otto Beck's sweetheart holding a hand to her mouth.

"Fair Maria, don't upset yourself," Durer begged her.

Maria Kohl stared up at Durer her expression a mixture of alarm and confusion.

"Do not allow this knave distress you," Durer continued, "he and his unkempt band will be dispatched soon enough." His words were meant to be reassuring.

The mystic leader's eyes narrowed when again he turned his head so that he was once more looking directly towards Durer now in conversation with Maria.

"I was searching for my mistress," Maria Kohl whispered, self-consciously, all the time drawing back and behind Durer. Her words were uttered as fragments and she lowered her head so she was no longer confronted by the spectacle in the square. "We were separated by the rush of bodies," she gasped from behind the hand that hovered in front of her mouth – the other patted her chest as if to steady her rapid breath.

"They will be gone quick enough - if they have sense and wish to avoid the licks of the torch," Beck quipped.

Maria turned to him her eyes wide and her mouth falling open as if intending to speak but no sound came forth. When Durer glanced down at her he noticed tears welling up in the maid's eyes.

"That child … is it proper she's roaming the countryside in such company?" asked an old man pushing into the space vacated by Maria.

"Just a scrap of a thing," Durer replied. "I fear for her if she is a sinful child for then what would save her from eternal damnation if she does not live to seek her own baptism?" At his remark a woman standing in front of the artist turned to look up at Durer her expression heavy with disapproval.

"Maria!"

From behind Durer a startled Maria Kohl turned.

"I could not find you in this mob," Maria said quickly, grabbing at the speaker's hand.

Otto Beck put his arm around Maria and at the same time he prodded Durer in the back.

"You know Frau Wolgemut, of course, Albi," he said by way of introduction.

Durer's attention was drawn to a tall, dark-haired woman now joined by the hand to Maria.

Gudrun Wolgemut, for it was she, possessed the kind of face that might distract men from their duties while their wives might detect a sullen aspect to her mouth. The woman was of exceptional height with a lithesome figure and sweep of hair as black as ebony, plaited and coiled snake-like around her head, setting off a handsome rather than beautiful face.

The lady, like many of us, was both admired and disliked; for some the wife of Franconia's revered artist was a figure of sweet virtue but to others this was a devious wife with desires beyond her station. Durer studied the woman for there was something familiar about her yet he could not recall them ever having met. Just then a lanky beanpole of a man positioned himself next to Frau Wolgemut and appeared to be taking a keen interest in their conversation. Durer thought him an Italian for he was a swarthy-looking beanpole. Then there were two of them, the other as short as the first was long.

Durer leaned across Beck and picked up the woman's hand now released from Maria's.

"Frau Wolgemut! It is a pleasure to make your acquaintance. What do you think of this spectacle?" He gestured towards the circle of pilgrims and added, "Forgive me, but I feel certain we have met before but cannot think where."

The young woman smiled shyly back at him; she almost matched his height. With her hand in his Durer felt her fingers tremble, a sensation that often occurred when he spoke with women so he thought little of it as he pressed the pale hand to his own beautiful soft and shapely mouth.

"I... I... I do not recall," she replied and moved the conversation on by enquiring if Herr Durer's wife was present.

"No, my Agnes is abroad at Frankfurt with her brother, Frau Wolgemut. They hope to make our fortune from selling some of my humble prints," Durer volunteered. "And Herr Wolgemut ... I trust his health is excellent."

Frau Gudrun Wolgemut looked thoughtful. It was only a very few days since their paths had crossed on the great staircase at the Rathaus the Friday before Michaelmas. She was there on a private matter relating to her husband when she recognised Durer make his way in.

"Albi has Agnes running around here, there and everywhere trying to sell his pictures, don't you, Albi?" Beck said, adding, "there's no shortage of folk queuing up to buy them, so he would have us believe, which is as well for both Albi and his Agnes have expensive tastes to satisfy - as you can see." He tugged on Durer's mantle. "Mark my words she'll return weighed down by bolts of silks and velvets - and not all for her." His remarks were meant lightly so he was nonplussed when Maria nudged him on the thigh - and being a good head short of Gudrun Wolgemut, he did not see her face cloud over or sense a stiffening of her person beneath her drab russet Nuremberg garb.

Gudrun Wolgemut's marriage to the Franconian master and teacher of the gifted Albrecht Durer had taken place after the young painter completed his apprenticeship and left on his journeyman travels abroad. Wolgemut's workshop rivalled any in the western world for its prints and illustrations and Michael Wolgemut's copper etchings fetched handsome prices in markets far and wide. He retained a reputation for being the region's most prolific and successful artist until his precocious pupil ousted him from that position. Wolgemut struggled with acknowledging reputations can wane with age and fashion and the emergence of a greater talent.

24

When the young Durer was in Italy learning first-hand from that country's great masters his former tutor succumbed to bouts of ill-health which prematurely aged him and limited his production of pictures and prints further diminishing his reputation and damaging his earnings.

"Any man who turns holy images into profit and encourages false veneration should face punishment," shrieked the mystic.

Durer ran his carnelian beads through his fingers and contemplated the mystic's words. He surveyed the sea of faces around him; many familiar acquaintances and neighbours - their expressions ranging from horror to rapture. Among them was the wrinkled-faced nut seller from the Hauptmarkt and next to her stood a tall attractive girl not known to Durer. She was, he supposed, about fifteen years old with a complexion as fresh as a spring flower. Her hair was a shade of ivory and settled in curls about her slim shoulders as she nestled up against the nut seller, transfixed by the handsome pilgrim so that her mouth dropped open revealing teeth as even and perfect as two rows of pearls.

Durer was not alone in noticing this charming creature; behind her, stooped over a stout ash pole with his tongue poking out from between his fleshy lips, stood Umberto Müller. The man mountain pitched forward his one good eye, a shade of the most exquisite blue, running up and down the maid's body. Little happened in Nuremberg that escaped Müller's attention despite his being an eye short; the missing one cut out in a youthful brawl when the grain merchant was but sixteen years of age. Sensing he was being observed Müller raised the focus of his lonely eye till it settled on Albrecht Durer. A smile played around the fleshy mouth and a hand was raised in greeting that then dragged a faded red skullcap down over the smooth pink cat's arse where once his second eye had been.

"And my husband talks often of you. Perhaps you would be good enough to call on him, Herr Durer."

A distracted Albrecht Durer realised Gudrun Wolgemut was addressing him.

"He considers you his prize pupil. That's what he calls you - did you know that?" she asked. Gudrun Wolgemut spoke with a forwardness that was absent in their first exchanges but the words had scarcely crossed her lips when her resolve faltered and she dropped her gaze as she continued, "In truth he is not so well nowadays for his memory troubles him and he rarely wishes to leave the house. I am sure seeing you would help raise his spirits."

Durer's attention kept straying away from Frau Wolgemut for there was much going on in the square. So it was without any thought he heard himself agree to visit his former master, her husband, Herr Wolgemut.

"It would be an honour," Durer assured Gudrun Wolgemut, adding "by coincidence it is only days since I dispatched my boy, Günter, to Herr Wolgemut with a letter requesting permission for Joachim to sit for me that I might use him as a model for Adam in a work I've been planning but I have not received a reply from your husband."

Frau Wolgemut's face coloured and her mouth dropped open but just then the mystic let out a bellow that caused her utterances to shrink back under her tongue.

"Priests are not on your side," the pilgrim speaker waved an arm, "they condemn you for gathering wood from the forest, for taking fish out of the rivers and food from the plain. They say you must find contentment living in misery and hunger while all the time they fill the churches with luxuries and their bellies are never empty."

A flutter of parched copper leaves swirled overhead as a gust of wind blew hard and chilly from the north. Durer drew his coat tighter about him. Pirkheimer extended his arm, settling a hand on the painter's shoulder. A whispered conversation took place between them; guarded for they wished to keep private their thoughts about religion. The subject of man's path through this world and into the next was often a topic of debate between the two friends but likely to be misinterpreted in a city of strong and contrasting opinions. Both were critical of Dominican preacher Johan Tetzel's claim that absolution for sins was guaranteed in exchange for providing the church with gifts without any need of improving one's behaviour and in this belief they were on common ground with the mystic.

Durer stood with his hand resting over his heart; a pose he struck in a self-portrait painted four years earlier and intended as an emblem of hope at a time when black terror stalked the land amid prophesies that the end of the world was upon them. As fortune had it disaster did not materialise and Durer's handsome picture stared back, shamelessly, at all who paused to admire it. The painter plucked at the sleeve of his coat, the very one he wore in the portrait, and smiled remembering the rage created among his contemporaries at his audacity of presenting himself the subject of a picture in a manner traditionally reserved for the Saviour. He dismissed their stinging barbs for he was confident there was nothing unholy in challenging convention, especially from a talent as prodigious as his. He noticed Müller had moved away. Leaning towards Frau Wolgemut, he spoke directly into her ear for the noise around them was tremendous. "Perhaps I could call on him tomorrow?" There was something fragile about her demeanour, he thought to himself, and compared her to his wife Agnes who while diminutive in stature was strong and self-assured. Durer admitted something about Gudrun Wolgemut's meek nature was quite compelling. She smiled and nodded her response.

The mystic curled back his lips revealing white glistening teeth that drew gasps of admiration from women in the crowd, including Gudrun Wolgemut. The showman's grimace broadened into a wide savage grin. "We are surrounded by sinners. Sinners of every corruption," he roared, apparently sizing up his audience of fallible souls who clung to his every pronouncement. "Which of you is the glutton?" he demanded.

A space opened up around little fat-bellied Axel Marx who startled by his exposure toyed nervously with a string from which dangled the body of a fine specimen of hare; his podgy fingers working the line up and down. Sniffing at it enthusiastically was Axel's equally pot-bellied faithful yellow hound, Ulf. But as prepared as his fellow-townsmen and women were to brand him a glutton the agitator's rhetoric went further.

"Who among you ignores Leviticus where it tells us the hare is unclean for it cheweth the cud and has not divided hoof?"

Axel Marx looked at the limp beast clamped to his thigh.

The corners of the mystic's mouth softened and he seemed to feel the little man's discomfort at becoming the centre of attention and he looked away for a new challenge. "Where is the sloth lurking? And who admits to avarice? Who among you covets what is not his but is burdened by envy and jealousy." He lowered his voice compelling the crowd to listen harder, "you will be judged and your eyes sealed."

"Red hot iron shoes strapped to their feet so they dance to their deaths," rasped a woman caught up in the excitement.

"Hush," said someone nearby, "we are all guilty of a little jealousy from time to time."

"We are no worse than any other folk. What right has he to accuse us the good folk of Nuremberg of sinning? We are a pious people," a man called out.

"Yes, Nuremberg is a peaceful and industrious town. These people are nought but troublemakers creating mischief," cried another.

The pilgrim leader's head was bowed while his downcast eyes flitted like a beetle's from side to side, watching and listening to the crowd's reaction to his words. Finally, he struck the ground with the tip of his staff to drive his message home. "Those who lust and sodomise – are drunk with desires of the flesh - you will be known. Whosoever craves riches and knows not the value of truth will perish in fire. Sin is found at every level of rank so who among us is so bold to claim he does not transgress? Anyone?" Slowly, deliberately he wheeled around until once more he faced that portion of the crowd where Durer and his companions stood. "In flaming fire vengeance will be taken on those who know not God and do not obey the gospel of our Lord Jesus Christ."

"Quite a list he has there. Albi, you know Adolf Wolf our Town Clerk." Willy Pirkheimer had hold of a short bearded well-dressed man by the elbow.

"Yes, of course, I'm pleased to make your acquaintance again, Herr Wolf," Durer shook hands with the Town Clerk and noticed a handsome blue intaglio ring on the man's third finger. "What is your opinion of these fellows?"

Wolf dragged a brown woollen cowl from his head exposing a face of sallow complexion and heavy lidded eyes. "They bring trouble to the city, I fear." Wolf spoke softly, "It is many years since last we had such a display."

"I would say they also bring their own colour and what he has to say is not all bad, surely?" Durer responded.

Adolf Wolf looked thoughtful but offered no more opinion. Willy Pirkheimer meanwhile had turned his attention to the women alongside Otto Beck.

"Otto, I have been so taken up with Herr Wolf I hadn't realised we were in the company of your fair Maria and Frau Wolgemut - enchanting."

He took hold of Gudrun Wolgemut's free hand and pressed it against his moist eager lips; her other hand clutched a tiny Venetian reflecting glass. As Pirkheimer reached for Maria's willowy fingers his eyes explored the v-line of her bodice with its black kirtle revealing a hint of linen chemise and he was about to kiss the hand when Frau Wolgemut addressed him.

"You are familiar with my maidservant, Herr Pirkheimer?"

"Maria and I are acquainted," Pirkheimer agreed, nevertheless he released the girl's hand for the sake of propriety while his gaze shifted to Maria's rosy dimpled cheeks.

Maria Kohl had been employed in the Wolgemut household for a few short years. She was the youngest of five children all, save a single brother, died before reaching adulthood. Her parents had been master iron smiths at Spalt and while it was unusual for a woman to follow such an occupation it was not unknown for a widow or daughter to learn a craft and continue the family business on the death of a husband or father to keep the family from starvation. Maria's surviving brother had shown no wish to be a tradesman but was so taken with the scriptures he left the family home to preach God's word. He and Maria occasionally corresponded by letter; his being mainly dull sermons while Maria's were long and gossipy recounting incidents involving people she met and were so well-drawn her brother might have identified each and every one from her descriptions of their characters.

When Maria's father died her mother continued to work the forge assisted by Maria for the girl had inherited something of their clever hands but then Maria married a youth by the name of Kohl who turned out to be a wastrel who expected his young wife to work so he could enjoy himself hunting and drinking and whether by good- or ill-fortune he was killed one night in a drunken fight. The shame felt by Maria drove her from the village and so she found herself in Nuremberg where she was hired as Gudrun Wolgemut's maid. Soon she encountered Otto Beck whose interest in her grew on discovering her mechanical dexterity and quick mind for he was a man of ambition who saw her arrival as providential.

A lean figure dressed head-to-toe in red velvet worked his way through the crowd until alongside Durer's party where he lingered directly behind Gudrun Wolgemut. He had the beginnings of a stoop which gave the impression he might be whispering into that lady's ear. Durer stepped back and had to apologise for treading on a foot he discovered belonged to Prince Ernest's Chamberlain known as Slobberer due to a squint mouth that leaked (said to be the result of injury inflicted by a dagger). Slobberer's other attribute was his acquaintance with all that went on in the town for he maintained a network of informers that fed him information on anything that might be of value to the castle.

"Isaiah warned – the man who does not resist corruption shall face retribution for his sins."

"Suffocation in human excrement," came a shout.

There was a collective intake of breath with people exchanging horrified looks then someone giggled which set off more laughter in the crowd. The mystic's eyes narrowed as he fought to reassert control over his audience.

"Turn to the person next to you. Can you read vanity in their appearance?" And more forcefully he proclaimed, "In Adam we all die but in Christ we shall all be made alive again."

"This fellow," Pirkheimer, whispered, "is cut from a cloth that is not easy to decipher.

Adolf Wolf who was not given to intellectual theorising snorted. "Well, Herr Pirkheimer what do you recommend we do with these characters? Shall it be the torch? Or should we have them drummed out of the city?"

Pirkheimer was about to reply to him when Maria Kohl stifled a cry of alarm. She was pressed in behind Albrecht Durer, peeking around him from time-to-time at the firebrand mystic but hardly daring to engage him with her eyes.

"Whoever lacks humility is guilty of self-love. He who sets himself up alongside God denies the Lord his rightful place - that is above nature. To that man I say, fear Lucifer!" The agitator raised his arms above his head hoping to silence a mounting hum of insolence from his audience. "You all know of the angel who fell from heaven through a misplaced sense of his own importance but do you know that here among us today his earthly agent skulks?"

Heads turned expecting to recognise the guilty party.

"I fancy I have seen him before, Willy, for there is something familiar in his appearance," Durer said.

Pirkheimer leaned in close to Albrecht Durer. He told him all he knew of the fellow – that his name was Thomas Hut and he had a reputation throughout Franconia as a harsh critic of the church for its detachment from the common people and its attachment to princes. And as if prompted by the Councillor the mystic agitator damned again the powerful for their greed and cruel indifference to the suffering of the poor.

Albrecht Durer pushed back a lock of wind-blown hair screening his forehead. The sun had come out and Durer felt hot in his heavy woollen mantle though it struck him the mystic's polemic might be causing him discomfort more than any warmth produced by the sun's late appearance. He was a true and devout Christian but the preacher's words pricked him, nonetheless. The way the mystic kept looking his way planted a seed of doubt in his mind and increased his unease so he resolved to defend himself - his abilities and successes. Durer bit on his lower lip. He looked away from the exhibitionist making him question his life and observed three foreign-looking gentlemen dismount from magnificent chalk-white chargers at one of the entrances to the square. The mounts kicked exhaustion from their powerful limbs and shook their necks glistening with sweat as steam streamed out of their distended nostrils. Their riders stretched saddle-weary backs, crouching and shaking loose stiffened knees they stamped life back into their feet. One of them pointed to the multitude gathered in the square and leaving their animals in the care of a stable boy the trio sauntered towards the focus of the crowd's attention.

"A man's talent is God's gift and given to carry His meaning in everything mere men do so they better understand Him. Anyone who misuses his talent to sever his connection with God must be condemned and his works destroyed. And any person who creates images for the admiration of others should be condemned as vainglorious; guilty of misplaced pride."

Beck tugged on Durer's sleeve. "Albi, I'm convinced he means you. I doubt even your Agnes would succeed in persuading that one to purchase one of your portraits."

Durer looked Beck in the eye. He was fairly sure his leg was being pulled but Beck's words were loud enough to be overheard by others so Durer was obliged to defend himself in the same manner.

"That imposter," he nodded towards the pilgrim leader, " is no more a man who speaks for God than my fine fox here," and stroked the pelt draped across his shoulders with an air of certainty he did not possess for the nature and venom of the attacks stung home.

"I'd say you're right, Otto," Pirkheimer said. "There's no-one else here who fits that description more aptly than Albi and see how the man's attention is forever in our direction." He chuckled. "Yes, Otto, I'd wager my best hat that our insolent visitor had Albi in mind when he led his disreputable little band through our city gates. But at least, my dear little Otto, we are both off the hook," he said with a wink. "Never fret, dear Albi, there are many theologians who would reply to his charges with their fists until the sweat drips off their noses."

The mystic was now silent, standing stock still, his eyes shut. His followers gathered around him and a woman taking hold of the young girl by the hand fell in behind her leader. The mystics then quietly filed out of the square, the crowd opening up for them.

Despite the ferocious accusations that had been hurled their way and Nurembergers' natural intolerance of foreigners there were a few, quite a few, among the throng who thought there was something in the mystic's words - especially his condemnation of greedy princes who punished the hungry for gathering food from wild places.

With no more entertainment on offer the people drifted away – several making their way to inns for there was yet time to sup on this Feast of Saint Michael.

"What should we make of that?" Gudrun Wolgemut asked, dabbing an eye with a lace handkerchief and checking her appearance in a small looking glass.

"Do not alarm yourself, Frau Wolgemut, they are all noise," Durer said to reassure the lady who he thought was shedding tears.

"They do not trouble me, Herr Durer. It is only my eye that waters a little."

"Your handkerchief is very pretty," Durer remarked.

Gudrun Wolgemut smiled. "It was a gift from my sister in Augsburg."

Despite her reassurances Durer was sure his former master's wife was troubled by the scenes in the square but he dropped the thought from his mind.

"Those rascals came here to torment us for their own amusement and criticised us taking ours," Beck complained then stuck his thumb in his mouth and nibbled its nail.

Maria glanced about furtively following the mystics' retreat but did not venture to speak.

Otto Beck poked her side with his elbow, "I've already wasted too much time here." With that he was gone.

Pirkheimer bent over and picked something up off the street.

"Frau Wolgemut, I think this is yours." He held out a handkerchief worked with fine embroidery that the lady had dropped. "Such delicate needlework - a violet I fancy. You must keep it safe."

Gudrun Wolgemut mumbled her thanks as she tucked the handkerchief into her bodice.

Chapter 4

It was the Monday following Michaelmas and Albrecht Durer was listening to the old nut seller in the Hauptmarkt complain about the city guard opening the gates to the mystics rather than escorting them to prison.

"The Löch is where that lot should be - locked away in the gaol under the Rathaus with the rest of the vermin residing there," the nut seller snarled.

Hers was not the only voice raised against the city's slackness in detaining the mystics for many among the good folk of Nuremberg the heretics were as welcome as leper's spit.

Durer neither agreed not disagreed but listened to her give vent to her fury. Only when her anger was assuaged did he ask if she might let him have a few of her wormy and inedible chestnuts to press for oil (that he might use for thinning his pigments.) She had often obliged him in the past making him a gift of nuts she could not sell but today her ill-humour led to her brushing aside his request with an impatient flap of her small hand as wrinkled as the walnuts she hawked. Durer took this to mean she intended slipping one or two poor specimens of walnut in with every sale. It was of no consequence to him and not a reason to fall out with her but he did watch closely to what went into the scale pan when she weighed out his purchase and he bridled at the price she asked which he considered steep. It sometimes occurred to Durer that the nut seller charged according to how wealthy she considered her buyers to be and it was a wise master who sent his servant to the market for the best deals. With that in mind Durer regretted being in his best cloak and fox while on so mundane an errand but cheered himself with the knowledge his appearance could not be faulted. As it happened he observed that after weighing his walnuts the seller slipped him one or two extra of the more miserable specimens in addition.

***

35

The meticulous care with which Albrecht Durer dressed was little shared by the majority of his fellow-citizens and came not out of affectation so much as his own nature. As a child Durer had been sensitive to what others thought of him and he grew up determined to present himself to the world at his best in all things. Durer the Elder saw his son's streak of independence and recognised his determination to make his own way in life and supported him even when it meant him abandoning the family trade to follow his ambition of becoming a painter; lowly as that craft was. And so it was settled that young Albrecht would be placed under the wing of Michael Wolgemut, Nuremberg's finest master artist and printmaker.

During his apprenticeship with Michael Wolgemut the boy learnt the art of woodblock cutting so well his skill soon surpassed that of his master. He was quick to absorb lessons and new techniques of working and discovered for himself that Wolgemut's press was never at a standstill but continually turning out volumes of prints so that a single image when printed would return a prodigious profit when sold through a web of agents up and down the country.

A lesson eventually learnt by his master, Wolgemut, was that no style of print or painting survives indefinitely and by the time Albrecht Durer left his workshop the older man's popularity was already waning. The onset of old age and illness added to the great man's woes and a decline in his workshop's output led to rumours that the elderly artist's household struggled to make ends meet.

Young and supremely talented Albrecht Durer was an innovator keen to learn from the best which is why he travelled to study in the workshops of Flemish and Italian masters and how he came to perfect his clever imitation of nature in his works. None of Albrecht Durer's contemporaries could match his penmanship for he was the most painstaking of men in the attention he gave to the smallest detail of his drawing and in painting to the application of layer upon layer of pigment to enrich the brilliant appearance of his pictures. The rise of such a bright star in the firmament of Franconia's circle of painters attracted attention from both admirers and rascals seeking to exploit his talent for their own ends. Yes, young Albrecht Durer discovered that eminence was frequently accompanied by envy; a lesson he was reluctant to learn.

Durer thanked the nut seller and was about to take his leave when the fair-haired maiden he had seen with her the previous day appeared and engaged the old woman in conversation.

"We can't avoid each other today, Albi."

Durer transferred his gaze from the pretty girl to Willy Pirkheimer's florid rotund face.

"Albi, dear friend and companion you are reduced to purchasing your own victuals I see. No Anton?" Willy Pirkheimer slipped an arm about Durer's shoulders. "I trust you slept soundly last night and did not permit those scoundrels to disturb your beauty sleep, my kindred spirit."

"My indulgent friend," began Durer, "how good to see you. Don't be concerned for me for I had an exceptional rest whereas you look like you have had scarce a wink – but tell me are you able to advance me a thaler or two?"

Pirkheimer pouted as if disapproving but dug a hand into his leather purse and pressed a few coins into Durer's outstretched hand at the same time shifting his attention to the youthful flaxen-haired Fraulein alongside the nut-trader.

"Have you recovered from being the focus of yesterday's spectacle, my dear Albi?" he asked almost absent-mindedly. "Those heretics made for some amusing sport but I fear one or two of our more gullible brethren will pay too much heed to their ideas. Hallo, who have we here?" he purred.

The maiden smiled shyly and her eyes flitted to the large man but it was on Durer's pretty face they settled.

Observing this Pirkheimer sighed, "Ah, I understand. It's not food for the belly which brings you here, Albi, but this attractive nymph."

Albert Durer shook the ringlets rinsed that morning with water to which he had added a squeeze of lemon juice to bring out their golden highlights. Agnes liked to chide him for his conceit and would advise him to imbibe rather than apply the juice but her husband cared little for her counsel on such matters.

The walnut seller placing herself between the men and the maiden scowled at Pirkheimer.

"You buying or just looking?" she brayed. "If you're not buying you can take yourself off and pester someone else, I have customers to attend."

Pirkheimer looked round at the near deserted market and saw the diminutive Axel Marx approach with Ulf at his heels and a leg of ham secured under an arm.

Axel made elaborate play of raising his hat with his free hand. "Forgive me folks and Frau," he cooed, bowing to the old woman as he scurried by.

The nut seller hardly looked in his direction but repeated her reprimand of Pirkheimer with a wag of her finger. "Buy or get lost and you can cut out the lewd behaviour or I'll report you to the Council," she snapped.

Pirkheimer opened his mouth to speak but was interrupted by Durer.

"I'd like to hire the services of this handsome young woman, if she is willing," he asked.

"She most certainly is not," the woman replied.

At this the girl's face lit up. "What did you have in mind, Sir?"

Durer drank in the deliciously velvet tones that sprung like water trickling over warm pebbles from between her plump rosy lips; his imagination could not have conjured up a more perfect Fraulein to be his muse.

The nut seller's jaw was by now as wide as a hay loft so Durer lost no time in explaining his purpose.

"I seek Eva ... a pretty girl to be Eva ...as in Adam and Eva ... which I'm anxious to begin ...," his fingers extended to touch the girl's silky locks. "Master Botticelli's Venus is less fair," he sighed and took out a thumbnail sketch from his purse. "I carry these as way of introduction," he explained to Pirkheimer not the girl.

"To sit ... for a painting? You mean you want to get her to take her clothes off?" the woman whinnied, "you can just get lost."

"Albrecht!" Pirkheimer roared. "You're making a start on your *Adam and Eve* at last! And this pretty young thing will be Eva? Excellent choice, Albi." He reached out and grabbed hold of the giggling girl's hands and smothered them with moist hungry kisses.

"She will not," protested the old woman.

Pirkheimer rounded on the stall holder. "Albrecht does not see a woman as any ordinary man might. To him a woman represents God's handiwork on Earth. He ... "

"Don't try that hogwash with me. Els! I forbid you to consort with these lechers." With that the nut seller lifted her apron in an attempt to shield the maiden from the corruption confronting her.

"My dear Frau you are most mistaken. It will be the greatest gift to the world for this child to represent Eva ...," Pirkheimer began.

"To represent a fallen woman! No Sir. Away with you!" the grandmother squawked.

"My dear Frau! That is blasphemy," Pirkheimer insisted, "you risk being dragged off to the Fleischbrücke and having your tongue torn out - not that I approve of such barbarous behaviour." He held up his hands to emphasise how much he condemned such cruelty.

Albrecht Durer troubled by the sinister twist of mood appealed directly to the tender creature in their midst. "Els...how charming a name for such an enchanting young beauty."

"Grandmother, these gentlemen mean no mischief, I am sure," the girl insisted in a quiet tone.

The old woman clamped her mouth shut and shook her head.

"And why have I never cast my eye on you before pretty one?" Durer asked.

The girl's smile vanished. "I lost my mother and father to the plague, Sir, and my grandmother has kindly agreed to let me stay here with her in Nuremberg."

Durer's immediate impulse was to withdraw his offer. Had he not fled Nuremberg when the city was ravaged by plague? Yet this girl looked the picture of health. Casting aside his reservations he enquired where she had come from.

"Schwäbisch Hall," she replied.

"When was it your poor parents were carried off?" he pressed her.

"Some little time ago, I stayed a while with an aunt but she could not keep me so I came here to Nuremberg."

Satisfied he was in no immediate danger Durer was persuaded Els would make a perfect Eva for his engraving. He laughed and threw up his hands that this fortunate encounter had brought him face to face with the fairest Eva he could hope to engage - whose expressive face and shapely body had won him over so completely. It was true he had considered making his Eva a mature woman like the fleshy *Nemesis* he engraved a year or two before but Els struck him as the very incarnation of Eva and he saw this unexpected good fortune as a good omen for the success of his picture.

Els fingered the thumbnail she recognised as the Henkersteg, the bridge crossing the river Pegnitz where Hans the city's Löb lived in its strong tower protected from those who wished harm on the hangman. Durer watched as she turned it over and mouthed the words written on the other side.

"It gives my name - which is Albrecht Durer. Do you read?" he enquired kindly.

"A little," she admitted, "and I hope to improve my skills yet." She slipped the sketch into a pocket.

Once out of earshot of the grandmother Pirkheimer poked Durer in the ribs.

"I think you're due me a favour, Albi, for charming that old crone into silence," he chuckled, "what say you that you make me your Adam?" To emphasise his point he jutted out the first of his chins and turned his head in profile.

"You are an incorrigible old lecher, the crone wasn't wrong about you. That poor innocent child is but a kitten while you, Willy, are a rapacious old dog. I, by contrast, am yet young and lithesome and quite a maiden's idea of perfection. Besides I have my eye on Wolgemut's pupil, Joachim," Durer replied.

"It's been noticed Albi," Pirkheimer stretched his large mouth into an enormous grin. "Is there a fine looking youth in Nuremberg who has escaped your attention? And young Günter – doesn't he feel edged out for Adam?" Pirkheimer patted Durer's shoulder.

"Joachim is a strong handsome lad who will be perfect for Adam while Günter is such a little runt, likeable and a promising painter, but he hasn't the kind of physique that sells prints," Durer said.

"Well you can expect trouble from both Günter and Wolgemut," Pirkheimer cautioned.

"I've sent a request to Herr Wolgemut for his permission to borrow the lad for the picture and as for Günter he will do as he is bid." Durer looked at the girl and her grandmother. "Please believe," he cleared his throat, "my intentions are strictly honourable." Then for Pirkheimer's ears only he whispered behind his hand, "As honourable as matches yours, Willy. If the old witch comes along you will have to entertain her while I work on Els, after all she is closer to your age. It's a small thing to ask of the man I look upon as nothing less than a father."

"I'll pull my hat down over my eyes and think of Athena," Pirkheimer snorted as he tugged on his cap in a gesture of farewell.

As he made his way home Albrecht Durer recognised the clerk Adolf Wolf in conversation with Frau Wolgemut and two cloth merchants whose brocades and silks were attracting interest from Nuremberg's women whose usual attire comprised of dowdy weaves. Durer stood and watched the group, observing that Frau Wolgemut was also taken by the

41

dealers' bolts of richly coloured fabric and spoke a good deal with them. At the edge of the group was a small woman, hunger-thin and with a look of deep longing in her dark eyes as if transfixed by the vivid colours and patterns that contrasted so much with her own worn and much darned dress. She gazed longingly at the rolls of exquisite embroidery, her thumb tracing their exotic patterns. He saw her move away from the stall then stop and rummage around in her apron pocket. She picked out a coin and weighed it in her hand as if establishing its worth then returned to the foreign mercers and pointed to a coil of narrow blue silk ribbon exchanging her coin for a length of it.

Chapter 5

Durer stood in front of the house near the Laufer tor and brae leading to the Imperial fortress generously provided by Willy Pirkheimer's family for him and Agnes. The two families were close friends and the Pirkheimer's own home was but as short walk away. It was occasionally said of Albrecht Durer that he would do well to remember he lived at the foot of the Tiergarten hill and not the top - for his self-confidence brimmed to a level above the usual arrogance of men.

Head tilted back Albrecht Durer watched a spindly straggling skein of gaggling geese navigate a glowering pewter sky, his mind on Agnes and how she might be faring on the river journey between Bamberg and Frankfurt. A practical man Durer had bartered a set of his woodcuts for travel passes for Agnes and Susanna from the Bishop of Bamberg in expectation they would ease their passage at customs houses along the way.

Durer sighed for despite their constant squabbles he missed his Agnes; her sharp tongue and wilful ways - and hoped his outlay of six gold florins apiece for hers and Susanna's living expenses would prove a wise investment. The annual journey to Frankfurt's art market was a strain on Durer's pocket and there was no certainty his prints would sell in sufficient numbers to cover the outlay but it was a chance both were prepared to take to reach new buyers and establish his name as an artist. In any case Agnes enjoyed the freedom the voyage provided for she was armed with confidence - a proficient businesswoman who rarely returned from such expeditions without her purse bulging with coin. Her husband recognised her ability as an agent for his prints, as competent as any outsider he hired for that purpose, and more trustworthy. He was certain she would not return with any of the quarter sheets of prints for Agnes Durer understood her market and the popularity of little printed illustrations as prayer book markers and new year cards. At Frankfurt she would use what remained after the boatmen's expenses along with a portion of the profit from sales to purchase a length or two of fabric to make into pretty blouses to brighten winter's dark and dreary months and return home with sufficient in her purse to impress her husband. The couple's fondness for fine garments was their major extravagance; Agnes would tease Albrecht that he should have been born a hercinia, the bird whose glowing plumage lights up the forest.

The Durer's unconventional marriage was occasionally the subject of tittle-tattle in Nuremberg, as was to be expected in any small place where lives were shared with the whole community.

***

The keening wind winding between Nuremberg's tall buildings tousled Albrecht Durer's long fair hair. Leaves swirled over rooftops like flurries of golden snow. It was predicted winter would come early to Nuremberg this year, chasing away its few remaining merchants before they got trapped in the snows of Franconia. Nuremberg's popular markets, a lodestone for traders from every corner of the earth expected their numbers to thin during the last quarter of the year and become mainly local again, until better weather returned in late spring.

Commerce was an important source of wealth for Nuremberg for it was her good fortune, and her misfortune, to stand on the crossroads of Asia's trade routes. The little city nestled into a valley on the sandy and unnavigable river Pegnitz attracted people of every hue and belief to buy and to sell: goods from near and far - trinkets and trifles; spices and silks. The markets were very popular with people from the Low Countries who came in vast numbers seeking curiosities from the Orient. But for every honest man and woman who arrived with honourable intentions there were others intent on mischief – aspiring and sharp-eyed rogues lured by tales of riches, real or imaginary. Nuremberg attracted those with a flair for enterprise and others with a trick or two up their sleeves so that in every inn and concealed within street corner shadows lurked brutality and wickedness avenging grudges and plotting reprisals. But for all the stir and suspicions of a busy merchant city Nuremberg's prosperity came less from trading imports out of wagons and off the backs of pack horses than from goods produced by her own craftsmen along with strong government led by learned men and prominent humanists.

Günter was not where he ought to have been preparing Durer's workshop for the day ahead; indeed, the shop was unusually quiet for the apprentice's presence was normally advertised by much tuneless whistling or off-key renditions of popular drinking ditties. Durer called twice on his pupil before he appeared - quite out of breath.

"Overslept this morning?" Durer asked but without waiting for his reply enquired if he had taken breakfast.

Only then did Durer spy a loaf of bread and dish of cheese abandoned on a side table and crawling with black flies. Swiping them aside he summoned his manservant, Anton, to remove the food.

"Where have you been, Günter?" he demanded roughly, "and why are you wearing my blue jacket?"

The boy hurriedly removed the offending garment.

"I was preparing charcoal sticks, Sir," he replied, wilfulness in his tone. He pulled the top off a blackened tin box lined with woollen rags and filled with pieces of broken charcoal.

"Are they birch?" Durer demanded sharply. He rubbed one of the twigs between his fingers and snapped off an end, satisfying himself of its dryness.

When Günter went to put away his master's jacket a small shiny carved green pebble fell from it and clattered along the floor. Durer's quick eye was on it.

"Is that my jasper?" he demanded.

"It was in your pocket - there must be a hole in it," Günter said with a sly grin.

"Because you insist on wearing it and carrying stones in the pockets," Durer snapped.

"I carry only your special ones, like this grass stone," Günter picked up the pebble.

"Out of fear you will be possessed if you do not."

The boy squirmed but said nothing.

Durer's man servant, Anton, had slipped into the room and was clearing away the bread and cheese when Herr Wolgemut's pupil, Joachim, bounded in from outside.

Making for Günter he held out a folded bronze-green paper. "How goes it Günter?" he asked brightly then noticing Albrecht Durer, "Oh! Herr Durer ... I didn't see you ... this is for you ... from Herr Wolgemut," offering the missive to him.

"Put it down there." Durer was wiping charcoal dust from his fingers with a rag. "Come, take some refreshments with us, Joachim, and give us your news. Been brawling again I see. Who has taken a fist to your eye?" Durer reached out and stroked the youth's bruised face.

Joachim turned down the offer of food but offered no explanation over the state of his eye.

"I haven't congratulated you on taking the apprentice prize," Durer continued. He looked the boy up and down - the long lithesome limbs, firm and pleasingly rounded. He longed to have the youth agree to pose for his engraving.

Joachim's blushed and a smile stretched to his ears but his attention was on Günter apparently deep in concentration preparing charcoal sticks.

"Are you certain you will not take something to eat or drink, Joachim?" Durer asked again.

Anton, on his way out of the room with the food, looked at Joachim. The boy shook his head. Durer dismissed Anton and watched the two young friends engage in conversation. Their heads were close together so little of what they exchanged was overheard by him except for a mention of the mystics. When Joachim turned to go Durer suggested Günter might like to accompany him for part of the way back to Wolgemut's but Günter shook his head and carried on arranging charcoal sticks.

46

"I haven't the time, Herr Durer," he protested making no move to follow his friend even to the workshop door.

Once Joachim had left, Durer looked at Günter. "I wasn't aware you'd seen those nuisance mystics. Were you in the Hauptmarket?"

Günter's cheeks flushed. "I hardly saw them for I wasn't out for long," he said., defensively.

Durer chuckled. "As long as you don't bring shame on me you are free to do what you like when not working, Günter. Just don't get into scrapes like young Joachim does, for I know the two of you are as thick as thieves." Then noticing the boy's troubled expression, added, "Günter what is it that ails you child?"

"I was only out a very short time," Günter repeated.

"Yes, you said, did you secure the workshop door this time?" Then Durer remembered Wolgemut's note and he turned his back on Günter.

Chapter 6

Michael Wolgemut's modest dwelling and workshop was tucked into a dip in the hillside where the Kaiserburg overlooked Nuremberg. The Franconian master's residence, one time Albrecht Durer's second home, was partly screened from a well-trodden track by a belt of pallid-bark birch saplings. Despite the bitterly cold wind tugging exasperatingly at his mantle and hat and the steepness of the hill Durer took pleasure in rediscovering once-familiar landmarks.

At the sparse birch wood he chanced on the shepherd, Widukind, surrounded by his flock of sheep; bells around their necks clanging and jangling they grazed on the coarse undergrowth. The shepherd was always known by the one name; if he possessed another the folk of Nuremberg had long forgotten it. Widukind's black and white hound balancing on three legs scratched at an ear with the fourth and eyed Durer. His master returned the artist's hallo. The two became friendly when Durer was at Wolgemut's workshop but more recently their paths seldom crossed. Widukind spent his entire life in the district where he was a familiar figure in his long brown habit that protected him from piercing winds and thorny barbs as he wended his way around and through the Sebaldus forest. He rarely left the confines of the forest, having turned his back on both city and the land to the south with its Laurenzius Forst where his twin brother, Wedigo, was swineherd. Inseparable as children the brothers were said to have competed for the hand of a girl who in the end rejected them both for a shoemaker from Rothenberg ob Tauber. Following an ill-tempered quarrel the two agreed to work the land above and below Nuremberg and from that time never again spoke to each other. Occasionally Widukind would be seen buying bread and eggs in the Hauptmarkt or one of the small markets near Am Ölberg but his forays into town were of the briefest as though he was fearful he would happen upon his brother - not that there was likelihood of that for Wedigo forsook

Nuremberg entirely from the day of their parting and scavenged the plains and the forest to satisfy his simple needs. Wedigo's existence depended near entirely on the oak carpeted Laurenzius Forst whose acorns fed his beasts, giving them the sweetest flesh in all of Franconia. Wedigo occasionally traded a porker for supplies of fruit and vegetables from the Knoblauchsland where most of Nuremberg's food was grown but over time he made himself into a stranger who preferred the company of loathsome beasts and spirit-dwellers within what Nurembergers regarded were dreadful and cursed woods - home to evil elves and pixies. So townsfolk avoided Wedigo and cared nought when Nuremberg's youths teased him with their tricks.

A stranger encountering both Widukind and Wedigo north and south of the city might imagine they were one and the same but locals could tell one brother from the other. Dark-eyed Widukind clad himself in garments as brown as winter's bare earth while Wedigo's habit was as blue as the waters of the Pegnitz on a summer's day, like his eyes, but his tranquil appearance belying his flint-like temper.

Durer bade farewell to the shepherd and completed his walk to Herr Wolgemut's home. There he encountered his former master's excitable hound with its teeth bared and straining against a leash in the hands of Wolgemut's manservant, Schmeichler.

***

Frau Wolgemut was reading to her husband when Schmeichler showed Durer into the low-ceilinged hall smoky from a recalcitrant fire of crackling birch splits. She and Durer acknowledged each other shyly; their third meeting in almost as many days, before she withdrew leaving him and her husband to their discussion.

Michael Wolgemut and Albrecht Durer had not spoken since the latter completed his apprenticeship and for several moments there was an awkward silence as they took stock of one another. Durer was surprised at how Wolgemut had aged in the duration and struggled to recall people and situations once familiar to him. But as for Wolgemut's renowned eye for detail – that proved as acute as ever. On presenting him with a small sketch of grasses Wolgemut held it close to his screwed-up eyes, examining the drawing for quite some time, enthusiastically discussing its fine strokes and delicate tones with great eloquence.

The mood changed after Durer congratulated his host on Joachim's success in that year's apprentice boys' contest; a compliment that was first received with a mixture of pride and caution but then Durer went on, "My lad Günter is most envious for he had expected to come away with the prize."

Wolgemut fell silent and his eyelids flickered as though overcome with fatigue. He raised one of his legs that appeared to pain him and placed it on a stool at the very moment the door opened and Gudrun Wolgemut entered carrying a tray with a nösel of beer and two silvered beakers. Without a word she filled each beaker, handing one to Durer before assisting her husband by wrapping his arthritic fingers around the other cup and steadying his free hand whose fingers thrummed the chair arm. The three looked up at the sound of Schmeichler's shuffling gait.

"Leave us," Herr Wolgemut growled into the fire; his eyes narrowed into slits," and you, Schmeichler." Gudrun Wolgemut glanced towards Durer and coloured a little.

Schmeichler and Gudrun Wolgemut closed the door behind them when they left.

"He turns up when he's not wanted and is nowhere to be found when he is," Wolgemut mumbled. "Insists he's a heavy sleeper and he can hear nothing at the back of the house but I wonder what he gets up to when he's out of my sight." The old master's voice was splintered with age. He gave a start as if suddenly conscious he was speaking aloud and turned his attention towards Durer. "I sent for you because some ruffians have stolen one of my pictures," he announced matter-of-factly.

"What?" Durer echoed stupidly, "stolen?"

"That's what I said," the older man replied. "Such a thing has never happened to me in all my years. What do you have to say?"

"When was this? What has been taken?"

Wolgemut cleared his throat. "It was on the feast of Saint Michael when there were many strangers in the city. Nuremberg is not the place it once was which is why I rarely venture out these days." His words dried up, as though he had forgotten he was talking.

The room fell silent except for the sizzling and sparking of logs in the hearth. The old man turned his gaze to the walls lined with paintings and prints, as if to draw reassurance from all that was familiar to him there.

"Could it be you are mistaken? Perhaps it was mislaid ...," Durer began.

A low rumbling laugh emitted from Wolgemut's throat. "The knaves left me a correspondence ... they say they will destroy my picture unless I pay them a bounty." The old man clawed his thigh, cat-like.

"Destroy one of your pictures? But why? They are asking you to pay money? Is it a trifling sum?"

Herr Wolgemut met Durer's eye as he battled to contain his emotions.

"The sum is immaterial. You would not care to lose a work of yours in such a devilish manner. And I may say this picture was intended for an important patron. No, young Durer, if this is allowed to stand then what is there to prevent others suffering a similar fate?" The words rattling off his tongue seemed to exhaust him for then he slumped down into his seat.

"Herr Wolgemut," Durer leaned forward a hand resting on the old man's forearm, "if I can be of any assistance ...," he began – disturbed by the blank look Wolgemut's eyes had taken on. He got to his feet intending to summon Gudrun. "Perhaps it is best if I call on you another time."

Wolgemut reached out for Durer.

51

"You, Herr Durer, were named in that note, so yes, I expect you will see to it my picture is returned."

"Me?" Durer asked, horrified.

Wolgemut shook his greying head. "I do not accuse you of the theft but of a connection with it that is all ... and command you to secure ... recover my property ... you are in my debt, are you not? Those years you spent under my roof - learning my trade ... you must help an old man. Will you deny me, Albrecht Durer?" He examined Durer's face. "But say nothing to anyone of this. Not to my wife. Schmeichler knows, of course ... he is the thread connecting me to the world ... but not one other person, you hear? Not a single soul."

"Can Schmeichler not ... " Durer began.

"Schmeichler is not concerned with this matter. It is you who are named and it is your responsibility to bring this disgraceful matter to an end," Wolgemut barked.

"But I have not stolen any of your pictures. I know nothing of the matter, I assure you. This is a great shock to me."

"The mention is not that you took the picture but that you can be the means of its safe return," Wolgemut said.

"This picture - what is it about it that has attracted a thief?" Durer asked.

Herr Wolgemut considered Durer's question. "Tis a study of a rabbit, as I recall."

"You recall? A rabbit?" Durer echoed. "This is not at all your usual subject, Herr Wolgemut." He fancied there was much that was strange about this whole affair.

"What has that to do with anything you impudent wretch," Wolgemut fired back at him.

Taken aback by the old man's temper Durer repeated his intention to leave. It rankled with him that he had been drawn, unbeknownst, into this affair but consoled himself with the conviction he was wholly innocent of any involvement. Nonetheless, his name associated with a theft was alarming. Muttering words intended to be reassuring he told Wolgemut he would do whatever he could to rescue the stolen work.

On his way back to the city, Durer struggled to comprehend both the theft and the subject, a rabbit; not a subject associated with Herr Wolgemut. Indeed, Durer had often heard the older man sneer at his own fondness for depicting 'coarse brutes, as he called them. And Albrecht Durer remembered his own watercolour of a field hare, much admired by his mother, who strongly hinted she would like it for her own home. Her taste was unusual for most people with an interest in painting preferred their art to contain biblical content or at the very least to honour a temporal personage of merit, such as a prince. Durer ruminated on his conversation with Herr Wolgemut and his rashness in agreeing to help retrieve the stolen painting. It occurred to Durer his former master could be suffering from a malady of the mind since his claims seemed so outlandish. But most troubling for Albrecht Durer was the prospect of being drawn into the wicked world of thieves and rogues, placing him in danger. With that in mind he chided himself for having impulsively agreed to aid Wolgemut knowing a change of heart was all but impossible.

Durer looked out for the shepherd, Widukind, but there was no sign of him as he retraced his steps back into the city but sauntering, unhurried, along a track that fringed the birch forest he chanced upon a profusion of Krötenstuhl, a good handful of which he plucked for Anton to boil into a tasty toadstool soup for supper.

Chapter 7

"You took your time," Otto Beck complained as he shifted along the bench so Durer could sit down beside him.

Durer drank down a good measure of beer, savouring each mouthful then leaned his elbows on the table before he answered Beck. "It's usually me waiting for you to turn up and when do you ever hear me criticising you for your tardiness?"

"Quite a lot now that you ask," Beck was quick to reply, "something up, Albi? You look like you've swallowed a fish with your beer."

Albrecht Durer examined the inside of his krug then clearing his throat he recounted the strange meeting with Wolgemut and the man's assertion he was involved in the theft of a picture. Durer studied Beck's reaction. There was very little.

Beck admitted he'd already heard about the missing picture. "Maria told me before I came in here. "They were all probably listening outside the door. You should have taken me along, Albi. I also heard Wolgemut lost his temper with you." The locksmith laughed. "There's nothing more enjoyable than a good spat, Albi, but picking on an old man is a bit low to my mind."

Durer shook his head, denying there had been any quarrel.

Beck belched. "Well, that's not what I heard."

An awkward silence descended between the two men, breached when Beck landed a hearty slap against Durer's back.

Durer took a deep breath and watching the fire hungrily feeding off smoking logs, appealed to his friend's sympathy. "The thing is, Otto, I'm also a victim of these rascals."

Beck stared at Durer, detecting a slight tremble in the painter's hands. "You? When? What?" he solicited, unable to disguise his disbelief.

"Er ... when I arrived home from Herr Wolgemut's ... I discovered ... the door was ajar ... it was discovered one of my pictures had been removed from its frame and is gone ... we've searched the place from top to bottom ... no-one saw or heard … it is quite vanished." Durer's words melted away and he swallowed a long measure of beer.

"In your house? Who would be in your house but Anton and those employed at your workshop? "Beck asked.

"That is a mystery. Perhaps foreigners for when I was walking along Bergstrasse I passed two unusual-looking fellows who ran off at my approach, " Durer explained.

"Ran off? Were they in possession of this picture you say has been taken?"

"I cannot say," Durer replied.

"You cannot say! Was it a very small picture?" Beck continued, unable to mask doubt in his question.

Durer shook then nodded his head.

"And where was Anton when strangers were making off with your handiwork?"

"Everyone was out but Günter who was in the yard boiling a rabbit for glue for a panel …," Durer's reply slunk away. "I found the door open and thought first of Agnes's jewel box and couldn't find it then recalled she's taken it with her to Frankfurt. I must have called out for Günter came running up and it was from him I learned the picture had been cut from its mount and the frame discarded in the workshop. I went down and saw it with my own eyes. The boy swears he heard and saw nothing. He's so excitable nowadays … he's been very down lately … since the apprentice prize … and now this." Durer lowered his head and sighed. "Heigho! Otto."

Beck's mouth gaped open. "What has the apprentice contest to do with a theft?" he asked.

Durer pulled a face. "There is nothing to connect them … I was only explaining that Günter has been troubled … then and now."

"Upset that he didn't win the prize or you were robbed?" Beck's round face crumpled in bewilderment. "You haven't told me what it is that's been taken."

"My study of a field hare … cut out from its mount. A pretty little thing," Durer said.

"The mount?" Beck asked cheekily.

Durer glared at him.

"The painting."

"A field hare?" Beck asked.

"Yes, and a remarkable coincidence – for the study stolen from Herr Wolgemut was very similar."

Otto Beck stroked his chin. "My own thoughts, Albi."

"But my picture is of a hare while Herr Wolgemut's is a rabbit, as I understand. I can honestly say I am the unluckiest person in Christendom," Durer insisted.

"Oh I don't know," Beck said. "If these are the same fellows that made off with Wolgemut's rabbit then it should be a simple matter to track them down. After all it's unusual to see a fellow walking about with a painting under his arm and these villains have one apiece … if two there are - fellows I mean not pictures." He sneaked a peek at Durer. "Albi - ," he continued, "Albi - are you really sure about this? It sounds quite far-fetched."

Durer rounded on his companion. "What's far-fetched about it? You happily accepted Wolgemut was robbed but not that I'm also a victim of ruffians?"

Beck scratched his chin. "Seems a lot of trouble to go to for pictures of - well … rabbits and hares. Who would want any such picture? I can see that someone might want a fine oil panel of say … a crucifixion or … a deposition … but … are you certain all they took was a common hare?"

Otto Beck was correct in his observation that hares were not most peoples' idea of a subject worthy of portraiture. The mystic preacher, Thomas Hut, had mentioned that very creature and its base reputation when his band of mystics invaded the Hauptmarkt on Michaelmas. The hare was much derided as a beast - frequently found carved into the backs of church benches and secretly fashioned in clerestories – allusions to Eve; the first woman whose disobedience, licentiousness and sly nature led to the downfall of man.

"A study of a field hare" Durer said curtly, "I've told you. We hunted up and down but it's nowhere to be found. Am I to believe you are now an authority on painting and my judge at that? I can tell you think I imagined my misfortune." Durer sprang to his feet toppling the bench as he did so and attracting the attention of fellow drinkers.

"Sit down, Albi. Sit down. All I'm saying is ... this is a strange coincidence and you've never before had a work stolen then the moment old Wolgemut loses a picture ... suddenly you do, too ... and one very like it. Imagination never sleeps like judgement does. You've got to admit it takes a bit of swallowing, that's all I'm saying. Now calm yourself and sit down." He helped Durer right the bench. "What does it matter, Albi, hey, drink up and I'll buy another. Ana, over here."

Ana Brauer hurried across. "I thought you were about to leave us, Herr Durer. You don't look too happy with life at the moment. Here, I have something that will cheer you up," and she handed him a portion of spicy gingerbread before pouring him more beer.

Albrecht Durer who was nearly as well-known for his sweet tooth as he was for his draughtsmanship took the sweetmeat and thanked Ana but the moment her back was turned he informed Beck, through a mouth sticky with cake, that he was for returning home as soon as he finished his drink and true to his word he drained his bierkrug, slammed it down on the table and had an arm down a sleeve of his coat when he blurted out, "You were there when I got the hare."

A surprised Beck belched, "Oh yes, when was that?"

"One day we were running hares with our hounds and we came upon a particular beauty - which you were all for killing there and then but I insisted we trap instead." Durer said.

Beck's brow wrinkled as he struggled to recall the occasion for he and Durer often hunted hare in the garlic lands. Then it came to him - an incident when Durer insisted on taking the creature alive - bright-eyed, limbs swollen with life. He recalled, too, that later Durer told him Agnes was for boiling the animal with leek, barley and sage leaves.

"Did you sup it after you were done with the poor brute? You never told me." Beck brandished his bierkrug above his head for beer. "If it's that hare I found for you," he said, "then by rights I can claim it as mine. So, where do we stand on its ownership, Albi?"

Albrecht Durer shook his head. There were times when Beck's humour proved too much for him.

"Couldn't you have got your beer at the same time I topped up Herr Durer's, Otto Beck? And saved my poor legs. And what's this, Herr Durer, my gingerbread is not reason enough for you to stay?" she remarked while refilling Beck's krug.

Durer's coat remained half on.

"I heard you mention hares, Otto," Ana continued, "you should have offered it to Prince Ernest - they say he cannot satisfy his craving for the creature – did you know he has a grotto in the castle grounds where he worships them? Keep it to yourself, though. We're not supposed to know such things happen up there." Ana Brauer nodded in the direction of the Imperial castle.

Albrecht Durer slipped off his coat and sat back down on the bench.

"The hare is a noble creature." He smiled at Ana. "Did you know, Ana, that the Jill hare was the ancient's goddess Eaostre, a symbol of fertility and spring?"

"I would say they are full of evil, Herr Durer, though fine flavoured in a marinade of vinegar and stewed in a pot with onions, a sprig or two of rosemary and good handful of juniper berries. My customers are quite partial to a helping of rich hasenpfeffer - but here am I talking about hares when I should be away to fetch Kläuschen." And so Ana Brauer left Durer and Beck to their squabble and by the time her sister Klara served them with dinner there was harmony of sorts between the two men.

***

"Here we are my cherished regulars. I hope you have brought your appetites with you. Herr Pirkheimer not joining you today, gentlemen?" Klara relieved herself of the heavy platter and an extra dish she was holding, placing them down on the table. Crossing herself, she thrust the blade of her knife into a steaming-hot pork knuckle and dropped it onto the spare platter. "Maybe it was that body that's just been dug out of the shit heap or the appearance of those penitents – but someone's put my customers off their vittles, though not their thirsts. Here take these - save them going into the swill." She tipped out another three joints onto the dish.

Durer and Beck gawped at her then at each other.

"A body ... what? ... in a shit heap?" Durer asked.

"That's what I said. Body of a man, it's said, with his limbs cut off - and his head," Klara confirmed.

"Where?" Durer asked in horror.

"Here," she gestured with her thumb, "at the east corner."

"In Am Ölberg?" Beck asked.

"Yes, that's what I'm telling you; here in Am Ölberg - by the scavenger. A man is all I know. They say it's the work of those mystics. I said to Ana that no good would come of them being here. You heard their bearded leader threaten and condemn us in the Hauptmarkt. We're all witnesses to his charge that we're all sinners." She again crossed herself, leaned over and in a voice reduced to a whisper, added, "That Müller," she glanced over her shoulder towards the grain merchant, "always knows everything before it happens. Heard it from him. Wouldn't surprise me if he was in league with them." She straightened up and stepped back from the table. "His mother was the same, knew everything, or thought she did which might be why she ran away - the burden of guilt she carried got too much. Mind you, she wasn't always like that. Frau Müller was once a pretty young thing, always nicely turned out - neat with her mother's gold locket around her neck. I often admired it. The prettiest trinket and she was so proud to own such a precious object; we were all surprised her husband didn't sell it. Maybe he tried. Maybe that's why she left. Do you remember her, Herr Pirkheimer?" Klara asked.

Willy Pirkheimer looked down on the diminutive woman from his great height. He had missed the earlier conversation and before he could think how to respond Klara continued.

"Leaving her child to be brought up by that father of his – God rest his soul," she crossed herself again, "but good riddance. Turned the boy into a chip of the old block."

Klara's words were true. With his mother away the Müller child became a virtual appendage of his father. He had no siblings or rather none that survived and it was said that having lost so many babes the mother turned half-mad and her careless indifference towards her young son and disrespect for her husband meant that when she went away few were surprised and the lady was soon forgotten.

Chapter 8

"Willy! How are you my noble friend?" Otto Beck asked, squeezing up against Durer to make room for Willy Pirkheimer. "Have you heard what Klara's been saying?"

"What have I said? I was speaking about Frau Müller's necklace," Klara frowned.

"Not that, about the body, Klara," Beck said, "though telling everyone won't do your trade any good."

"I'll say what I like in my sister's inn, Otto Beck. But if there's one thing around here that puts our customers off it's our friend over there," she side nodded towards Müller. "He'll shoo my customers away quicker than any body in a midden. But pray tell me, Herr Durer, is it this that's troubling you or have you worries of your own for your face says you've lost a stiver?"

"He's had a shock, Klara," Beck began.

"Well drink up, Herr Durer, a belly full of beer will help you forget and today is a day for forgetting." With that she went off to attend to her other customers.

"Willy, have your heard about the murder?" Durer asked.

"I have, Albi, I have - but only the bare facts. It's being dealt with now, as I understand," Pirkheimer spoke softly.

Klara had scarcely left them when she was back at the table with yet more cooked hock swathed in thick soft fat and floating in gravy and a bowl of millet with peas. "They're well peppered, the way you like them, Herr Pirkheimer. I've barley bread just out of the oven, I'll bring some over."

Willy Pirkheimer smacked his thick lips, "Thank you, Klara."

Klara loitered; hands clenched into fists against her broad hips. Her face full of concern. "Those men back there swear the body had no head. No head, nor legs, nor arms and was all cut about and bloodied so. A short man - that could be several around here - but then Axel's hound, Ulf, was fussing about it and Axel is nowhere to be seen. They say the dog had to be dragged off the body. God rest his soul." She crossed herself.

"Surely not Axel!" Durer gasped, "Willy? Is this true?"

"I don't know, Albi. I heard the body was all but destroyed so it's hard to put a name to it," Pirkheimer replied.

"And you a Councillor - I would have thought you knew all about something as important as this," Beck said with a shake of his head.

"Ah well, gentlemen. I must get on and fetch that bread. Don't forget to eat up. I don't want to hear about three more corpses later today," Klara snorted, "but I hope poor Axel is alright."

Durer, Pirkheimer and Beck sat on in silent contemplation for a short interval. In truth the whole of Brauer's was more reserved than usual. Klara delivered the bread in a basket then rushed away again.

"A devilish business. Someone will pay for it." Willy Pirkheimer stared at the hock glistening and inviting and he breathed in its distinctive aroma.

Otto Beck coughed. "Willy, Albi's lost a picture," he announced, keen to lighten the mood. "And before you get going again, Albi, of course I believe you. There I've said it."

"Lost? How?" Pirkheimer asked.

When Durer gave no response Beck spoke for him.

"Stolen! He's had a picture stolen - just like Herr Wolgemut. Isn't that bad fortune?" Beck said in a singy-songy voice.

"Herr Wolgemut? What is this?" Willy Pirkheimer asked, picking at the hock.

Durer shrugged and remained silent so the Councillor looked to Beck for an explanation but Beck was preoccupied carving himself a piece of joint which he swallowed before answering.

"Herr Wolgemut claims he's had a painting stolen and that whoever's behind it is demanding he pays them for its safe return. And – and now the robbers have also taken a painting from Albi's workshop, or so he says."

Pirkheimer stopped chewing and stared open-mouthed at Durer before helping himself to a spoonful of millet. "If Albi says he's been robbed then robbed he's been, Otto. Why do you doubt him?" he asked, millet spraying out of his mouth.

The locksmith shrugged. "I don't doubt him. But, on the bright side, Albi always signs his pictures so unless the villains burn the thing they can't sell it off as someone else's."

Durer looked forlorn. "I usually sign my work, yes, but hadn't got round to doing that on this picture."

Beck pointed his dagger at Durer, "Which means if a painting of a rabbit or hare, if anyone can tell the difference, turns up it could be said to be yours or Herr Wolgemut's," Beck said.

"Herr Wolgemut's - why would it be his?" Durer berated Beck. "We're talking about my picture ... not his. There have been two pictures stolen," he insisted.

Otto Beck cleared his throat. "Willy, you are the brains among us. What do you say?"

Pirkheimer listened attentively to Beck's fuller account of the missing paintings but his troubled expression upset Durer.

"You believe me don't you my most faithful friend?" Durer implored Pirkheimer.

Willy Pirkheimer made a sucking sound through his teeth and clasped his giant hands behind his head. "Your predicament is not an easy one to swallow, Albi. I only say this because I am much fond of you - but it strikes me you have not been yourself lately ... are you worried over money? You asked me for a loan at the Hauptmarkt. Remember?"

Albrecht Durer blushed and he looked away. Beck coughed nervously. Pirkheimer picked up his krug and drained its contents. Across the inn the grain merchant was singing loudly, encouraging others to join in. Though initially reluctant a few indulged him with a rendering of *Josef liber neve min*. In their corner Durer, Beck and Pirkheimer sat on in uncomfortable silence until Beck could stand it no longer.

"Albi, Willy is right - you've not been your usual self since Agnes left ... drinking too much. And tell me have you been picking those mushrooms again? I know you're partial to them - to help fire up your imagination ... "

"Yes, I have," Durer admitted. "Anton made me a broth from the toadstools I gathered near Wolgemut's earlier but they've had no harmful effect on me and before you run away with the idea my stolen hare is a figment of my imagination let me say you are mistaken." Durer glowered at his companion and his words crackled like splintered ice.

"Oh my goodness," Pirkheimer exclaimed, on looking up. "Gentlemen."

A voice smooth as rancid butter trickling off a warm tongue paid its respects to the table. It belonged to Herr Wolgemut's lapdog, Schmeichler. Schmeichler's distinctive stooped figure was a familiar sight around Nuremberg but he usually kept himself to himself, rarely leaving Wolgemut's residence outside the town. A shiver rippled over Schmeichler's bowed frame as he declined an invitation from Durer to join them. Instead, he hovered awkwardly making it necessary for Beck and Pirkheimer to twist round to face him. Schmeichler was by no means a small man but neither was he tall. In build he was neither plump nor lean. He was one of those remarkable people who defied the usual signposts of ageing: his hair retained the colour of his youth - all that was observable to the eye for he kept it tucked under a faded, none-too-clean green and red striped linen skull cap worn over a bandage that protected an ear for the man was plagued with earache; a straggly beard, shot with grey followed the crevices of the servant's pale slack-skinned face before nestling under a protruding lower lip; not his best feature - although in the view of some it may not have been his worst. The severity of the cap laid bare Schmeichler's face with its clumsy mouth, bulbous ox eyes and pronounced Roman nose which ended in cavernous nostrils. In Durer's opinion it was a face which embodied ignorance and corruption. Schmeichler bent over so his mouth with its crooked teeth pressed against Durer's ear; the servant's words oily and his breath rancid.

"Frau Wolgemut's uncle, in his generosity, has provided the entire sum needed for the safe return of Herr Wolgemut's animal study which you have agreed to administer. It is now your responsibility to meet the guilty party and pay over this sum for the picture's safe return," he told Durer.

Durer nodded and Schmeichler slipped a hand between the folds of his cloak drawing forth a leather purse. Placing it down on the bench next to the artist he picked up his lantern and made for the door, hesitating only when Ana Brauer called out to him, "Herr Schmeichler won't you let me stiffen your wick before you set off?"

Durer, Pirkheimer and Beck watched him disappear into the night. Willy Pirkheimer blew out his breath. Albrecht Durer stared down at the purse entrusted into his care. Beck prodded him.

"Well! What do you make of that?" Beck asked, "let's see what's in there," and reached out for the purse.

Albrecht Durer swatted his hand away and slackened the purse strings.

Willy Pirkheimer adopted a thoughtful expression and adjusted his felted hat on his head. "Let's take a look at it then, Albi," he urged.

Durer pushed the hock platter aside and the three put their heads together to peer into the purse for it would be foolhardy to let it be known they were in possession of so much coin.

"Sink your teeth into one or two of them," Beck urged, "check they're real."

Durer picked out a paper-roll of coins. "They have a good weight," he said and peeled back the paper confirming the coins were genuine. To make quite certain he bit into one and nodded. He felt the other rolls then dropped them back into the purse.

Pirkheimer watched him, his eyebrows raised in scepticism. "So much money for the recovery of - of what sounds like a very ordinary picture. I can make neither head nor tail of this business. Why doesn't Herr Wolgemut just let the painting go? He wasn't commissioned to paint it by the sounds of things and so what difference does it make if it's lost? And why, Albi, has he involved you of all people? The two of you haven't spoken, as I understand, for several years. Now to top it all you have suffered a similar misfortune but at least I trust you're not tempted to pay out any money to recover your missing common field hare?"

"Albi doesn't like it called a common field hare, do you Albi?" Beck said.

Albrecht Durer grimaced. "It's not the subject that matters, for I'm very fond of this innocent creature and I have created a true likeness – it is a mastery of naturalism that is not matched anywhere else. I will not pay for its return, however, as I have not the means to do so."

"And you haven't been asked to pay, have you?" Beck asked.

"That is true, Otto, no-one has yet made contact with me but I'm sure that will happen in time," Durer replied.

Pirkheimer pulled off his hat to scratch his head. "It's all very odd. Albi, are you quite yourself my young friend? As for that wretch Schmeichler ..." Pirkheimer stopped talking on noticing Durer's thunder-black expression and his slender fingers reaching for the hilt of his dagger.

Durer plunged his knife into the hock. "You are both unworthy of my companionship. How is it you doubt my word when I have been nothing but a faithful friend to you both all my life?" he complained.

Beck and Pirkheimer shifted uneasily, avoiding meeting Durer's eye for fear of fuelling a fire that might engulf their friendship. Durer had the appearance of a man betrayed and instead of attacking Klara's flesh, peas and millet he prodded his food with the point of his dagger. As for Pirkheimer and Beck their appetites rarely let them down and they ate heartily. A further silence breached their discussion during which Durer realised how implausible the account of the stolen picture was, immediately following the theft of Wolgemut's. In any case he was in need of Beck's and Pirkheimer's assistance, for he had a plan to retrieve Wolgemut's picture which involved them and so with that in mind he affected reconciliation.

Immediately the discomfiture between the three fell away and their conversation took on its usual level of levity. Soon they were singing along with everyone else some of Nuremberg's most popular drinking songs led by a table of craftsmen from Am Ölberg, despite the day's grim event – the untimely and brutal death of Brauer stalwart, Axel Marx. The uneasy jollity all changed with the appearance of the three horsemen who turned up during the mystic's gathering on Michaelmas. Inn regulars speculated on what brought them to Nuremberg so late in the year when most foreigners had already left. And, they whispered to one another, was it not an odd coincidence that following their appearance in town poor Axel Marx was done to death?

Gradually interest in them abated. Albrecht Durer treated Pirkheimer and Beck to a wan smile before sinking his teeth into what remained of the ham. He tore off a piece of barley bread, using it to mop up gravy which was congealing to the colour of old ox blood. But when he glanced back to the foreign trio Beck caught his look.

"Them?" Back asked. "Are they the fellows you've been talking about?"

Durer's quizzical expression forced Beck to explain himself. He nodded towards the horsemen, asking again if Durer suspected them of being the strangers hanging about his house. Durer shook his head before getting to his feet and disappearing out the back door to relieve himself.

"Phew! Glad of that," Beck said, relieved. He drank a mouthful of beer then continued, "The tall, dark one," he indicated with his thumb, "is Collado - a fearless Spanish gentleman and great hero in his own country. All of them are men of substance with no need for thieving. It's my desire to interest them in ... well ... in something ..." he added, coyly.

"What's this Otto? You're inventing again. Out with it," Pirkheimer demanded.

Otto Beck grinned sheepishly. "'Tis an improvement on the firing mechanism of a gun ... maybe I should be getting along I'd quite like to ..." His words ran out of explanation.

"Improvement - what sort of improvement," Pirkheimer asked, helping himself to a scrap of flesh then running his fingers along his dagger to clean it.

"Oh, just some alterations." Then, changing the subject, he told Pirkheimer he had reassured the Spaniard of their safe passage to these parts for the last time they were in Nuremberg two people were murdered. "Do you remember it, Willy? When our people were attacking foreigners, driving many out of the city and fearing for their lives."

"Everyone falls under suspicion when evil is abroad," Pirkheimer said, stretching his long legs.

Otto Beck grinned, uneasily. He never thought of himself and his fellow-Nurembergers in the same way he did strangers with no roots in the city even though he sought their custom. Collado the Spaniard's eyes met Otto Beck's and he raised his krug to him.

"What do you make of Albi's story, Willy?" Beck asked under his breath. "This yarn of losing a painting hot on the heels of old Wolgemut's - doesn't it strike you as a strange happpenstance?"

Pirkheimer pulled a face. "I don't doubt Albi's word, Otto, but I fear he is missing his wife a little too much and swear the reason he's taken to wearing the vixen about his neck is because it reminds him of her. It may be his sweet Agnes has sold the picture and kept the money for herself for I think she is capable of such. And as you know, my short friend, I have little time for that wench - but here he comes, say nothing more of your doubts, I implore you, Otto." He steered the conversation onto other matters, extolling the excellence of Klara's well-spiced hock and buttered millet and engaging with Durer on Konrad Celtis's discourse on ancient paganism. Aside from his interest in hock and millet Otto Beck had little to contribute to the conversation and so his mind drifted away to matters concerning his craft and some practical difficulties he had in satisfying the Spanish man-at-arms.

Collado, who stood a good head and shoulders above most of Nuremberg's stocky little inhabitants, was of a dark complexion with lank inky-black hair worn just below his ears. Most striking about his appearance were his eyes; unfathomable and asphaltum, that never appeared to miss a trick. He was quick to laugh and equally quick of temper that expressed itself in the delight he took baiting Ana Brauer's customers over the merits of their respective lands. Collado being no stranger to Franconia and its ways understood the welcome that accompanied an open purse, even when that purse belonged to a foreigner. He was not so feeble a man as to allow trivial prejudices to thwart him dealing with the city's excellent craftsmen and in any case his own intimidating presence plus that of his two companions - both men near as talented with blade and firing weapons as he, lent him greater assurance of safe passage.

Otto Beck's workshop was the reason Collado made the long journey from his home in Andalusia to Franconia; an arrangement Beck hoped would continue. The locksmith knew that if he ever failed to satisfy him his Spanish patron would go elsewhere to purchase his weapons and in such uncertain times when death plucked the little folk of Nuremberg like so many feathers off an old hen, foreigners were inclined to scurry away at the first sign of bother. When Collado failed to appear in Nuremberg, as expected, that spring Beck worried he had abandoned him so wrote to the Spaniard (in truth his Maria did the writing for Beck was not handy with a quill) informing Collado of the great progress he was making with his hand gun's reliability. The letter had the desired impact as Collado's late arrival in the city confirmed. His eagerness to get his hands on the most efficient weapons available persuaded him to undertake the long and difficult journey from Lebrija in far-away Andalusia to Nuremberg despite days becoming short and the weather unpredictable.

Nuremberg's reputation for the accuracy of its weaponry was unrivalled and a consequence of an abundance of copper and tin on its doorstep, together with the town's accomplished artisans. Excellence was the quality Collado demanded as a master in the art of war. It was critical he out-armed his opponents for he was a devout man who recognised combat an essential means to eradicate evil and instil God's truth into laggard minds. The strands of his convictions, therefore, threaded pastures, crossed mountain ranges and strung the lengths of riverbanks from the plains of Andalusia to the uplands of Franconia and its civic nugget - the fair city of Nuremberg, for the suppression of heresy and to seal deals for the purchase of reliable arms.

Yes, there was no doubt Collado believed his was a worthy cause and as a zealous upholder of the faith he was proud to shoulder responsibility for exposing and eradicating heretics wherever he encountered them. He valued no role more important than that of soldiering for the Lord and to that end was ever mindful of looking out for evil wherever it lurked and his ears were ever open to whispering which exposed God's enemies. It is worth saying that the zeal with which Collado pursued his mission while lauded by some was regarded as cruel and oppressive by others.

And so Collado was again in Nuremberg for the single purpose of buying Otto Beck's newly adapted hand guns such was the esteem he had for that city and its phlegmatic citizens; patient to a fault in the pursuit of perfection. Had Collado an eye for fine art he might, too, have recognised equal precision was to be found in Albrecht Durer's workshop where every leaf and blade of grass, each fine hair or filament of feather was keenly observed and replicated in all their intricacies and second only in perfection to the hand of God.

***

"Well, Albi this is an ill-fated state of affairs - strangers taking advantage of our hospitality," Beck said, picking up on their earlier conversation.

"Now you believe me?" Durer asked.

"Yes, of course, Albi. I was merely toying with you."

Heartened by Beck's support Durer voiced his own prejudices. "Italian, I suspect - they will cheat man and beast.

Some of them are the biggest tricksters, liars and scoundrels that ever walked this earth." Squinting at his reflection, faint and distorted on the lid of his krug he continued, "When I come face to face with the thieves, I'll demand they return my own poor hare to me, also."

Willy Pirkheimer tutted. "I was seven years living in Italy, my dear Albi, and I cannot agree with your sweeping portrayal of the whole Italian people as being shady but then I have not had your unfortunate experience."

"It isn't right for strangers to swan in, steal our property and, generally, take advantage of our generous nature," Beck leaned over and picking up twigs from the hearth tossed them into the fire. "Now then, I must be off."

"Our property?" Durer asked.

Beck looked at him. "Yes, we Franconians must stick together. When one of us is injured, we all are."

A dish of ham; piping hot, pungent floating in a small lake of rich dark gravy landed on the table with a clatter. Klara nudged it towards Durer.

"Stop it going to waste. For all of you, Otto," Klara called back.

Beck hesitated and looked down at the ham. Pulling his dagger back out from under his belt he wiped its blade along the leg of his hose then sliced himself a hefty wedge, dipping it into the sauce. His two companions watched him devour helping upon helping; his gaping mouth steaming like chimney smoke for the ham was long boiling in the pot.

"I thought you were leaving us," Pirkheimer goaded him.

"Nothing would stop me finishing off this ham," Beck hissed through his teeth. "Phew! This is hot. Come on, Albi, dig in."

Pirkheimer stroked his chin. "Nothing puts you off your meat, Otto."

Beck prodded Pirkheimer's swollen belly with the end of his dagger.

"I haven't noticed you go hungry, Willy." He pulled out a plug of gristle from between his teeth, brandishing it in Durer's face. "My anger at the villains who've divested my friend of his painting has whetted my appetite."

"Divested?" Durer asked, pulling a face.

"You'll be reporting it?" Beck pushed the gristle back into his mouth.

"I did think I might," Durer replied.

The fire hissed and a shower of red-hot sparks scattered around Beck's feet. He ground them out with the sole of his shoe. "Look, I've been thinking," he said, still chewing, "I see it as my duty to you, Albi, to get Herr Wolgemut's picture back to him - and yours too, hopefully, and deal with the villains responsible for stealing them." He spat what was left of the gristle into the fire.

"I will report the theft to the Council," Durer said.

Willy Pirkheimer opened his mouth but before he could speak, Beck piped up.

"Let's face it, Albi, you've no intention of taking it to the Council so why say it? Eat up." Beck wiped his mouth with the back of his hand.

Durer studied what remained of the ham - the few shards of flesh that escaped Beck's dagger and he swallowed a mouthful of beer.

Beck picked up the bone and began nibbling it. "Maybe we don't need to drag the Council into this matter." Beck leaned forward so that his nose was a hen's egg distance from Durer's ear. "You won't sort this mess out by yourself, Albi, but I'm here to give you a hand," his words sticky, hot and sweet.

Chapter 9

Earlier that day

A deputation made up of magistrates, members of the city guard and the Löchwirt's head gaoler, Jodocus Franke, dispatched to investigate who was responsible for murdering and stuffing a body into a midden were to a man mystified by the incident of the truncated corpse. Their duties were made more difficult by Axel Marx's dog, Ulf, who followed them to the midden and would not be shooed away but repeatedly attempted to get at the corpse; barking crazily till he was dragged off and secured to a tree so the remains could be dealt with.

Two surgeons summoned to study the burnt body argued over the evidence and left as bewildered as every other man for not only was the little corpse headless but all four limbs were absent also and the trunk so hacked, slashed and blackened by fire it represented little more than a burnt offering of meat. A bad-tempered Jodocus Franke went away, complaining he had too much to do without wasting his time on an over-fired hog-roast, which drew murmurings of disapproval and reproach from those around him.

"Axel Marx did not deserve to be insulted so disparagingly in death," complained one Councillor.

His protest met with support from locals attracted by the gory spectacle - all of them acquaintances of Marx who were disgusted that his corpse was compared to that of a common boar. Someone mentioned sorcery; if men could be changed into beasts then it was possible to change pigs into men but he was ordered to shut up by Herman Kalb, leader of the city's militia, who growled that he would not tolerate such talk for he had known Axel Marx all his life.

When the body was pulled from the dung heap over fifty rats scampered out and were duly chased by club-wielding spectators who bludgeoned them, kicked them to death or threw them to a pack of hounds, attracted to the smell of roasted meat, who shook the life out of them.

Murder is always an act of devilment but the disfigurement of the corpse in the midden was deemed particularly repugnant and there was a clamour for retribution for poor Axel. The words of the pilgrim leader, Thomas Hut, aimed it was believed at Axel were fresh in their minds for his condemnation of gluttons who everyone knew were punished by being fed to rats.

As the truncated corpse was being tied to a plank so that it might be carried away for burial, the hound, Ulf, whined and barked pitifully, straining hard on the tether that secured him to a tree. Uncertainty over the victim's identity fell away in the absence of Marx and Ulf's frenetic behaviour, for surely everything pointed to it being poor little Axel Marx. While it was acknowledged that Marx enjoyed a hearty appetite it was questioned if that could be regarded as gluttony. And even if it were surely being slaughtered and buried in excrement was excessive punishment?

"Let the creature be with him one last time," Kalb urged.

The moment Ulf was untied he bounded straight away to the corpse, licking and nibbling at it so determinedly that even the sternest-hearted there was touched by his fondness for his master.

The assembled Councillors put their heads together. They feared that if word of such an appalling act spread across Franconia the city's status would be harmed and so agreed to waste no time in capturing Axel's killer to limit any lingering reputational damage to Nuremberg – and to satisfy their duty as Christians in countering evil. A priest enjoying a meal of bread and smoked duck was dragged, somewhat unwillingly, out to the horrifying scene and in no time the murdered soul was laid to rest.

Of course, no amount of speedy action could stop common gossip: Axel had been seen taking the path to the Palace, it was said; Axel had been spotted entering the Laurenzius Forst near the mystic camp; Axel was seen talking to strangers on horseback riding out from the city.

Perhaps all the tales were true - perhaps none. What surely could not be denied was that Axel Marx had been no match for any average-sized man intent on attacking the little tailor.

Chapter 10

Albrecht Durer stumbled when his toe found a loose stone on the path to his workshop and he fell dropping his lantern which crashed to the ground extinguishing its flame and plunging him into total darkness. He groaned, chiding himself for having drunk too much at Brauer's and wondered if Otto was not right that Anton's dish of Krötenstuhlsuppe might have unsettled his mind, as was often the result of consuming certain toadstools.

He discovered the workshop door was locked which was unusual but then he remembered having scolded Günter for not locking it and groaned again. Sinking to his knees he groped around the yard till he located a key concealed beneath a stone. The key was cumbersome and cold and awkward in his fingers as he struggled to insert it into the lock. It slipped from his grasp.

Retrieving it once again Durer found his legs were not up to standing so was obliged to crouch and from this position he worked the key into the lock at last. Pulling himself upright he was resting all his weight on the handpull when the door suddenly swung open, propelling him forward with such force he landed face down on the floor of his workshop. Sprawled on all fours Albrecht Durer found contentment and was in no hurry to test his legs again so closed his eyes and drifted off to sleep.

A cushion of rose-scented air held him aloft; gently buffeting him hither and thither. Someone giggled and he thought it might be himself but then he doubted it was. He heard music and a head appeared; partly concealed beneath a grey hood. A long curling tapered finger summoned him as heavenly voices sang, *Albrecht welcome home;* their inflection suggested a Romance language rather than his own guttural Franconian dialect. Durer fancied he recognised some Venetian in the articulation.

A second figure materialised in a turban of exquisite brocade, his features obliterated by a single beam of light. The shorter of the two figures Durer took to be Axel Marx but of that he could not be certain. Durer stretched out his arm to touch the pretty brocade but the head vanished and he felt himself glide into the air higher and higher, rocking from side to side with increasing urgency. He seemed to roll over and over and far below he spied a field where sat a hare, ears alert, or so it appeared though he could not be certain it was a hare, for it might have been a painting that passed before him; a painting of a field hare. He screwed up his eyes to make sense of it but the image dissolved into perpetual gloom from which voices trilled, a high-pitched, lute-like chorus.

Where is the thief, Albrecht Durer? … When will he be exposed? … The great and respected Herr Wolgemut is much troubled by Durer's scheming … He is being persecuted by the rascal Durer

These words were emblazoned across a frieze held by coiling lute strings that entangled his arms and his legs and pegged him to a dense ashen cloud. The singing drifted away and just when it seemed the pitching and tossing would ease Albrecht Durer was sent hurtling into the inky void where another banner flew past emblazoned with the message *Durer dēceptiō*. The lute strings tugged at him, they screeched and scraped and they wound around the floating banner till stretched so thinly they ripped it asunder with such a din Durer was forced to shield his ears.

A rich baritone voice grew louder till it, too, shuddered and cracked and out of the dark Durer stirred, blinded by a radiant glow lighting a mouthful of familiar-looking teeth. A grinning Otto Beck leaned over the bewildered Durer.

"Look who I've found," he shouted as he put down his lantern.

Willy Pirkheimer's familiar square head bobbed into view.

"What have we here, Albi?" Beck chuckled, toeing a scattering of blackened toadstools, "little wonder your legs have given up on you. Here, let me help you to your feet. What is this?"

Albrecht Durer rubbed at his eyes and tried to focus on what Beck held in his hand.

"Give it to me," Durer demanded. "My father's rabbit foot for smoothing and polishing his gold and silver works." He stuck out a hand to take the truncated limb from Beck.

"My father had one of those, too, only it was cleaner," Beck said drily, placing the foot on a windowsill.

"It's old," Durer retorted, groggily.

"So am I but I'm not dirty," Beck said, "not very."

"So why are you here?" Durer rubbed again at his eyes.

"Why are we here? You hear that, Willy?" Beck asked.

Pirkheimer waved his arms about in a dismissive gesture.

"It occurred to me," Beck continued, "that you might need us with you when you go to fetch old man Wolgemut's picture. You'll be remembering about the picture, sorry pictures, no doubt, Albi?"

Albrecht Durer sat up dusting down his clothes.

"And you might want this." Beck passed Durer's discarded lantern to him.

Durer scrambled to his feet, albeit unsteadily, looking around, desperately. "I've lost it! What am I to do? I've lost it!" he wailed.

"Oh, I wouldn't worry. I'm sure it'll turn up. Most things do in the end," Beck said.

"But I've lost it," Durer gasped, tugging at his hair.

"I put it on the windowsill," Beck nodded in that direction.

"Not the rabbit foot!" Durer screamed, "the bag Schmeichler left with me – containing Wolgemut's gold!"

"You mean Frau Wolgemut's uncle's gold," Beck tutted.

"Help me look for it!" Durer pushed past Beck and out into the dark yard kicking at a straw heap and scattering it.

"Well this is indeed a fine mess, Albi. Willy, what do you say?" Beck winked at Willy Pirkheimer.

Pirkheimer who had been a mere observer pacing up and down took Durer by the elbow and led him back indoors.

"Since Otto was pretty well drunk and incapable, I thought it would be best if I took possession of this - to ensure its safe delivery," Pirkheimer explained with studied casualness.

Albrecht Durer stared at a purse in Pirkheimer's great paw. He turned to Beck. "Why did you let me leave without it?"

"My fault ... of course - it's Otto's fault. Albi, I know I'm your friend but I didn't think that involved being responsible for your memory, or lack of one. Never mind a word of thanks to Willy and me. We'll take that as being intended by your insolence."

Durer threw up his arms above his head then clapped his chest. "Willy - Otto - I am indebted to you both." He bowed then reached out and tenderly touched each man.

"That was surely why they were here when I returned ... to take the purse and its contents. It was lucky I forgot it."

"Who returned?" Pirkheimer asked.

"Yes, who returned?" echoed Beck.

Durer looked at them both. Had he been dreaming? Had someone been in the house waiting for him - waiting to get their hands on the purse of gold coins? He would say nothing else to Otto and Willy for they would no more believe him now than they had at Brauer's.

"It's nothing," Durer dismissed the conversation.

Beck picked his teeth with his thumb nail. "I was saying to Willy on the way here you can't trust anyone nowadays. Don't know what the world is coming to, Albi." Having succeeded in extracting a thread of ham from between his teeth he licked it off his nail. "You only have to keep it safe until tomorrow night. Think you can manage that, Albi?"

Chapter 11

Nuremberg's festival of hunting, Schutzenfest, fell on the first day of October when shrieking hunting horns and bugles both day and night guaranteed little peace for anyone or any creature.

There was always great anticipation over who would be crowned the year's Schutzenkonig, King of Marksmen, from the foresters, tinsmiths, bakers, brewers and men from every other craft competing for the honour of parading before hundreds of his cheering *subjects*. For those not so adept at hitting a target there were other diversions best enjoyed in their most colourful attire and there was much dancing and singing around streets specially decorated with garlands of foliage for the occasion.

Schutzenfest was a favourite with Nurembergers for it was held late in the year when few foreigners remained in the town, making it a very local celebration. Each year found it grow more and more raucous with entertainment from exotically-dressed performers and minstrels flitting from square to square plucking the strings of their instruments or blowing pretty melodies through flutes and enticing the city's children to follow them in procession. Yes, Schutzenfest was an opportunity for much jubilation, loud trumpeting, drumming and, of course, over-eating and drinking.

Albrecht Durer stood at his open window breathing in the cool morning air sweetened with the aroma of bread freshly baked. The city's bakers had forsaken their sleep to prepare special loaves and small rolls studded with poppy seeds and walnuts which were always popular with revellers. Such Schutzenfest creations were weeks in the planning: apple cakes; almond bread pudding with plum puree; date and raisin tarts; elderflower custards; lebkuchen baked in every shape and size; cherry pastries; honeyed breads topped with egg and cream snow; sweetened-preserved orange peel; marzipan dainties. Well before daylight stallholders and traders were dressing trestle tables at street corners from Am Ölberg to Lorenzkirche.

This Schutzenfest, however, found Albrecht Durer a trifle out-of-sorts. His sleep had been disturbed by outlandish dreams so he woke, disturbed and exhausted at the tolling of the prime bell. Remembering it was Schutzenfest he proposed to doze on for there was no urgency for him to rise but despite the comfort and warmth of his feather bed he could not calm his agitation. What if he failed to recover Herr Wolgemut's picture? His torment was interrupted by the sound of voices drifting up to his chamber from below. Günter, he decided, was adding to his tribulations and wearily he threw back the covers and stepped into his clothes.

Holy days and festivals usually found the boy up early and out on some mischief with Joachim but lately Günter had become withdrawn, reluctant to leave the house, preferring to loiter in his room under the eaves or skulking about the workshop.

Durer picked up the hunting jacket he had looked out the previous evening then put it down again. He had little enthusiasm for riding out to the Knoblauchsland with Beck and Pirkheimer to watch the archery contest; indeed, he had no interest at all in who might be crowned this year's Schutzenkonig. His indifference did not stretch to his appearance, however, and he studied his reflection in the looking glass before leaving his chamber. His foot no sooner touched the stair landing than he realised one of the voices belonged to a woman.

Günter ran into Durer as he descended the staircase. "Els says she might sit for me," he burst out excitedly, wiping his nose on his sleeve.

There, looking up at them was the girl from the market, and prettier than Durer remembered.

"Els! This is a pleasant surprise!" Durer began, his weariness forgotten.

The girl smiled up at him. "I'm sure we arranged I would come here on Schutzenfest. My grandmother has already gone off with her friends. They all love to watch the archers battle it out … it gets quite thrilling, according to her, although I've never seen it for myself."

Durer laughed. "And you don't want to go with them to find out how nail-biting the match really is?"

"No. Though I love her very much I see quite enough of my grandmother. She's lovely and kind but I don't want to be with her all the time. So, I'm all yours for today, if you still want me. I am nervous, I admit for I've never posed for a picture before but I'm looking forward to it." Her eyes sparkled, then as if tempering her enthusiasm she covered her mouth with her hand.

Durer, by now downstairs, stood in front of her, smiling. "Has your grandmother decided I'm not about to corrupt you?" he teased. Then taking her hand in his he led her along a short dark lobby and into his workshop. "Günter if you're not going out you might help arrange my bits and pieces so I can get started."

Günter, who had been following on behind realised he would not be drawing Els and pulled a face. "I was going to watch the archers," he muttered defiantly.

Durer ignored him so taken up with Els was he. "I've long been planning an oil panel of the parable of Adam and Eve in the Garden of Eden and if I get a picture that pleases me I'll make print copies from it. Just think, Els, if fortune smiles upon us you will become celebrated by people across this land."

Els gasped. The room was wide and airy, its interior bleached with the bright sunlight streaming in through large windows. Her eyes darted in all directions for the chamber was filled with every manner of strange and unusual things. There were lengths of freshly sawn timber, neatly piled; a discarded wood saw; large and small stoppered flasks; rolls of coloured papers; uneven pieces of vellum; wooden easels; jars and bowls containing the colours of the rainbow; a pot of twigs next to what Els thought might be a dried curd which crumbled when she dug her fingernail into it; between two windows was a shelf containing a row of sharp-looking knives, arranged by length. Wherever she looked Els was confronted with unfamiliar or unusual items littering every surface: every bench, every window ledge, every shelf and hanging from hooks affixed to walls. And brushes - more than she could count - light bristled and dark and cut into neat points or straight edged.

Tentatively the young woman pressed a finger against a tiny blade projecting from a willow handle and flinched at the keenness of its edge against her soft skin. There were wire implements made out of coloured metals and a buffalo horn, Durer explained before excusing himself to fetch something. Els ran her finger across the horn, smooth to her touch. She squinted at a plaited hat which Günter laughingly told her was woven from the bark of an alder tree and she admired a shining polished green stone carved into the likeness of a dog. Els prodded a tiny cap-like object with regular scratch marks cut into it - her fingers tracing the lines and feeling its hardness. She cupped her hand over it delighted by its silky feel.

Günter watched her as he set a fire in the hearth. "It's the shell of an animal," he explained, piling logs into a pyramid.

Els's eyes grew large and she snatched her hand away.

"A tortoise," Günter added, laughing. 'They live to be very old. Master was given it when he was in Italy."

Tentatively, Els turned over the shell, glancing towards Günter.

"That's all that remains of the creature. The rest was probably eaten by some fat Italian painter," Günter remarked, flicking ash off his sleeve and sneezing.

Els pressed the cool shell against her face.

"And this is what they call coral. It's very rare." Günter came alongside Els, offering her a piece of bleached rock, "it's an animal too, I believe."

By the time the fire had taken Günter was describing something of the process of engraving to Els and that one day she might be in an image pinned to a wall in a stranger's house. He chatted away non-stop while sorting tools – pointed metal styluses, long twigs of charcoal and a whetstone which he carefully arranged on a bench heavily scored with cuts and stained by ink and pigment.

Durer came back into the room carrying squares of grey and pale nettle-coloured primed rag paper he had cut for the cartoon. He instructed Günter to drag an easel in front of one of the tall windows and clear away stools that lay abandoned around the studio.

"Günter, fetch a pitcher of beer and some bread and cheese for I've not breakfasted and am quite famished."

Durer led Els to a cleared area of the workshop where he spent a little time putting her into one position then another before apparently finding a pose that pleased him. It was not long, however, before he pulled a face and began creating little angular windows with his hands and peering through them with narrowed eyes. Els noticed how he bit on his lip when concentrating. Durer inhaled – a long, deep breath then worked his shoulders up and down to help himself relax. He repeated this performance until his face softened in contentment.

Günter returned carrying a tray of food and drink which he placed on a bench before setting up an easel for his master.

Durer clapped a hand on the boy's shoulder. "Günter I must have a branch that will do for the tree. Not any branch," he insisted, "it must be a fine specimen of mountain ash with all its leaves or a few at least."

Günter threw his master a quizzical look.

"For the Tree of Knowledge and Good and Evil," Durer's tone was sharp for he was keen to make progress now that he was about to embark on the picture.

Günter dropped an easel peg which clattered across the floor. Durer paid it no attention but wolfed down a wedge of cheese while his apprentice retrieved the peg and replaced it in its hole before reaching for the door. Through a mouthful of food Durer warned him not to get shot by any of the hunters plying their crossbows.

"You don't have to hurry back, after all it's a holiday but don't take all day," Durer told him.

Els was happy but tense. With Günter out of the way Durer found the simplest way to settle the young woman's nerves was with a kiss or two and some pretty words and soon the two were at ease with each other.

Helping himself to more bread, cheese and beer Durer considered the young woman standing before him and once satisfied he ran a hand over a greyish sheet of paper fixed to his ash leaning-board and with a shard of charcoal roughly established positions for each main element of the picture. Pausing to assess his initial outlines, he nibbled again on his lip then discarded his first effort and replaced the paper with another. So the process began all over again.

Eventually and with an almost imperceptible nod of his head, Durer indicated his satisfaction with the latest version; that it might well work up into an etching suitable for pressing. Amidst the quiet industry in the room the fate of the *Field Hare* was all but forgotten and when Durer's concentration did waver, it was his forthcoming Council commission for the Charlemagne and Sigismund panels that preoccupied him, for he was aware he should be preparing them and not his *Adam and Eve* composition. As Agnes would doubtless remind him on her return he had to get his priorities right - *money in the hand*, she was fond of telling him, must determine his working schedule. But Agnes was not at home and an emboldened Durer pressed on with his study of *Adam and Eve*; his hand diligently marking and smudging till not one corner of the sheet escaped its attention. When once more he found himself pondering the civic commission, it was from annoyance that so much of his time would be spent for so small a reimbursement. Had it not been for Willy Pirkheimer's coaxing he might never have put his name forward for consideration for the work but Willy was persuasive, and his dearest companion, aside from Agnes, and he would never set out to vex him. The painter needed no reminder that he was blessed at having the friendship of such a great man for there was no stauncher ally in the whole of Nuremberg. That truth aside it did not alter his abhorrence of public commissions for their encouragement of *grovellers* and *hangers-on;* cravers after civic patronage.

Albrecht Durer wished only to be able to create according to his inclination, uncompromised by the whims of patrons and their prescribed terms that curtailed his liberty as an artist. All that preparation; laying and scraping the ground, not to mention the half stiver it cost for each porpoise bristle brush and another two stivers to the boy to grind down pigments - extortionate sums – as much as twelve florins for a single ounce of ultramarine - he shook his head in disgust; the drain on his time and the paltry payment for works that would be seen by a mere handful of people - albeit a handful of important people - confirmed his prejudice against commissions still further. An etching, he considered, carefully drawn and copied several times over was, by comparison, a valuable source of income. The Eden picture at a florin a sheet could make him four hundred florins in a single year compared with the measly sixty ducats for the Council's commission and since his trade must support his whole household he could scarcely be criticised for favouring one over the other. And then his *Field Hare* slipped back into his mind; for many a mere low animal of the plains and an unworthy subject for a picture when there were holy parables to illustrate. And while Durer venerated the Virgin Mary most highly he could appreciate beauty in brute nature as well. The painter of Nuremberg would not conceal his admiration for this handsome creature, if not its reputation. It was a marvel to him that hares were born with their eyes open, like the greatest painters. He laid down his charcoal stick and after rubbing its dust from his fingers he assisted Els off with her cloak.

"Not too cold now, I hope?" he enquired kindly while pulling apart a crust of bread.

Els shook her head but nonetheless ran her hands up and down her arms for the spacious room was distinctly chilly.

"Sit here for a bit." Durer cleared aside books taking up room on a wooden settle. Els picked one of them up, staring at its cover board. She opened it.

"The writing is Latin," volunteered Durer, "it's Nicholas de Cusa's exploration of the coincidence of opposites."

Els stared at its title page, *De Docta Ignorantia* then turned over several of the book's thick pages. "I wish I could read books like this; full of clever men's ideas," she sighed. "I can read a little and I can understand pictures," she added quickly, "my grandmother lets one of her customers pay for spices by teaching me reading."

Durer looked at her, concern clouding his features. "Who is it that tutors you?"

Els laughed. "A kind lady who was taught by her own father - she bakes me apple cakes and we eat them while I practise my words. It's very nice."

She caught Durer's eye and began giggling. Durer popped the last of the cheese into his mouth and washed it down with a mouthful of beer. The grandmother, he was certain, was too fly to allow her granddaughter to fall into *that man's* evil trap. In any event the girl was strong-willed like his Agnes - though without Agnes's good fortune to have been born into relative affluence. Still, the child had survived the pest which claimed her parents and she was entering adulthood armed with a healthy curiosity about the world and determination to learn what she could.

Anton shuffled into the apartment as if he had been loitering behind the door waiting for Durer to finish his food. Without uttering a word he gathered up the remnants of breakfast. Not once did he look in Els' direction. Or, at least not perceptibly so. Els, however, appeared to shrink in his presence, her eyes fixed firmly to the floor.

With Anton gone and the chamber now a little warmer, Durer coaxed the book from Els's hands and the girl out of her remaining clothes and back into her pose. Recognising her embarrassment, he smiled to reassure Els before canting her head a little to one side to give the impression of Eve in conversation with Adam who would eventually stand left of the tree on her left, as convention demanded.

Els noted that when Durer referred to her role he called her Eva not Els. Everything was confusing for her in this strange world of painting. The musk-scented oil she had applied to her long fair locks that morning mingled with the harsh odours of linseed and gum Arabic, which she found unpleasant. Els tried to think of herself as Eva occupying a corner of Eden – mainly to overcome her embarrassment at being naked. As a distraction she went over the story of Paradise and Eve in her head; at how eating the forbidden fruit unleashed God's wrath resulting in hers and Adam's banishment from Paradise. She reasoned that since nakedness only became shameful after the forbidden apple was eaten and Herr Durer's picture represented the moment before biting into the apple her unclothed state was no cause for shame.

Els watched Durer like a hawk. For long spells he stood motionless except for his long finely boned fingers constantly labouring and his eyes flitting from paper to her and back again. Occasionally Durer crossed the room to adjust her pose –the direction of a foot, her head. Then his retreat. He would reflect on the change, advance once more and make another alteration, retreat, screw up his eyes, give a shake of the head, step up, lower an arm, narrow his eyes, snort, lean forward, touch her shoulder, bite his lip. This rigmarole was repeated until, finally, Durer appeared content and from behind his drawing-board an arm then another extended and his hands formed more rectangles through which he observed her ... not Els but Eva. Ideal beauty.

***

Red rags fluttering from the boughs of trees, bushes and stakes identified Nuremberg's hunting grounds; where prey were funnelled to make the hunter's task of increasing their tally of kills so much easier. Branches were painted with tar and lime so that birds alighting on them were trapped, unable to fly off.

The excitement of Schutzenfest was no less this year with the air rent by non-stop blasts from hunting horns – it seemed every man and boy carried one and blew it while pursuing every class of creature from both land and sky. In every district of the city - above the town by the Kaiserburg and across the garlic lands, sportsmen and spectators revelled in the thrill of the chase. Contenders for becoming King of Marksmen were both confident and nervous as they competed across a number of disciplines – combining their scores from fixed targets and game shooting; greater value being placed on the diversity of animals and birds felled.

A very few participants were armed with firing guns to shoot their prey, for not so many townsmen were as practised with these weapons as with bows and arrows. Being something of a novelty, gunmen proved popular with spectators – among them, Otto Beck who had manufactured several of the hand guns in play and being tested by his friends, for accuracy mainly, before being refined to make them suitable for sale to military gentlemen such as the Spaniard Collado. Beck's hand guns had their detractors; traditionalists who preferred Schutzenfest remain true to its origins and others who complained Beck's weapons were too pricey – much more so than crossbows and slingshots so not for the common peasant. Still others were able to imagine a time when a hunter might prefer a handgun if it could provide greater accuracy at a distance than an arrow so affording man yet more advantage over quarry.

Aside from the competition for King of Marksmen entertainment was the order of the day with cock and dog fights most popular among Nuremberg's menfolk who were prepared to risk a stiver on their animals. Street gambling always attracted sizable numbers of men and youths but being illegal required lookouts at every close and corner for Hans the hangman was on the prowl, and anyone caught was liable to find themselves in the care of the Löwe in the city gaol. Little pleased Hans more than getting his hands on an illicit gambler unless it was a good hanging for he was a pious man determined to clear his home city of its wrong-doers. But gamers were their own worst enemies for wherever they gathered, whether to roll dice or speculate on a fight to the death, they always made lots of noise and so were easy targets.

Pieter, a fisherman, abandoning the river Pegnitz for the day had taken the road to Green Wood close to the Kaiserburg. He was accompanied by his twin sons and they were out for a spot of dog baiting.

"Isn't that Axel's hound, Ulf?" Pieter asked. "Better be off Ulf, if you value your neck." He kicked out at the little dog to frighten it with no intention of hurting the nervous animal.

"Can we keep him?" one of his boys asked, "he's a fine little fellow."

"We've no need of a further mouth to feed and that one never stops eating … be off hound," roared the fisherman. He turned on hearing Klara and waved a greeting at her approach, hand-in-hand with little Kläuschen.

"Go Ulf," Pieter's sons echoed and together with Kläuschen they clapped their hands until the little dog took to his heels and vanished from sight.

***

Once he had screened Els's face from a dart of sunlight which made her squint, Albrecht Durer continued with his essay; his fingers rhythmically forming shapes with a sliver of charcoal on the ashen paper. "This way," Durer prodded Els's left knee with a finger until she relaxed and her weight was thrown onto her other leg, giving her the appearance of stepping forward. With a shake of his long mane of hair which had a tendency to fall over his eyes, Durer then tapped Els's left arm. "I'm not happy," he made a sucking sound, "Els, try it this way," demonstrating with his own arm.

Els copied him, holding her arm slightly proud of her body and her hand cupped as if she were about to pluck an apple from a tree. Durer retreated to the farthest corner of the room and considered her position then returned to his easel and attacked the composition again. The workshop once more grew silent, save only for the faint rasp of charcoal on paper.

After a time in this tranquil setting Els found herself day-dreaming about thousands of pairs of eyes that one day would associate her with Eve, the first woman. She liked that.

Harmony and tranquillity are seldom permanent states and in Albrecht Durer's Eden peace was rent asunder by the squeal of hunting horns. Durer fussed and grew impatient with the racket but for Els the distraction was welcome, for she was growing bored of standing stiffly in the cold room and longed to be outside, clothed, and sharing in the merriment of Schutzenfest. She attempted to attract Durer's attention in the hope of him realising how she felt with some unsubtle clearing of her throat. When this failed to work, she hummed a tune. Durer looked in her direction and their eyes met but instead of inquiring if there was anything amiss, he merely tapped the end of a stylus against his easel to quieten her. Els complied, watching him, somewhat irritably, pick up a fresh sheet of paper, scribble on it, stare at it for what seemed to her was an eternity before casting it aside. She noticed he was again biting on his lip as he picked up another leaf of paper, then another - each time marking them with charcoal between glances up at her, past her and through her without registering her growing restlessness and the appeal in her eye for him to pack up for the day.

Durer had other ideas and he still was not content with how she stood and made more adjustments to Els's right arm to have it look more natural in how she cupped her hand to hold an apple. At one point, Durer spun round. There was no apple. He went to the door and was about to call on Günter when he remembered the youth was away in search of a leafy twig and that everyone else from the household was off celebrating Schutzenfest so he took himself out into the yard and returned with a warm duck's egg which he handed to Els as a surrogate fruit.

Els relaxed the moment Durer went out so he had to rearrange her position before resuming his drawing. Being Durer he quickly settled back into making those familiar deft strokes with his nimble fingers, gradually filling up the blank spaces on the paper attached to his board. His facial expression was a study in absorption in a task.

Els could not stop thinking about how she would never again be simply a nut seller but an emblem for the whole of mankind once the drawing was completed and copied onto a copper plate, inked and pressed. The prospect of being forever preserved for as long as people bought the print excited her despite her growing boredom – that people would be able to see her, even after she was long dead and her flesh shrivelled, her bones bleached and broken asunder, and in that manner she would become immortalised. And she smiled but wished Herr Durer would get on with it.

"I don't want you smiling." Durer rat-tat-tatted the end of a silverpoint against his drawing board.

"I'm not comfortable and it's cold," Els felt brave enough to grumble.

Durer studied her, as if realising she was flesh and blood, for so caught up was he seeing her as Eva. "Sorry Els but if you could hold that position a little longer, I will release you from your torture very soon. I must first get this right - showing Eva, you, reaching for the apple - or egg as we have here from - the egg tree." Laughing, he tucked a loose lock of hair behind his ear. "You look the very essence of purity before that evil serpent tricked you and I'm near ready to stop. It was my fortune, and yours dear Els, that we met at the Hauptmarkt for you are the nearest woman I've seen that resembles a Greek goddess - or will do when I'm finished, so if you don't mind, hold that pose."

Durer worked on - neatly multi-hatching, his pen running back and fore, each line accentuating the youthful rotundity of Eva's form. He made her figure stand out by darkening the background, creating depth on the flat paper and heightening the sensation of threat and mystery represented by the sinister forest behind her and Adam.

Els was happy. Harmony resumed. No longer did she mind the ache she felt in her extended arm supporting the cupped hand cradling the duck egg or the crick in her neck from gazing so long over her shoulder.

A composition pleasing to Albrecht Durer gradually emerged under his deft manipulation now of a goose quill; his elegant fingers making tiny precise movements; eyes darting between model and paper; the absent Adam now a faint cylinder - more or less mirroring Eva, holding a branch of the Tree of Life - or about to be when Günter returned with a twig of mountain ash. Durer raised his hand signalling to Els to stay put while he disappeared, returning with a parrot.

"This is Papagei," he told a wide-eyed Els. "He belongs to my mother but she's away visiting my brother and I've been looking after him. He's going back to her today but I think I must include him in the picture for he's such a handsome creature, although I admit he has the coarsest of manners. Never mind he won't be able to talk from my picture and will make a fine symbol for wisdom - despite his base vocabulary - won't you Papagei? Els, this simple creature has an unusual talent for language," he explained. "How many men of your acquaintance can claim to interpret bird whistles, far less communicate in them?"

Els considered the bird with misgivings. He was colourful and handsome but she did not like the way he cocked his head and looked at her with his beady eyes. After checking out his surroundings Papagei grew restless. He hopped off his perch to the floor, resisting Durer's entreaties to stay still, squawking up at him, which Els interpreted as bird laughter. By now she was none too happy at having to share a space with the creature, insisting that she did not care for feathers and neither did she approve of the parrot's manners, for he was showing off his talent as a wordsmith and the words he spoke were wholly vulgar. Els could not believe Durer would consider featuring such a bird in a holy picture and her jaw dropped open in astonishment when a belligerent Papagei vented his opinion on the matter in a stream of foul-mouthed shrieks. Just then a contingent of Schutzenfest trumpeters and drummers from the children's parade passed-by close to the house and the racket both inside and out became deafening.

Durer tried to ignore the ensuing chaos. Neither he nor Els saw the long procession of children skip past led by two small boys dressed as hunters in frog-green and toad-brown tunics with green felted caps stuck with long pheasant tail feathers. They were accompanying the Schutzen princess who rode a long-coated short-legged pony. She was a pretty child clad in a milky white shift laced with coils of ivy leaves and soft azure-blue feathers and on her head was her princess's crown - a garland of ivy secured to her mane of curls of the palest ginger by a length of pale blue silk ribbon. The children giggled, self-consciously, as friends and neighbours walked alongside, calling out their names.

By the time the procession had passed Durer's house Papagei was throwing himself against the window in his excitement and liberally defecating into the bargain so that Durer was compelled to confine him to a broom closet to the doubtless satisfaction of Katze, Agnes's ginger tom cat, who was not fond of the noisy bird and who had appeared in the workshop to present Durer with the limp corpse of a mouse, dangling from his jaws.

Having dealt with Papagei, Durer discovered Els engaged in stroking the cat and leafing once more through his copy of Nicholas de Cusa's book. He picked up the lifeless mouse and was about to throw both it and Katze into the yard when it occurred to him that Katze would be ideal to represent the choleric temperament, bile, in his Eden engraving. And with a little imagination he might have Katze communing with the little mouse - signifying the harmony of God's world before Eva bit into the apple that still was an egg at this stage.

The chaotic events were beginning to worm into Durer's concentration. Try as he might his thoughts kept returning to his missing *Field Hare* and Wolgemut's rabbit. Trying to put all but the drawing out of his mind, Durer stared at his Eva. The girl was a beauty and he congratulated himself on having found her, and in so inauspicious a manner. But still the hare intruded and there and then he made up his mind, somewhat mischievously, to include a small hare in his Eden and have it nuzzle up to Eva to impute a relationship of temperaments between them - for he missed his little *Field Hare* so. It was, therefore, out of turmoil Durer found inspiration and while Els sat quietly looking over the book he quickly sketched in the small creatures next to her leg.

***

The combination of a small armoury of weapons and highly inebriated handlers not infrequently led to misfortunes during Schutzenfest so the good folk of Nuremberg were vigilant when taking to the roads, fields and woods lest they encounter a stray arrow from a crossbow or even a ball shot from a hand gun. But nothing that Schutzenfest was expected to match the discovery of a headless corpse in the great midden at the Spittlerthurm, for no-one could recall anything of the like happening before in the good city of Nuremberg.

It was at times impossible to distinguish the squeal of hunting horns from the squeal of hunters; their blood racing between heart and head. For any geese flying overhead the overwhelming perfume that rose from Nuremberg and its forests and plains was of blood with a trace of brimstone.

A woodman who was friendly with Günter invited him to help skin and gut a hind. But the boy found the task too difficult and stood aside to observe the woodman's dexterity with blades larger than Günter was used to as he cut into the magnificent beast, stripping away its hide and innards. The deer being dismembered was chopped and sliced and pieces distributed to those gathered there - the choicest part presented to the man of highest esteem while the woodman had to make do with the chine – though that seemed to satisfy him well enough for he declared the backbone would boil up nicely to sweeten his pot of vegetables.

A great steaming pile of the hind's bowels were quickly washed and laid aside or else roughly hacked up and mixed with bread and fed to the yelping hounds. The throwing away of the corbyn bone caused a raucous skirmish among crows, with much flapping of wings and shrieking.

Chapter 12

Brauer's was crowded. Klara, her face flushed from the effort of serving so many packed into the inn, had little time to chat with her regulars. She gave the briefest of nods to Otto Beck working his way towards Willy Pirkheimer and Albrecht Durer.

"You're lucky we kept a seat for you, Otto," Pirkheimer spluttered, his mouth stuffed full of green cabbage. "Called away on urgent business, were you? Our stomachs were becoming impatient and crying out for sustenance."

"When is your stomach not? It has a life of its own," Beck said, smacking his own extended belly. Then sucking in air between his teeth, admitted, "I've not a stiver on me."

"You'll expect me to keep topping up your beer then, as usual?" Pirkheimer muttered under his breath, and more loudly, "hunger and this crowd meant we couldn't sit around chewing on our tongues before Ana or Klara threw us out for not paying our way ... I'll call Klara now." Pirkheimer used the back of his hand to rub a trickle of grease from his chin. "Hallo, hallo, over here," he cooed across the inn; his great arm signalling for service.

Klara acknowledged him with a back nod as she waited behind two arrivals who were shaking the wet from their coats and hats before finding them a space at an already cramped table. Müller pulled at her apron for attention so she served him first before attending to Durer, Beck and Pirkheimer.

"If only those mystics would turn their minds to that one - though it's wicked to say so - for all of you mind," Klara half-turned in the direction of Müller before setting down a helping of pork knuckles. "Has no-one been caught for Axel's killing, Herr Pirkheimer?"

"Not that I've heard, Klara. There are a few in our city who are not strangers to every kind of perversion and pagan practice but I cannot comprehend them being involved in cruelty such as that." He shook his head sorrowfully.

The murder of Axel Marx was still the main talking point in Brauer's despite the excitement over the competition for Schutzenkonig. Principal suspects were the mystics, not only strangers but who had openly maligned the city's good character. Contented, corpulent little Axel Marx might be dead and buried but it was less easy to bury suspicion of outsiders that dwelled within the heads of people of the town.

The death of one of their own naturally created an atmosphere of unease within the city, especially with a killer was on the loose. Was Axel Marx but the first of them to be judged and made to suffer a horrible death? Could such a small weakness as Axel's gluttony be taken as a denial of God's word? Could God have commanded retribution on such a gentle soul as Axel for so slight a misdemeanour? And if so, how many more lives of townsfolk were at risk?

"Eat up, Otto," Pirkheimer coaxed but Otto Beck had turned uncharacteristically green in the face and shook his head.

"You'll have to finish it, Willy, for I have a fearsome belly-ache."

"Get stuck in Otto Beck and you, too, Herr Pirkheimer, for men must eat. I know it's a disturbing time but your bellies are like mine," Klara winked at them, "they don't like to be starved no matter how much the Devil threatens us. When we're thirsty, we must slake our thirst. And we eat because we have to. Whoever has done this to Axel has not acted from righteousness but from evil. Come along now - don't let your appetites spoil. Otto Beck you would normally eat the very fingers off my hand if I didn't move fast enough and there's nothing wrong with that. And you, Herr Durer, you must keep up your strength." She turned around and yelled, "Kläuschen - over here now!"

The small boy was giggling at some remark from Herr Müller.

"Come over here and stick by me - you've been told." The child obeyed and Klara placed a protective hand on his shoulder; glaring disapprovingly in Müller's direction.

From beneath his faded red cap the grain merchant's eye engaged with hers.

"Like father like son," Klara muttered. "Look at him - will drink himself into an early grave will that one. I'm not surprised his mother abandoned him – was always no good."

Just then the inn door was thrown open by a group of rowdy revellers, among them a very drunk Herman Kalb - newly crowned King of Marksmen; as might be fitting the chief of the city's militia.

A cheer rang out when the news got around and there were calls for more beer to celebrate Kalb's success amidst much foot stamping and impromptu singing.

"I must attend to my customers, gentlemen. Herr Durer you've scarcely supped enough to satisfy a mouse. Hope it's not catching. Very glad to see you are again hale and hearty, Otto." With that she was gone, steering the boy between boisterous patrons.

Pirkheimer swallowed back his despair and was making good work of gnawing the pork bone down to the shine. Beck had overcome his belly-ache and was also squaring up to the food.

"The Spaniard Collado is impressed by my latest hand gun," Beck began between bites, "insists it's the most accurate weapon he's handled. How's that for praise?"

Pirkheimer looked at Beck. "Well done, Otto," he said, "one day you'll make your fortune from those firing machines. You'll have to teach me to use one the next time we go hunting."

The three friends drank a great deal of beer but the more they drank the more morose Otto Beck became. Then he was on his feet, shouting.

"I tell you these mystics mean to destroy our quiet town with their accusations of vice and depravity. They are the ones doing the Devil's work and should not have been given free passage on Holy Michaelmas. If our Council will not protect us then we must protect ourselves from their mischief. Who's with me? Who's willing to find Axel's assassins and get him justice?"

A great hullaballoo ensued with knife handles and bierkrugs banged on tables. Several of Brauer's patrons also stood up intent on immediately starting out to confront the mystics but when the inn door was thrown open it was found to be raining hard outside and Brauer's lamp-lit hospitality, not least the fire roaring in the grate, made them think twice about their proposal - there was beer to drink and good gravy to soak up with bread that shouldn't go to waste and so every man sat back down, apart from Otto Beck.

Schutzenkonig, Herman Kalb, strained open a bloodshot eye, dragged himself up to his full height and pointed a none-too-steady finger at Beck.

"Sit down, Otto Beck and stop making a fool of yourself," he bellowed, promptly dropping down as his legs gave way from under him.

Beck sheepishly obeyed the order signalling an end to the Beck revenge campaign.

"Pity you've found an Eva, Albi," Pirkheimer said, his eyes following Ana working the tables. "for Ana Brauer has the figure of a goddess - although her face might not be quite so suitable. How's the latest magnum opus coming along?" he asked Albrecht Durer.

"There's progress in that direction, Willy," Durer declared, "and Els is everything I'd hoped she'd be."

"Before or after the apple?" asked Beck, now calmed down. He eyed Durer mischievously, his words indistinct for they were churned up with pork and splashed with gravy.

"I think you'll find that's sacrilege, Otto," Durer said.

"I think you'll find it isn't, Albi. It's a question."

"Els is everything I could have wished for in my Eva."

Beck winked at Pirkheimer. "I don't doubt it." He raised his bierkrug to his lips and washed down another mouthful of food. "But this is not catching the rabbit. We have to make plans for snaring our rabbit's poacher," he grinned.

Durer looked downhearted. "I was born to suffer bad fortune," he said to no-one in particular.

"When will we make our move?" Beck asked excitedly?

100

Durer ran a hand through his hair and said nothing.

Beck thrust the point of his dagger into the table, his eyes trained on his friend. "Come, Albi, what do we intend to do to get them back?" he asked.

Willy Pirkheimer rubbed his ample stomach while Durer inspected the ridges carved into the table by a thousand knife cuts.

Beck sidled up to him. "What we need is proof that our hare was taken on an order from Wolgemut," he whispered.

Durer groaned. "I was wondering if Agnes really has sold it to him ... before she left," he said.

"No, Albi," Beck said, "she would have told you if she'd done that. Even Agnes speaks to you occasionally. And she would have entered it into your sales ledger. Is it there?" He smacked the dagger's hilt making it vibrate.

Durer shook his head. "No ... but ..."

"No but," Beck mocked him. "If it isn't there it's because it didn't happen. For goodness sake, Albi, Agnes is proud of every picture she sells and would have announced it to the world if the rabbit was one of them. And she wouldn't have removed it from its frame, would she? You did say it was taken out of its mount? She wouldn't have done that - reducing its value ..."

"Alright, that's enough Otto," Pirkheimer cut in, "let's calm down and think about this. I agree with some reluctance that Agnes is usually organised but there's just a chance..."

"No chance," Beck interrupted.

Pirkheimer raised his hands for quiet. "Albi, did you ask Herr Wolgemut if he'd bought the *Field Hare* from Agnes?"

"No, it didn't occur to me and anyway he insinuated the picture was his."

"Well it would have been if he'd paid for it - and you can't ask Agnes now," Beck said with a snort," and by the time she's returned from Frankfurt it'll be too late. The question is, has your picture really been stolen, Albi? or are we talking about one picture?"

"You know it has. Albi has said so," Pirkheimer insisted.

"I have," Durer insisted; his eyes narrowing.

"Why, Otto, do you impute Albi is lying?" Pirkheimer demanded.

"No," Beck barked back.

"You have."

"Asking the question … that's all I'm doing … we have to be clear," Beck said, defensively. He raised his hand as though fending off further criticism. "From what Maria's told me the Wolgemuts won't keep quiet for long and if word gets around implicating you, Albi, your reputation will be tarnished and no-one will buy your work."

"What's she been saying?" Durer demanded.

"Maria?" Beck asked.

"Yes, Maria."

"Only that the delightful Gudrun suspects you may be out to damage her husband's standing." Beck again flicked the dagger handle so it sprang back and fore.

"Why would she think that?" Durer asked.

"The remarkable coincidence of both you and old Wolgemut losing two very similar pictures - and the Council commissioning a pair of oil portraits from you - the very ones she expected her husband would be hired to do." Beck arched an eyebrow to emphasise his misgivings in the matter.

Durer's brow furrowed. It dawned on him why Gudrun Wolgemut had appeared familiar to him. "She was at the Rathaus Friday last," he muttered under his breath.

"What was that?" Beck asked.

"It's of no consequence," Durer replied. "What were you saying, Otto?"

"Frau Wolgemut was very interested in your pictures according to my Maria," Beck replied. "Maria notices everything. She's often compared your pictures to Herr Wolgemut's – she even remembers your *Field Hare* from one of the times we were in your workshop, for it struck her as unusual - and not altogether appropriate for a painting. She's quite conventional, is Maria and prefers images that are holy rather than common vermin. I expect that's how Frau

Wolgemut got to know about your little hare. Like I say, not much gets past my Maria."

"Maria should learn to hold her tongue," Pirkheimer snarled, "Frau Wolgemut is a woman of good character and it ill becomes her maidservant to indulge in gossip about her mistress - especially when that mistress has taken her in - an outsider." Pirkheimer pulled his hat down about his eyes as he conjured up an image of the lady in question and when he looked down at the table he found Beck's outstretched fingers ready to pick up a morsel of bread from the poplar charger.

"Remove your filthy hand, Otto." Pirkheimer clipped Beck's wrist with the haft of his dagger.

Otto Beck turned on Pirkheimer. "That's not dirt you silk tail – it's what years of working metal does to the skin. Not every man can laze around with his nose stuck in a book all day. Some of us must shoulder the burden of toil."

"But," Pirkheimer scolded, "take note Albi; he doesn't rush to the defence of his woman. Be assured good Beck your own contribution to Nuremberg's industry is greatly appreciated yet gluttony is a deadly sin, even for a craftsman of your talents and I see you've guzzled the rest of the bread. I would say it's by mere good fortune the murderer chose poor Axel over you."

Otto Beck looked aggrieved. "I used it to soak up the gravy," he whined.

"Then you must have had too much gravy," Pirkheimer fired back.

Otto feigned hurt. "It's the style nowadays to be well-proportioned."

"For Silesian oxen, perhaps," spluttered Pirkheimer coughing into his handkerchief. "What ails you, Albi?"

Durer roused himself. "This whole business with the pictures is worrying me sick."

"You're taking it all too seriously," Beck said.

Durer rounded on him. "It's all very well for you but I'm the victim of a picture thief. Now it appears my good name is being blackened as well. Should I not take the matter seriously?"

"We will devise a fool-proof scheme to get Wolgemut's picture back, Albi. You won't be alone for Otto and I will be looking out for you to make sure nothing goes wrong." Pirkheimer sounded like the Councillor he was. "Otto clean that mess off your face and say nothing." Pirkheimer pulled Beck's dagger out of the table and handed it to him.

Three heads came together. Johannes Brauer's was a first-class location to rehearse the evening's arrangements for it was near impossible to overhear a word quietly spoken with all the uproar of Schutzenfest making for some of the noisiest merry-making heard within its walls all year. With the onset of evening the racket intensified with blasts from hunting horns ever more frequent so that normal conversation was all but impossible.

In a far corner of the inn a party of fleshers, noisier than most, aired their opinions of Prince Ernest and his fondness for worshipping heathen gods; Pan in particular - that licentious creature born in a hare skin who spurred men on to indulge their lusts. It was common gossip that the Kaiserburg played host to bizarre ceremonies with men dressed in hare pelt coats.

Of all God's creatures it was the hare the fleshers held in greatest disdain: *wasn't it dangerous to indulge in crazes involving those devils on Earth? Meddling with enchanted animals could lead to a man being broken on the wheel. What is a hare but a creature imbued with dissolute and magical powers?*

Had it not been for the commotion within Brauer's the fleshers' conversation might have remained private but having to shout to be heard their words carried a good distance across the room ... to Councillor Pirkheimer whose commodious ears rarely missed a rebellious expression made in his presence so he was compelled to caution the fleshers against such reckless talk. Moments after Pirkheimer resumed his seat two men took up occupancy of a bench immediately behind the raucous butchers.

"I know them," Durer said.

Pirkheimer and Beck turned their heads and found themselves looking at two stylishly-dressed merchants, not at all typical of Nuremberg or any part of Franconia. A lanky grey-haired hound settled beneath their table; one eye alert the animal snapped whatever morsels the pair dropped on the floor.

"Italian, I'd say," Pirkheimer suggested. "Dark, like Italians with that hair, I am certain I am right."

Durer and Beck agreed. They recognised them as the pair next to Gudrun Wolgemut watching the heretics in the square. One wore his blue-black hair swept back clear of his almond eyes but for a single lock that fell about his forehead and which he habitually wound round an ear suggesting he was straining to hear. His associate was a good head shorter; his dark hair cut close to his scalp and his lips formed pale rosebuds; a feminine feature counterbalanced by a day's growth of beard around his jaw. The taller of the two who had been eating one of Klara's knuckles stopped chewing, dropped the ham bone onto the stone flags where the hound's mouth stretched open, then looked up and found Durer's eye.

Chapter 13

With dusk came strong winds whipping up dust scraped loose by hundreds of feet hurrying along Nuremberg's earthen streets, sending it into the air only to fall back down as showers of dry rain. Flying high above the stoor, near invisible to the naked eye, raucous geese navigated a flight path across a dramatic turnsole sky.

Durer recalled reading that the Ancients believed the goose of all Earth's creatures was gifted with the most acute sense of hearing and smell; no mouse could stir but they were noticed and for the sensitive goose the stench of humans compared with a putrefying dog carcass to man's nose. He spotted them; glinting white in the moonlight - flying powerful and free. Freedom that would last four more weeks for then it would Schlachtmonat, slaughter month, when the geese of the skies, Widukind's sheep in the pastures and Wedigo's pigs in the forest would be butchered, smoked, salted or dried so that Nurembergers might survive the lean months of winter. Albrecht Durer tried to shake off a picture of Axel Marx butchered like a beast and roasted.

Albrecht Durer intended being at his mother's house well before curfew bell but he was running late and Papagei's cage was bulky and awkward for him to carry. His mother insisted on getting her parrot back the instant she returned home from visiting his brother Hans for she did not trust her bird in the same house as her son's cat, and Durer was none-too-keen on the bird either and glad to be rid of it. He planned no leisurely gossip with his mother about Hans and his family for this evening was dedicated to retrieving Wolgemut's stolen picture and he was sore pressed for time.

Barbara Durer first fussed over Papagei then persuaded her son to make her fire safe for the night. Impatiently Durer shovelled up its warm ashes, putting them into an iron pot which he emptied in the yard. At the same time he called on his mother to fetch the leather purse he left in the house for safe-keeping. It transpired his mother had returned home, seen the purse bulging with coin and moved it to an even safer place. Her difficulty was remembering where that safe place was. Durer's increasingly urgent pleas to locate the purse only agitated his mother the more so that she even questioned if he had, in fact, left it in her home at all. They bickered and an emotional Albrecht Durer implored her to recall where she concealed it for he was already late and he had to confess to his mother the money was not his but belonged to another who entrusted it to his care. At this point Barbara Durer looked her son square in the face and demanded an explanation as to why any man should trust his purse to another.

Durer briefly recounted the story of the picture theft and his former master's insistence he should help recover it. Barbara Durer looked at him askance before reminding her son of an incident that took place soon after he went to Wolgemut as his apprentice. He came home one day with one of his teacher's paintings under his arm to show to her but without asking his master's permission. The episode long forgotten by Albrecht Durer planted a seed of doubt into his own mind for he had been much preoccupied worrying about work and finding buyers for his prints and Agnes' absence, and his fondness for toadstool soup which occasionally blurred his thinking. His head got so confused he thought it just possible he was, unwittingly, mixed up in the disappearance of Wolgemut's picture. But he dismissed the idea as preposterous though it continued to trouble him. It also troubled him that his mother might mention something of it to others. That would play badly for him.

"Is this it?" Barbara Durer held up the elusive purse which she discovered when she went to fill up a jug with oats from her meal chest.

A relieved Durer slipped on his coat, dragged a hat onto his head and immediately set off in the direction of the Schöner Brunnen fountain in the Hauptmarkt. The curfew bell's insistent ringing in his ears reminded him how late he now was and he ran with his lantern swinging to-and-fro in his hand. The jerking movement made the flame flicker so much he was compelled to slow his pace to prevent being plunged into complete darkness.

By now most of Nuremberg's citizens were safely tucked up in their beds with only a few stragglers sharing the night with the painter; one man dressed in a long striped woollen cape staggered towards the artist like a moth drawn to his lamp's flame before vanishing as quickly into the gloom. Nearing the fountain Durer spied figures - no more than smudges of dark ink on lapis Venetian paper at first – a trio of women chatting while they filled their pitchers with water for morning. At Durer's approach they hurried off, back to their homes.

Durer could see no-one else as he waited by the Schöner Brunnen but he heard the familiar creaking of the city scavenger's cart on its laborious course along Nuremberg's dark, deserted streets, loaded-up with abandoned dead and diseased animal remains; sometimes, though not on this night, there was an unclaimed corpse, perhaps a suicide to be burned outside of the city walls. Durer scolded himself for having lingered so long in Brauer's and then that business with his mother. He heard more geese flying overhead and allowed himself a moment to consider how Nuremberg's distinctive smells assisted their navigation; its vapours belching out from forge and furnace chimneys, wood smoke, the pungency of boiled cabbage, decaying fruit, animal dung, the stench of human flesh all carried upwards into the heavens aiding the birds' passage across the city on their flight south.

Following Schmeichler's instructions he circled the richly painted and gilded illuminated fountain without noticing its familiar magnificence. This means of identifying him to the picture thieves made him feel foolish, for he supposed he was being watched by them or else there was no point in the exercise, but looking about him he could detect no other living soul.

Durer had scarcely gone any distance from the Schöner Brunnen than the candle in his lantern began popping and guttering so much he was obliged to clean it. Laying down Wolgemut's pouch Durer opened the lamp's shell casing and with a finger he gouged a dip in the congealed tallow to expose the tiny rush wick so it might burn more efficiently; his nose wrinkling at the disagreeable stink of burning fat which unaccountably conjured up an image of Klara's pork knuckles.

Darkness clung to Nuremberg like a widow's veil and on hearing a noise Durer pulled up mid-step - a trickle of moisture tickled his armpit. The brutal death of Axel Marx unnerved the good folk of Nuremberg; even the most learned and rational of city scholars was not immune to the parasite of panic. Slipping the cover back into place Durer sighed at what remained a darkling gleam through the lamp's pierced brass body. There was nothing else to do but pick up the purse and continue on his way. He slipped a finger through the lantern's D-hold so that it swung gently to the rhythm of his step as he made his way along the silent and dark street.

In an attempt to calm his nerves, Durer turned his mind to his *Adam and Eve* and more particularly to Els, regretting his impatience with her when she complained of the ache in her arm from having to hold up the duck egg for so long but a rasp of metal on stone brought Durer back to the present. He tipped his head, listening - for what he could not tell. He was not familiar with this part of town with its nooks and dens and steeply pitched houses creating ghostly channels and his feet slipped on the earth paths. He had no need for geese to discern the fetid nature of the air around him; sickly sweet like rotting apples. Pausing to scrape the soles of his boots, he wondered how much farther.

There would be no heroics; he would keep to the instructions set out by the villain or villains who stole Wolgemut's picture ... with one exception. Beck and Pirkheimer would approach the rendezvous from intersecting lanes so that Durer would not be alone during the exchange.

However, unknown to Durer, neither Otto Beck nor Willy Pirkheimer were where they should be. Beck had only meant to drop in by his workshop for a trice to try out a possible solution to a difficulty he was having with a mechanism - a solution suggested by Maria - but then became absorbed in the task. Elsewhere, the usually reliable Pirkheimer had also been side-tracked by different matters.

***

Adolf Wolf let himself into the house that had been his home and where his mother still lived in that district of Nuremberg that was home to the city's most miserable specimens of humanity. He was a good son, reliable and caring in his own way. He would have done more for his mother but she was a proud independent woman who disliked being beholden to anyone, even when that anyone happened to be her own son.

Frau Wolf's husband died of the pestilence when Adolf was an infant. She escaped from the city with their child at the first appearance of the pest and returned a widow. From that time her main goal was to find a means of educating the boy so he might improve his standing in the world and to that end she used every means at her disposal to supplement her income, including laundering and operating a boiling oven. While she could not afford to hire tutors to teach Adolf reading and counting she entered into an informal arrangement with a man of sufficient competency in numbers and letters to be able to instruct her son to a satisfactory level. The arrangement usually included the instructor's weekly bathing pfennig, paid as cash. For his part the young Adolf proved himself an able scholar who was taken under the wing of another gentleman, a learned man who once taught at Heidelberg University. By his thirteenth year, Adolf Wolf found himself apprenticed to Melchior Pfinzing, provost of St Sebaldus, who introduced Wolf to several of Nuremberg's most eminent citizens, including the magistrate Willibald Pirkheimer.

During his sixteenth year, Adolf Wolf eventually secured a position of clerk with Nuremberg Council. The promise of the precocious child reached its pinnacle within this fine though stilted institution. He did rise a little in rank as an official at the

Rathaus before his ambition extinguished and there he remained, contentedly on course for middle-age. Wolf never married and was rarely seen in the company of women, save his mother, but nor was he tied to her to any unnatural degree. Frau and Herr Wolf lived quite separate lives; he in a smart area of Nuremberg, in a fine townhouse of three stories with attics, and she in her single room in a shared building in the labyrinth. Of friends he had one or two of the type who might better be described as acquaintances. He never introduced them to his mother. It was not that Wolf was ashamed of her but she had so little time for anyone but her son it never occurred to him to bring them together.

It surprised both Willy Pirkheimer and Adolf Wolf that they should bump into each other in quite such an unremarkable quarter of the city. Wolf was quick to explain that he had been calling in on his mother, although that was not the complete truth. He had seen his mother, it was true, but the assignment he was planning took him to another part of the labyrinth, right by its edge.

Willy Pirkheimer, as Wolf's superior in all manner of ways, hardly felt any need to explain his presence in the Latin district so late and after curfew. Nevertheless, he loitered to exchange a word or two with Wolf, thereby delaying himself and then knowing he had missed the agreed meeting between Durer and the thief he decided to return home where pressing matters of state awaited his attention.

***

Durer cursed when he stumbled over a rock protruding from the path. Believing both Pirkheimer and Beck to be nearby he did his best to dismiss the apprehension that rattled his nerves. What with the wind and his imagination the painter's ears were assaulted by sounds; all of them threatening. He held up his lamp level with his eyes to see better through the gloom for now a steady drizzling rain was falling. A shimmering presence advanced on him. With quickened breath he prepared for the exchange of money for Wolgemut's picture and, surely, his old master's eternal gratitude – and perhaps become a hero in the eyes of Gudrun Wolgemut.

The shimmering presence turned out to be nothing more than distorted light from a lantern suspended from a balcony entangled with a creeper plant. This was the place. Durer recognised the distinctive cut-away gable mentioned in the ransom note. His heart pounded under his shirt and he fought to calm his rapid breathing. He wished it was not so dark, for neither the pendant lamp nor his own light produced much illumination, though he was able to distinguish two taper-like vennels, entirely unlit, stretching both to the left and right. He thought again of poor Axel Marx for no good reason and silently recited a prayer - *God willing - God willing, all will be well.*

It occurred to Durer that the thief might have given up on him since he was so late in arriving and the plan that seemed straightforward in Brauer's now looked as leaky as a cook's sieve cloth. Durer willed someone to appear.

If corruption had a voice then the wind wailing along the thin alleys on either side of the rendezvous was it. And if corruption had a body then Durer suspected he was looking at it right then. Straining his eyes, he peered at a murky casement in the building opposite and decided or hoped what he saw was nothing more than shadows sporting with lamplight or moonshine.

The wind howled along the labyrinth's narrow winding passages making it difficult to distinguish it from the other sounds that pricked his nerves - subdued laughter; coughing; a throat being cleared; humming. Durer felt threatened by each and every sound drifting from and rebounding the labyrinth's nooks and crannies. Scarcely daring to breathe, he discerned a man's voice and something about it was familiar. Joachim? Was it Joachim he heard? He fancied it might be. Durer called out the youth's name - raspily - as if afraid to disturb what should not be disturbed. Receiving no answer, he repeated the call - louder this time. The wind fell silent. The drizzle that kept falling grew more hushed. The laughter stopped, the humming, too. It was as if every person and thing packed into that crowded part of Nuremberg waited for the answer. And in that frightful silence Durer sensed his bowels grumble and shift.

Albrecht Durer retreated into the shadows, watched he imagined, by whoever dwelled behind the filthy escapements overlooking his position, for he suspected that behind those tiny gaps in its walls eyes were observing him for vague shapes came and went. He commanded his own eyes to stop feeding his imagination and looked instead along one of the twin alleys where a coiling serpent of smoke was advancing – a sharp foul odour dispersed by the wind as it neared.

The gable lamp swayed on its bracket, grating like a choleric crow. Durer crouched down, setting aside his own light and Wolgemut's purse so he could fasten up his mantle against the cold. The crow flame extinguished. Durer jumped to his feet and the hem of his heavy coat knocked against his lantern, toppling it and sending a ripple of yellow starlight along the length of the brass tube. He was about to retrieve the lamp when Durer noticed the door under the gable stood ajar. Then the yellow starlight went out and in his consternation Durer stepped back onto the lane searching his pockets for the flint striker he knew he had left at home.

"What!" he yelled as a stocky figure barged into him.

A woman; one hand clutching a glimmering lamp, the other gripping a basket secured under an arm and piled high with laundry cried out in alarm. Items from the basket tumbled to the ground and after putting down her lamp the woman adroitly picked up the lost aprons by their strings, stuffing them back into her basket. She ignored Durer's offer of help and with no word exchanged she hoisted up the load, balanced it against her hip, snatched up the light and went on her way; listing to one side as she disappeared down the crooked lane that led in the direction of Müller's granary. Durer thought it was strange that an old woman should be going about her business beyond the curfew but the wail of an infant brought him back to his current predicament.

A yellow striped cat rubbed itself against Durer's legs. He stooped down to tickle its head as the cat circled him; echoing his own circumnavigation of the fountain. As it sniffed Durer's boots its ears pricked up - its attention drawn to one of the dark alleyways then it was off as if Lucifer himself was on its tail.

A trick of the wind or whispering? An agitated Durer strained to hear. His mouth was so parched he could scarcely swallow. Was the whispering coming from behind the door beneath the balcony? He pushed it open and peered in. He could see nothing and hear nothing. Durer looked back over his shoulder. There was no one else in the lane yet he could not shake off the feeling he was being observed. A familiar figure then heaved into view; the washerwoman, her gait less laboured. Durer made himself visible to her but as before she refused to acknowledge his presence. Then from nowhere came heavy footsteps and young men yelling at the tops of their voices. Durer recognised them as barrowmen. They ran past Durer and the washerwoman, clearly drunk. Durer stared after them. When he turned to enquire if the washerwoman was hurt, he discovered she, too, was gone.

Albrecht Durer wrung his hands nervously. So much time had passed he thought it unlikely the thief would show up so straightening his cap he turned for home. At least the rain had stopped and with the moon shining more brightly he was able to see his way. He looked down at his feet, at his beautiful soft ox-leather Venetian boots, and saw they were smeared with what appeared to be squashed and rotten apple. Bending down to wipe them clean he mused on what his father would have made of his predicament. His poor father who had been so ill when he was working on *Young Hare* that the picture became linked with his memory, and a reason his mother was keen to own it. All who had seen the work declared the watercolour most excellent; its exquisite detail perfectly capturing the texture and movement of the animal's pelt through the subtlety of brush strokes and Durer's application of layer upon layer of soft colour. *A triumph of interpretation* was his friend Willy Pirkheimer's judgment of it.

It was as though he had been kicked by an ox bull. Durer's head slammed against a wall with tremendous force. By the time he had collected his wits his ears were ringing to the retort of retreating footsteps. It was impossible for him to detect which direction his assailant or assailants had taken for the moon had slunk back out of sight and what he took to be two shadows of different heights melted into the murk. Down on all fours Durer felt about for his lantern. He could not find it. Nor could he locate Wolgemut's purse.

Stumbling and tripping Durer worked his way along the warren of eerily dark alleys - in and out of shadowy dens until eventually he found himself back at the Hauptmarkt and, there, leaning against the fountain was Otto Beck.

"Where did you get to?" Beck snapped. "I'm soaked from hanging around here."

Durer slicked his hair back from his face with his fingers and felt them sticky.

Where was the picture? Why was Durer walking in the dark without a lantern? How long before they get out of the wet so he could get off to bed? Beck fired off several questions at once. "You're bleeding, Albi. What's happened?"

Durer steadied himself against the fountain, working the pump handle and drawing several hat strings of cool water which he splashed over his pounding head and shook his hair like a dog emerging from a river. "What's happened, Otto, is they've taken the money but forgot to give me the picture," he snapped.

Beck pulled a face in consternation.

"Where did they go?" Durer asked facetiously.

Beck looked vacant. "I didn't see anyone. It's so dark in there," pointing towards the labyrinth, "impossible to see much – and the cloud cover," he lied.

"I didn't see you," Durer barked.

Beck shrugged. "Like I said, it was too dark. I followed the plan," he added quickly.

115

"Well, where were you? I didn't see your light." Durer nudged Beck's lantern with his foot. "Your light is burning brightly."

"I was careful not to be seen," Beck insisted. "Those picture thieves would not have shown themselves if I'd been striding around like Lucifer, would they?" He threw up his hands expressing his exasperation.

"You were meant to look out for me," Durer protested.

"In case anything happened to you, Albi. That's what we decided."

Durer tapped his head. "Something did happen, didn't it?"

"And how was I to know that? Those alleys in the labyrinth are so tight and in the dark it's impossible to go about without exposing yourself. You've really messed up, haven't you, Albi? What's Wolgemut going to say?"

What Herr Wolgemut might say was also foremost in Albrecht Durer's mind. "Where's Willy?" he asked.

Beck shrugged. "Not a sign of him. It's been quiet ... apart from an old washerwoman... found her struggling with her basket so I helped her with it. After that I couldn't see you; there was no light so I came back here. Really thought you'd collected bunny and had headed off home. That's where I'm going. The sun will be up soon and me with it. You should go too, Albi – and get that head attended to. It doesn't look too good."

Chapter 14

Incessant knocking woke Durer. Pushing open his bedchamber window he called down. "Who's out there at this late hour?"

"I've been sent by Herr Wolgemut," came the reply.

Recognising Schmeichler's sickly tones Albrecht Durer reluctantly lit a candle and went downstairs to open the door.

"Good evening, Herr Durer. I hope it isn't inconvenient but Herr Wolgemut's anxious to be reunited with his picture," trilled the sycophant.

Durer's hand migrated to his cut head.

"I don't have it," his words cracking with tension. "They deceived me. Knocked me over and ran off without giving the picture to me."

"Oh dear," Schmeichler grimaced, "that is unfortunate." He shifted uneasily, "In that case I'll take back Herr Wolgemut's gold." A thin smile worked its way over Schmeichler lips as he extended his hand to take receipt of the purse.

Not for the first time that night Albrecht Durer was overcome by a heaving in his stomach and bowels. "There is a difficulty with that also," came his hesitant reply.

Then a third person emerged; the tall figure of Frau Wolgemut stepped up alongside Schmeichler. She looked at Durer's injured head, an expression of concern clouding her handsome face.

"You are hurt, Herr Durer. Let me tend to your poor head."

Schmeichler stepped aside for his master's wife. "Herr Wolgemut will have his explanation," Schmeichler said.

"Leave us now," Gudrun Wolgemut rounded on the manservant.

Schmeichler gave a hint of a bow and his mouth stretched into a broken twig of a grimace. "Very well, Frau Wolgemut, but I fear this twofold loss of his prize picture and purse of gold will gravely displease Herr Wolgemut."

"I will attend to Herr Durer's injury and when he has had time to recover he can accompany me home and speak directly with my husband. Leave us now."

Schmeichler hesitated then with a moist smack of his thick lips he retreated so Gudrun Wolgemut could gain entrance to Durer's house.

Herr Wolgemut's handsome wife did her best to reassure Durer that she would pacify her husband for, she explained, she was certain Durer was not to blame for the unfortunate outcome of the evening. As for her uncle's gold she told him that was of little consequence compared with the painter's well-being. Moreover, she insisted she check his house and workshop to make certain no more dangers lurked therein to take him unawares - even searching within his presses and stores; the lady made quite a game of it to Durer's amusement.

At the ringing of the matins prayer bell Albrecht Durer clambered out of his warm bed. Gudrun Wolgemut had nursed him well; she had washed the grit from his wound and removed every trace of blood from his hair and moustache. Having checked his premises the lady later sat quietly sketching on a fragment of paper she found in his workshop while Durer rested. The effort of drawing, however, appeared to tire her eyes for she frequently paused to dab at them with a handkerchief. At one point in the night she also slipped in beside Durer so that her body might warm his, for she said she noticed him shiver following his travails and she felt responsible for any harm he suffered because of her husband.

It was a serene Durer who left his house arm in arm with Herr Wolgemut's wife in the early hours of the morning when no-one else was about - at least none known to them - who might overhear two people conversing on the mystery of lost images of hares or rabbits and of servants who might not be trustworthy, for to Durer's surprise he heard Maria Kohl's name uttered in the same breath as stolen trifles. The remark had scarcely tripped off Frau Wolgemut's tongue than she begged Durer to forget her charges against Maria Kohl for fear, she said, the young woman might find herself on trial for her life.

Durer smoothed a hand over the thick green woollen coat he had purchased while in wind-swept Antwerp and which Gudrun insisted he wear against the night's damp chill. Frau Wolgemut had complimented him on its handsome appearance; its leather straps and decorative copper buckles, telling him how much she liked to see a man take pride in his dress - the inference being her husband took as little interest in his, as he did in her garments. Frau Wolgemut had been particularly complimentary over a well-cut green velvet outfit with slashed sleeves Durer had fetched out of his grandfather's chest - and a pretty pale blue linen under-shirt, the shade of rosemary flowers - worn beneath the Antwerp coat while his legs were clad in a decent pair of burgundy hose and his feet encased in the leather boots provided by his father and cleaned of the offending dirt from the labyrinth. Frau Wolgemut admitted she was no needlewoman able to sew a pretty seam and neither was Maria skilled with needle and silk thread. Having mentioned Maria Kohl again Frau Wolgemut shared further criticism of her: that she was poor company; that her manner was manly; her appearance was plain and that Gudrun pitied Otto Beck for having to put up with Maria. The vehemence of Frau Wolgemut's words surprised Durer and on voicing his own Agnes' affection for her maid, Susanna, drew from Gudrun Wolgemut an admission of envy for Frau Durer, in some ways, not least her independent spirit as well as her companionship with a trustworthy maidservant. Although curious to know Albrecht Durer did not probe what else about Agnes aroused Gudrun's envy.

Their conversation might have remained their secret but for another who was on the road late that Tuesday, secreted within the shadows of Kaiserburg hill.

Handsome Thomas Hut was at pains to conceal his presence for his own situation was precarious and there were many who wished him harm, notwithstanding he was forbidden from being in the city overnight. Hut knew capture would lead to his incarceration and likely torture in the city's gaol but he risked all for one with whom he longed to speak. And so, there were three persons making for Herr Wolgemut's home long after both curfew and matins bells pealed.

Durer and Gudrun arrived at a fork in the road – one track led to the Imperial Palace while the other passed the old master's property. Close to the fork stood a low-roofed hovel half-submerged in the earth and next to it a ramshackle shelter of rough timber, windowless, so that whatever lived within its walls was invisible to the outside world - an occasional rattle of chains the only indication of life therein. Albrecht Durer and Frau Wolgemut recognised the clanking irons as belonging to cripple Joseph's old brown bear.

A little distance on the pair were confronted by Wolgemut's watch-hound surprised at the approach of people at this late hour. The dog wound itself into a state of ecstasy at the advance of potential quarry and his disappointment was plain on recognising his mistress.

Gudrun told Durer how the hound, a rangy roan creature, was an excellent hunter and for that purpose was kept hungry by her husband. Not that her husband hunted anymore but he maintained the habit of sparsely feeding his dog. When they approached the cottage, the hound re-appeared standing legs akimbo and sniffed at Gudrun's skirt as she brushed past.

"Won't we disturb your husband?" Durer asked for the umpteenth time.

"He rarely sleeps. He'll be waiting for us."

"Won't he be angry that you've been alone with me?" Durer asked for the umpteenth time.

Wholly unexpectedly tears trickled down Gudrun Wolgemut's face and she emitted a sigh at the moment the cottage door opened a crack.

"You've made a friend, Herr Durer."

Schmeichler's reedy strains grated on the painter. Wolgemut's hound skulked around Durer's legs, poised to squeeze inside the instant the door opened wide enough to allow his lean body through.

"Away!" Schmeichler shooed.

Durer assumed he was addressing the animal.

"I'm returning Frau Wolgemut safely home but I won't come in as Herr Wolgemut will not be expecting me at this hour," Durer said, apprehensively.

"Oh, he will," Schmeichler assured him, "but wait here." He closed the door before even Frau Wolgemut could enter.

The dog drew a claw down the doorpost.

Albrecht Durer rescued his hat, a pretty creation of plaited elder pith which had slipped from his head, and he removed the kid gloves that had been a gift from the cousin of an acquaintance, Tomas Imhof, in exchange for a set of engravings. The door opened and Wolgemut's hound attempted entry.

"Here, here, out, brute!' Schmeichler commanded roughly, his foot nudging the animal's belly causing it to yelp.

"Who's out there abusing my dog? Rascal! Answer me!" Michael Wolgemut's ample figure filled the doorway.

"Albrecht Durer is this your doing?" The old man bent down awkwardly and stroked the hound's head. He cocked an indifferent eye up at Gudrun.

"What? No!" Durer refuted.

"He's so excitable, aren't you fellow?" Schmeichler flapped a hand timidly at the dog. The animal rolled back its lips and snarled at him. "Such a sweet temperament," Schmeichler tittered and stood aside to let Durer and Frau Wolgemut enter.

"I thought you might be asleep, Sir," Durer blurted out.

"I rarely sleep, pain is my unwelcome companion and seldom lets me alone," roared Wolgemut, his corpulent frame heaving to the left and right like some great ship at sea; a pair of applewood poles heroically bearing the strain. It was painful for Durer to see his former tutor toil in his movements which reminded him of the washerwoman in the labyrinth.

Wolgemut's dog scampered triumphantly around his master's legs as he progressed at a snail's pace towards his chamber; somewhere between the cottage door and there they had lost Gudrun. Durer looked about the room with its dark heavy furniture and walls busily hung with pictures and the pretty blue and white tiled stove that took up nearly a whole wall with chairs and a settle arranged before it.

Wolgemut dropped into one of the chairs, a cushion at his back, and he raised a leg, resting his foot on a stool before bending over to remove his slipper. He squeezed his big toe with thickened fingers then leaned back and drew a worn grey blanket across his legs. Noticing Schmeichler loitering at the door Wolgemut dismissed him with a wave of his hand.

"Can I just ...," began the servant.

"Hold your tongue," his master bellowed back. "Out ...out! I say! Out!"

A squeak of old timbers, the fall of a latch and the two artists were alone.

"Take off your coat and sit, Albrecht." Wolgemut's rheumatic fingers flapped crookedly.

Durer slipped off his coat and settled himself opposite the Franconian master.

Wolgemut came straight to the point. "Schmeichler tells me you have failed to get my picture back. Is this correct?"

Albrecht Durer took a deep breath. "They pounced on me. I didn't get a chance ..."

"They? You saw them? Who were they?" Wolgemut asked urgently.

"I can't be sure, Sir. It was dark and it all happened so quickly."

"And the gold coin, Durer, the money I trusted to you?"

"Gone, Sir."

"Gone you say?"

"I'm afraid so."

"Then there will be consequences, Durer. I'm not to be taken for a fool. You hear? This money must be found... or my picture. I won't be made a fool of ... not me ... not Michael Wolgemut. You remember who I am and what I am to you, Albrecht Durer. You were the youth I transformed into the fine artist I hear that you are today. And this is how you repay me? This is how your father raised you to respect your

122

elders? Where is the world heading that our young bear so little respect for their superiors? I don't hear your explanation, Albrecht." Spittle collected at the corners of Wolgemut's mouth splattering his chin stubble.

Durer feebly attempted to defend himself. It baffled him that one moment he was the toast on everyone's lips and the next a rogue. The door opened and Schmeichler crept in, a dish of lebkuchen in one hand, a flask of wine in the other. Placing the cake by the stove and the flask on a small table he took two beakers from a wooden press and filled them with wine. One beaker he offered to his master, waiting patiently for the old man's grip on the cup to steady; the other he handed to Durer.

"Leave us," Wolgemut growled; his eyes focussed on the ruby wine until the door latch clicked and he resumed his conversation with Durer. "You insult me, Albrecht. I will lay your behaviour at the door of the recklessness of the young but for all that matters cannot rest where they are. I must get my money back."

"Or the picture," Durer said.

Wolgemut considered the younger man as if trying to recall something. "Er, the picture," he echoed falteringly before urging Durer to partake of the gingerbread warming next to the stove.

Durer considered the portions of cake piled into a cobalt blue glazed bowl not dissimilar to the stove tiles.

"I remember that sweet tooth of yours, Albrecht. My wife makes a very good lebkuchen but I'm less partial to it these days than I once was."

The hound stirred, its nose sniffing the air. A morsel of lebkuchen offered by Durer was immediately snapped up. The dog looked up at Durer, imploring another titbit. Wolgemut's mouth dropped open as if he was about to say something then thought better of it and swallowed a mouthful of wine instead.

"Tell me, are you succeeding at your trade?" he asked.

Durer was unsure how to read the question for he sensed a sliver of hostility in Wolgemut's attitude towards him but having no desire to further inflame the older man's temper he replied matter-of-factly that he would be taking up an invitation to paint a pair of oil portraits for the Schopper House. Almost as an aside he spoke of the growing popularity of his print engravings. "There's a good income to be made from them. In fact, I would like to borrow young Joachim to sit as Adam for an engraving of *Adam and Eve* I've begun."

Wolgemut scowled at him. "I would have thought you had seen quite enough of young Joachim. Quite enough. People talk you know, Durer." His arthritic fingers smoothed out creases in the rug. "You haven't changed despite your marriage, I see. I will not have Joachim sit for your picture. I'm sure there's no shortage of youths who'd be only too grateful for that opportunity and," he waggled an inflamed finger in Durer's face, "if I hear that Joachim has disobeyed me he will be put out of my employment and there are few masters willing to take on a boy who is defiant. As for your boast about printing, I hardly need telling of the prosperity there is to be had from selling printed copies of woodcuts and engravings. I will remind you it was I who set up Nuremberg's first print workshop," adding under his breath, "how quickly the young forget."

Durer squirmed. He would miss Joachim if Wolgemut stopped the lad coming into his workshop. He enjoyed their conversations and Joachim's enthusiasm for his drawings and painting, comparing them favourably with those by Wolgemut. Meanwhile the hound having consumed most of the gingerbread nuzzled against Durer's knee and let out a sickening whine.

"Be silent!" Wolgemut roared sending the dog scurrying into a retreat behind Durer's legs. "It is common gossip I am told that you are wasteful with your money and spend more than you bring in Albrecht Durer," Wolgemut snarled.

Durer opened his mouth to defend himself but Wolgemut held up a hand to silence him. "What I will say is that if I find you have tricked me, have taken advantage of our friendship and trust, I will stop at nothing to get satisfaction. We are all answerable for our sins, Albrecht. That lesson I thought you had learnt but it appears it is not so."

Durer could contain himself no longer. "Sir, it is not you alone who has fallen victim to the thief. I, too, am a casualty of trickery – of a villain's deception. My workshop has been entered and a work of mine, not unlike the one you had robbed has gone. But perhaps you already know this."

Wolgemut threw him a quizzical glance. "I know nothing of the kind. What is it you are implying? Be clear in your meaning."

"A watercolour - of a field hare I'd completed two years past. A pretty piece, much admired. I thought your wife might have mentioned it...."

"My wife! what has my wife to do with this?" Wolgemut demanded icily. "Hare, you say? My picture was a ... er ... ."

Durer stared at the man opposite. Only a short time ago Gudrun Wolgemut told him she and her husband had discussed the theft of his *Field Hare* though how they knew of it he was unclear. Could it have been Maria had mentioned it after talking to Otto? he wondered. In truth he was so exhausted Durer could scarcely recall who knew what and when. "Rabbit I believe," he wearily volunteered.

Wolgemut knitted his brows. He, too, struggled to follow the course of the conversation. "Rabbit?" he echoed uncertainly. "Rabbit ... and you say your drawing was of a hare ... "

"A watercolour and gouache," Durer explained.

"Two pictures?"

"No," Durer replied quickly, "it was a combination of gouache and watercolour."

Wolgemut's eyes narrowed as he absorbed this information. "Tell me do you think the hare superior to the rabbit?"

"I'm not certain what you mean."

"I mean insolence, Durer. Insolence!" Froth oozed from between Wolgemut's cracked madder-pink lips.

Durer stared at him. Age, he considered, had turned Wolgemut into a crotchety and confused stranger ... frail despite his girth. Stooped. Paunch bellied. The once firm face sunken into a chin that wobbled when he spoke. The long aquiline nose that projected from deep-set malachite eyes was fleshy and Wolgemut's once luxuriant hair hung limp, its grey ends protruding from beneath a muslin bonnet like so many blades of dried grass.

Struck dumb by remorse over his bluntness Durer fought to conjure up words that might mollify the man for the face confronting him was livid: a palette of angry shades from which two observant eyes blazed with fury and a pink mouth opened and shut like a drowning cod's.

"Liar!" The accusation sizzled on Wolgemut's tongue. "Liar!" he repeated - spittle on hot coals.

Seldom had Durer witnessed such rage in the man. The hound craned his neck and gobbled down the last of the gingerbread while neither man was looking.

Wolgemut's knobbly fingers kept a tight hold of his rug as he dragged himself up into a half stance. With a face contorted with pain he thundered, "You are playing with me, fellow! Cat got your tongue Albrecht Durer? Thief! Scoundrel! You stole my rabbit and yet you have the gall to accept my hospitality and to claim you are the injured party! You think I'm too old but let me tell you I can still teach you a thing or two."

"If you have lost a rabbit then it's a strange coincidence that I've had my hare taken too," returned a defiant Durer. "Can there be a rabbit thief in our midst? No, not rabbits - I didn't paint a rabbit but a field hare ... there is a difference." Then stifling a giggle he turned at a sudden rush of cold air but could detect no obvious source for it. When he looked back at Wolgemut the old man's eyes had glazed over; the intensity of battle extinguished from them. Durer tapped his foot against the stove and waited, unsure what to do next.

With a hard crack Wolgemut's applewood crutch came down firmly on the flagstone floor. "Well, doesn't that just take the lebkuchen!" Wolgemut hissed. "Now I think of it my missing picture was also one of a field hare ... yes indeed, a field hare ... now what do you make of that, Albrecht Durer?"

Durer bit on his lip. He had a strong urge to pass water but did not wish to excuse himself in the circumstances.

Wolgemut's furious expression gave way to a smile and he leaned towards Durer. "It is possible the thief may be a moon worshipper. Or perhaps he is a man in concert with nature's lustful beast? For isn't that the reputation of the hare? It is a witch in disguise, is it not? And is it mere coincidence that dangerous cultists are camped outside the city wall? Is that where our culprit is concealed? Or might it be we are looking for a Herr Fox or a Herr Wolf with an appetite for hare? What do you make of that, Albrecht Durer?" Exhausted Wolgemut slumped back into his cushions and closed his eyes.

Durer sighed. "To tell the truth, Herr Wolgemut, I don't know what to think but be assured I am your dutiful servant at all times," he advised, "shall I call your wife?"

Wolgemut's eyelids slid open. "My wife? You insist on involving my wife. She knows nothing of this affair. This is no domestic matter. Why would you think to call on my wife?"

Durer's scolded himself for his insensitivity for he had often been told by Otto Beck that Wolgemut and his wife lived quite separate lives with her scarcely setting foot in her husband's workshop or showing any interest in his work. In the silence that followed Durer produced a thumbnail sketch from a leather pouch secured to his belt.

"Here it is," he cried triumphantly, "a miniature version of my picture *Field Hare* those faithless lying rascals stole from me. I experienced similar roguery when abroad, Herr Wolgemut. Venice is stuffed full of deceivers - all oily and ingratiating themselves the whole time they are going about their deception."

Michael Wolgemut was like a dog on a tight leash straining to get to Durer – his knuckles white from the effort of gripping and tugging on the arm of his chair as he endeavoured to pull himself up onto his feet and constrained by his infirmity.

"My picture, you rogue!"

"Your picture?"

Wolgemut flung aside the rug and his arms flailed about in fury.

"I have paintings and engravings, a great number – but I don't appear to have any of yours. If you would like to speak with my man, Schmeichler ... where is the fool when he's needed?" The old artist's head turned towards the doorway. "We can agree on a subject and a price and I will knock up a commendable image for you without any need for you to sneak in here to help yourself to the fruits of my labours so you can claim them as yours." His breathing came fast and his face turned as livid as Durer's burgundy hose, "Look around won't you ... do you see your precious picture anywhere, Albrecht Durer?"

Stung by Wolgemut's outburst Durer was up on his feet examining paintings and prints strung along the chamber walls. In the candlelight, however, it was near impossible to discern much of their detail.

"Fur was never your strong point, Herr Wolgemut," he muttered under his breath, "and your lines lack delicacy." The remark was unworthy of him and he regretted his words as soon as they spilled off his tongue but they were uttered so quietly Durer imagined they had gone unheard by the old man. They had not.

"That is a contemptible affront," spluttered a furious Wolgemut, "only recently I completed a very nice picture with well-defined fur that has been much admired. I would like to show it to you but unfortunately it was stolen from these very premises." The old master's rheumy eyes were defiant but as was the pattern with his moods the instant rage boiled over it subsided and with it the certainty of ever having created such a picture.

Too late to swallow back his careless words Albrecht Durer was ashamed of his own unpardonable rudeness to one who deserved only his gratitude. The hound opened an eye briefly then went back to sleep. Wolgemut settled back into his cushions as if exhausted. At the far end of the room a thin white line illuminated a gap beneath the door.

128

"You should go, Herr Durer," Herr Wolgemut's voice sounded tired out. "But don't think this is the end of the affair. How affronted your poor father would have been by your conduct. Now leave my house. Schmeichler!"

Instantly the door was thrown open and Schmeichler strode into the room. Grasping a flickering candle in one hand he took hold of Durer's arm with the other and pulled at the younger artist.

Durer broke free. "Please, Herr Wolgemut, do me the honour of demonstrating how you paint fur," he heard himself demand; again regretting his persistence for his tongue had become master over his reason.

"Show you? How flattering, dear Durer, but it is late. Show this rascal the door, Schmeichler."

Durer stood his ground. "Surely the matter can be settled here and now for my study carries my monogram." The words had scarcely left his mouth when Durer remembered that was not the case but chose not to correct his error.

"Of course, … young Herr Durer's affectation," Wolgemut sneered.

"You mark all your work, Herr Durer?" Schmeichler whispered the question into Durer's ear out of hearing of his master. Then more loudly he added, "Even with a signature or monogram it would be simple enough for any competent artist to paint over such a little thing or indeed a snip here and a snip there might do away with the thing entirely,' Schmeichler purred.

"Artists are my sole enemies for they copy my works and later insult them. Even when I was here as a youth in Herr Wolgemut's workshop another apprentice would claim my pictures as his and so I began to identify my pictures with my initials," Durer blurted out defensively.

That was the truth for Albrecht Durer's supremacy in his art attracted less able painters to go to lengths to claim his masterpieces as theirs.

Durer looked from Schmeichler to Wolgemut. The first returned his look impassively but Wolgemut's expression was thunderous.

"Your conceit is remarkable. God required no monogram on his creation but Albrecht Durer must have his stamp on every little daub he makes."

Schmeichler prodded Durer.

"If you don't mind, Herr Durer, it's this way out," he whispered as though choking on a mouthful of flies.

Albrecht Durer fairly ran from the house. He was desirous of passing water and relieved himself in the grass while the rain fell about him in a haze of small droplets that seeped into his fine coat. He had not gone so very far when he spied a figure emerge from the shadows.

"You are glistening under the light of the moon, Albrecht Durer."

It was Gudrun Wolgemut; her eyes dark from fatigue. "This theft has hurt my husband deeply. Please, Albrecht, pay no heed to his fierce words for his mind can be a trifle wavering." Gudrun Wolgemut slipped her slender hand into Durer's. "But he admires your work ... and so do I," she cooed in a tone laden with rapture.

Whether it was the beer he had consumed earlier, his fright in the labyrinth or a compliment from the lips of Gudrun Wolgemut - or indeed a combination of all three - Albrecht Durer's head swooned. He brought the lady's hand to his mouth and kissed it, delighting in the sweet rose perfume of her skin. She squeezed his fingers affectionately before modestly uncoupling his grip.

***

From the shelter of an ancient ash tree Durer watched Gudrun Wolgemut head home, a shawl protecting her head from the rain when he saw Maria Kohl approach the Wolgemut's from a different direction. He called to her but she ran off without a backward glance. Before he could turn again for home the cottage door opened and the hound was ejected into the night at the end of Schmeichler's foot.

At the crossroads he saw a magnificent goose hawk silhouetted against the night sky. Its presence furnished Durer with hope for the goose hawk represented truth and honesty.

Chapter 15

Next morning Albrecht Durer was in his workshop sorting, cleaning and repairing tools when he found a crack in his best bronze mortar and wondered if Otto Beck might repair it. The discovery did nothing to improve his temper following his nocturnal excursion and his guilt at failing to retrieve Wolgemut's picture and losing his gold. His head ached and he wondered how long it would be before he might be able to resume his everyday habits.

Günter, too, was subdued, taking his time with mopping up a spill of linseed oil and he bridled when Durer pointed out red traces on the sides of a mortar used to grind pigments, instructing the boy to clean it thoroughly. However, by the time the sext bell rang out across the city the atmosphere in the workshop had lightened with everyone profitably employed: one man prepared a waxed table; an apprentice sorted precious stones into terracotta bowls for crushing into pigments; two youngsters capered … attempting to hit each other's fingers while hammering out sheets of gold leaf and an elderly assistant pressed oil from the wormy chestnuts Els's grandmother had reluctantly supplied to Durer.

Günter sat next to a slight anxious boy of around ten years of age toying with a length of picture framing, superbly carved with intertwined oak leaves. The child's upturned pale oval face was fringed with thick black curls and his dark deep-set eyes were fixed on Günter arranging a bench for his lesson on brush and quill making. Durer stood behind them supervising as Günter fetched a bowl filled with water, an end piece of a stoat's tail, a sharp knife, assorted feathers, lengths of stripped and smoothed birch twigs and waxed linen thread for binding. Checking that the younger child was paying attention Günter pinched a tiny measure of fur from the tail tip and dipped it into the water, squeezing it to form a point. Transferring it to his left hand he sniffed as though to steady himself and sliced across the tail tip with the knife blade. He explained to the boy how to cut ends so they were uniform in length and repeated the procedure twice more. Then it was the boy's turn. The child dropped the piece of framing and picked up a fragment of stoat tail. Günter smiled up at Durer as they watched the child's first fumbled attempts - encouraging him with praise. Günter got him to repeat the exercise with different lengths and widths of bunched fur until the boy gained confidence and his fingers relaxed and grew more nimble. He got the child to break off some waxed thread and helped him wind it around the trimmed and dipped hair, securing it with a knot. They then prepared quills using a variety of birds' feathers. Günter tickled the boy's face with one when they cleaned and sliced the shafts to house the brush head. Finally, different birch handles were inserted into each hollow quill until all were matched. At the finish Günter had no need of a feather to tickle a smile out of his proud pupil. He looked around for Durer but his master had already left.

***

"I've just seen Otto. He says you lost ... er ... last night ... er ... you didn't get the picture back." Willy Pirkheimer threw down his hat and scratched his head.

The friends were in Brauer's about to take dinner.

"Where did you get to?" demanded an out-of-sorts Durer.

Pirkheimer settled his hat back onto his head and considered how to repair the rift in their friendship for he recognised his part in the failure of the plan to recover Wolgemut's picture and loss of the purse. He knew he owed Durer an explanation. "I chanced upon ... well someone and ... it was ... awkward ... in the labyrinth." The Councillor's expression revealed his revulsion for that neighbourhood and some of its inhabitants. "We fell into conversation and then I realised I was late and it was likely you had already exchanged the gold for the picture and were on your way home .... What can I say, Albi? I apologise most profusely for leaving you in the lurch."

"We had a plan and I was left to see it through and now Herr Wolgemut has neither picture nor his gold. It's all a mess," Durer whined.

"At least you had Otto keeping an eye on you all the while."

Durer shook his head. "Otto? No. I was left to face the villains on my own."

"But he said he was only gone for a short time," Pirkheimer insisted. "And the money ... it is all lost? Have you told Herr Wolgemut?"

"He knows and is not too content," Durer replied.

"Ah," was all Pirkheimer had to say.

"He's become feeble-minded," Durer said gravely.

"Albi, that's a terrible thing to say about one of our great master painters," Pirkheimer chided his companion.

"Yes, I know. He was a great artist - still is perhaps - but listening to him now ... he's not that same person, Willy. He is not always able to hold his thoughts together." Then Durer asked, "Who was it you met?"

Willy Pirkheimer ignored the question. "This is a serious business, Albi - attack and robbery. I would have you report it but there is something strange about the matter and I'm fearful how it will end."

Albrecht Durer studied the man across from him uncertain of Pirkheimer's meaning and the intent behind his remark but there was no time for him to dwell on the matter for Pirkheimer had already changed the subject. He told Durer that the mystic leader, Thomas Hut, was discovered in the city during the night has been apprehended on suspicion of the murder of Axel Marx and interrogated by the chief public prosecutor at the Rathaus gaol.

"Perhaps it best we put the events of last night behind us if we can, Albi, and not add to the dangerous frenzy that is taking hold in the town with neighbour suspicious of neighbour."

"Do you believe it was Hut that did for Axel?" Durer asked, relieved to shift the conversation away from his own troubles.

Pirkheimer shrugged his large shoulders. "He talked himself into gaol with his attacks on city folk on Michaelmas. It's

134

difficult to find a more obvious candidate responsible for butchering poor Axel, that's for sure."

"Maybe a term in gaol will transform his dismal view of his fellow-man," Durer commented.

"He is already free," Pirkheimer declared. "But he may regret his unaccountably quick release once it is known he has his liberty."

"But how has this come about? Not many emerge from the Rathaus dungeons ... has he a benefactor in the town?"

"I spoke for him." Pirkheimer coloured as he replied.

"You, Willy, but why?"

Willy Pirkheimer cleared his throat and rubbed his flabby hands together. Smiling wanly, he explained, "I was approached to intercede on his behalf."

Durer waited for him to say more.

"I was approached by Maria Kohl, if you must know," Pirkheimer added pulling a face.

"Maria Kohl?" Durer asked incredulously, "but why?"

"She asked me as a good Christian to speak up for him for she claimed Thomas Hut's words affected her on Michaelmas and she saw goodness in his soul." Pirkheimer spoke softly as if in confidence. "Of course, I would not act on the whim of a servant woman but there was no evidence of his guilt beyond his firebrand words and it cannot be right to condemn any man for speaking what is in his mind. Furthermore, I went among his followers who swore on the Holy Book that Hut was with them when Axel was put to death so following consultation with my fellows at the Rathaus it was agreed he should be released but watched."

"Is it not likely all the mystics were in on the murder?" Durer asked. "Surely even little Axel would need two men to work him into the dung – hacked into pieces that he was?"

Pirkheimer stroked his chin. "There's plenty that would agree with you but then you have to consider that the mystic preached against sin he did not advocate practising it."

"But he threatened punishment, vile and cruel punishment on any transgressors. I'm surprised at you, Willy, supporting the pilgrim's innocence."

"I admit I am not certain in my mind, Albi, but there is nothing to connect the mystics with this barbaric act and there were charcoal burners who also confirmed seeing them at the camp. To reassure our townsfolk the gatemen have been ordered to make absolutely certain that no zealot is able to gain admittance at night-time. Wolf," Pirkheimer said, changing the subject, "it was Wolf I chanced upon. His mother still lives in the brutalised world of the labyrinth. He moved out long ago but his old mother is stubborn and refuses to leave so he's always returning." Pirkheimer clapped his hands to break the slight tension between the friends.

"And you went off with Wolf and abandoned me to my fate?" Durer complained.

"It just happened. We were both discomfited being discovered there - although Wolf had reason enough … as for me - what else could I have done? What would you have done, Albi?"

Albrecht Durer wasted not one iota of his time considering how he might have acted in Pirkheimer's shoes. He had been let down by him and that was what mattered but he swallowed his annoyance. "I thought I might have seen Otto this morning."

"Otto will surely be here soon enough but pray, Albi," Pirkheimer implored, "say nothing to him of the matter concerning Maria for I don't believe he is aware of it."

***

Albrecht Durer led Els upstairs away from the workshop with its prying eyes. Within the privacy of his bed chamber she exhibited none of the inhibition that marked her first sitting and speedily fell into the pose she last adopted.

It was Durer's intention to have Eva represent the embodiment of womanhood but Els, while undoubtedly beautiful, was very young and in his view she hardly personified the perfectly proportioned ideal woman he originally had in mind. However, having become infatuated with his youthful muse a lithe and slender Eva would inhabit his Eden.

Els's eyes occasionally strayed towards the handsome artist deep in concentration, his fingers plying the silverpoint with fluid continuity. She became fascinated by the painter's eyelids flitting upwards then downwards and upwards again in perpetual motion between her and his drawing-board; his concentration centred entirely in a world apart from hers.

Cupping the fruit in her hand, the apple that was as yet an egg, a weary Els longed to rest, to lie out on a bed, as Durer promised, so he might capture her hair spread out as though blown by the wind. Still, she dared not speak out.

Durer's look of quiet absorption belied the exhilaration he was feeling working up detail on Eva's figure but content as he was, he could not banish entirely the thoughts crowding into his head. He pictured his father, ever patient, who instilled in him his meticulous approach to fine shading to create an illusion of depth in his compositions. And he contemplated how much hurt he caused his father when spurning his expectations to succeed him as a goldsmith; especially forsaking it for the lowly occupation of painter. This guilt, if that was what he felt, had driven him to transform painting into a respectable trade and if sales of his prints were any measure then he was making progress in that direction. *Adam and Eve,* when engraved would, he was confident, prove successful for the subject was popular as gifts to newlyweds with its allusions to love and passion and the first man and woman. With his head bursting with ideas for the picture Durer was able to shake off the last of the black depression plaguing him over Wolgemut's stolen painting. Even his missing *Field Hare* could not dispel the contentment that crept up on him when he observed Els; her beauty and the harmony of nature emerging from his skilful fingers.

137

Els's transformation into Eva was entire and the domesticity of the room transmuted into a Heavenly garden on Earth. Adam was as yet delineated by the merest of marks and it would be with him not Eva that the viewer's eye would begin the journey around Albrecht Durer's Eden - from Adam's hand touching a branch of the Tree of Knowledge where an uncustomary quiet Papagei was perched along the bird's tail and across Adam's shoulders to his outstretched arm and hand ready to receive the forbidden fruit from Eva.

Reflecting on the arrangement Durer decided to place a cartelino in as bold a spot as he dared identifying him as the artist and Nuremberg its place of origin. He would suspend it from the Tree of Knowledge next to Papagei who would deter the most cunning villain from claiming the work as his.

Els could see Durer's hand forming letters on a scrap of paper he had picked off the floor but was unable to read the message spelled out ALBERTUS *DURER NORICUS FACIEBAT* - *Albrecht Durer of Nuremberg.*

Having settled on the wording of his cartelino Durer gave a moment's consideration to Adam. Despite Wolgemut's opposition Durer was determined to have Joachim as his Adam. Indeed, he already had a collection of sketches of the boy made during his visits to Günther in the workshop. While disappointed Wolgemut would deny him permission to employ his apprentice, Durer did, at the same time, recognise his debt to the old master for providing the essential grounding of his trade; albeit his style altered following his time working with Italy's great masters. Durer suspected the old man of wanting to rein in his ambition and in an effort to shake off his irritation with Wolgemut, Durer attacked the background in his Eden composition, making it very dark, heavy with shadows - a menacing habitat for strange and dangerous creatures and spirits. With a shake of his head Albrecht Durer realised how long Els had held the pose.

"Put down the egg-apple, Els and rest your arm."

Els gratefully did just that with a slight groan as she shook numbness out of her arm.

"What was that?" she asked, looking up.

"What?"

"Outside. I can hear shouting."

Durer, too, then heard it. He leaned a knee on the window seat and peered out. Thomas Hut stood on Durer's doorstep employing it as a stage from where he was delivering a valediction on morality to any who would listen from among Durer's neighbours.

Wrapping her cloak about her Els stole up next to Durer. Together they observed the mystic. Durer could not understand the man's preoccupation with him for while he never claimed he lived an unblemished life neither could it be said it was tainted by malevolence. He was a staunch observer of the scriptures - as much as a man of flesh and blood might be expected to be - who employed his talent to broadcast the Gospel message.

"Adam and Eve were stripped of their angelic garments when they defied God and ate the forbidden fruit and were made to put on fig leaf aprons to conceal the shame of their mortal flesh."

Durer caught Els's eye. Her body froze as if she had taken root to the spot.

"And the Lord God planted a garden eastward in Eden; and there he put the man whom he had formed."

"What can it mean?" Els whispered. "Is he talking about us?"

"... but from the Tree of the Knowledge of Good and Evil thou shalt not eat, for in the day that thou eatest from it thou shalt surely die ... and she did eat, and gave unto her husband and he did eat. And God suffered the serpent to crawl on his belly and spread evil upon the land."

Els pressed a hand to her mouth to stifle a cry as Durer pulled her back from the window.

"Does he see the future?" she asked. "He can see that something awful is about to happen to me." She threw herself down onto the bed.

Durer tried to reassure her, dismissing the mystic as a fake prophet and troublemaker. It was he, Albrecht Durer, who venerated the word of God through his paintings and prints and neither he nor her had reason to feel shame. Still Els trembled uncontrollably and Durer was struck by her youth and vulnerability to men with persuasive tongues such as the mystic, Thomas Hut.

"Let's get you back to your grandmother," he said kindly.

"I fear he will harm me ... us ... like he did Herr Marx," Els cried, fumbling with her clothes. Durer left her to dress and with the firebrand's words ringing in his ears he descended the staircase.

"Eve made us all sinners in the eyes of God. When Adam slept God fashioned Eve from his rib. The two were innocent till Eve yielded to the temptation of the serpent and gave Adam the forbidden fruit."

Durer called up the stairs to Els that she should leave by the side door to avoid the preacher then he went outside where he discovered Willy Pirkheimer engaged in heated exchanges with Hut. A florid-faced Pirkheimer was accusing the mystic of hypocrisy and threatening to bring the whole civic authority of the town down on him and his sect if he did not desist from harassing the good citizens of Nuremberg.

"Where does your low opinion of human nature come from?" roared Pirkheimer so he might be heard over the mystic's continuing agitation.

Durer had rarely seen Willy Pirkheimer so angry.

"You attract nought but derision with your false charges against decent people who have granted you hospitality of this fine city. And think of the harm you are inflicting on this impressionable young girl?" Pirkheimer pointed to the child, the mystic's frequent companion standing by him; frail, anxious and under-nourished. As for the preacher he appeared none the worse for his interrogation by the chief prosecutor except for a cut beneath one eye.

Noticing Durer's arrival, the mystic's face lit up. "I have no low regard for my fellows only those swept along in a tide of falsehood and pretence. My words can open eyes to recognise true goodness amidst depravity and deception perpetrated by chatterers in those ships of fools - I mean St Sebaldus, St Lorenz and Frauenkirche. It is only by taking responsibility for our own salvation that we can win the battle against the wickedness of the world. You just have to listen to Christ's voice within yourself to discover truth." The agitator pointed up at Durer's house. "You will not find Christ in pictures or golden and bejewelled objects but in here," he pressed his hand against his heart."

Pirkheimer held up his hand for quiet. "You are wrong to come here and condemn the pious citizens of Nuremberg. We are not brute creatures like this little one," Pirkheimer bent down to stroke Katze who had followed Durer out of the house and sat cleaning himself on the step. "Man's nature is not set for he has free will, on that we can agree. My friend here," Pirkheimer pointed at Durer, "who I know intimately and who you dare imply is involved in false worship is a model of righteousness whereas you with your feeble theatricals prove your inability to grasp the fundamentals of God's existence in the hearts of men."

"You dare to suggest that man has the authority of God to choose his own destiny?" the mystic screamed.

"You say God is found in our hearts so it follows he is what we believe him to be. You object to priests but expect us to listen to your sermon, as if your ear is to God's mouth."

As Durer's neighbours became increasingly restless the mystic denied he interpreted God.

"Your objections are semantics - " Pirkheimer turned to Durer, "Albi, this fellow is becoming a thorn in your flesh, and a perilous enemy. I can see we were wrong to grant him and his band the hospitality of the city."

Hut appeared unnerved but pressed on. "Because you say a man is pious does not make him so. Man is consumed by self-interest and so is corruptible. He takes the gift God gives him and turns it against the Lord by choosing to present his own face to the world instead of God's image. It is through God we learn humility and truth, not man. And not through what is worthless: common nature - trees, wild mountains and lowly animals."

"But my work is a medium for the Gospel," Durer insisted. "My workshop is crammed full of religious images created by this hand," he said holding up his hand to emphasise the point. "My works are God's words rendered as pictures so that the humblest of men can understand them."

The mystic smiled ruefully.

"To the flames with him - murderer," came a shout from the street.

The mystic's eyes narrowed into slits, gauging the hostility surrounding him. "We have no need of pictures to interpret the words of the Lord. He speaks directly to us. Why confuse his meaning with symbols and artefacts? Why cloak God's meaning in mystery?"

The young girl at the mystic's side peered anxiously about her for she, too, sensed the growing intolerance of local people.

"It's blasphemous to give as much prominence to an ox as to the Holy family and Christ's apostles." Hut was looking up at the very window where a quarter of the clock earlier Durer had stood with Els. "Where is the harlot?"

That was the moment Els and Günter chose to emerge from the side of the house. They stood frozen to the spot. Ashen-faced Else wiped away a tear with the back of her hand while Günter, holding a leafy twig, stared uncomprehending at the mystic who extended his hand in a gesture of atonement for he appeared just as startled by their appearance. But he repeated the words, "Where is the harlot?"

The frail child was coughing and Hut drew her close in to him. Cat-calls rained down on the pair and with his arm around the child the mystic led her away. Willy Pirkheimer beckoned Els forward so he could accompany her back to her grandmother's house. Watching them go, Günter wiped his nose on his sleeve.

Durer sidled up to his apprentice, "Heigho, Günter. It's best we keep to our own company."

As he shut the door on the scene of his public humiliation Durer speculated on who Hut supposed was the *harlot* for by his expression of surprise it appeared it was not Els that he meant.

***

Willy Pirkheimer was about to enter Otto Beck's workshop when he became aware of voices from within.

"You will have twenty of these wheel lock firearms prepared for my return in late spring," commanded a man whose tongue struggled to cope with German words.

Beck was heard protesting that he was very busy but any excuse he was about to offer was dismissed by the foreign gentleman.

"You persuaded us to come all this distance, Herr Beck. If you will not provide us with the weapons we require you will provide instructions for their manufacture so they can be made up by another gunsmith."

Otto Beck's protests were silenced.

"If you do not agree to my terms we will take you back with us and hold you until you complete the assignment. You can decide for yourself which it is to be."

Willy Pirkheimer had heard enough and burst into the room where he found a giant of a man he recognised from Brauer's as Collado's companion bent over little Otto Beck whose back was pressed to a wall. Collado and the third Spaniard were seated but on Pirkheimer's entrance they jumped to their feet and a curved knife was held to the face of the Councillor.

Quick as a flash Otto Beck ducked from beneath his huge assailant and springing up onto his workbench he curled his fingers around the trigger of one of his new wheel lock guns and trained it on Collado. The Spaniard raised his hands in submission and his men copied him. The scimitar that threatened Pirkheimer clattered across the stone floor. With a twinkle in his malevolent eye and slow nod of acknowledgment of his situation Collado prepared his retreat.

Exchanges between the three Spaniards in their native tongue were partly understood by Willy Pirkheimer's cultivated ears. He picked up a reference to *Familiars* which Pirkheimer knew were spies within the circle of Spanish inquisitors and this intelligence must have revealed itself in some way to the mercenary who unleashed a string of obscenities or so they sounded for they shot so fast from his mouth they proved too quick for the Nuremberg scholar's comprehension.

"It is lucky for him he lives in this barbaric country," Collado thundered in broken German, "for if we could persuade him into ours how charmingly he would sing at one of our autos-da-fé but for now your little locksmith will be spared for I have yet to find another as talented in the making of a firearm as this sprite."

Otto Beck felt foolish atop the work bench and his round peasant face reddened self-consciously. Jumping down he grabbed hold of Collado's great hands and reassured him he would do his best to comply with his request. Collado pulled free of the handshake and avoiding Pirkheimer's eye he swept out of the room followed by his men; one retrieving the scimitar from the floor as he withdrew.

An abashed Beck grinned at Pirkheimer. "The sun - makes the Spanish hot-headed ..." he scratched his chin, "he is too important a customer to lose and it's a privilege for a valiant warrior such as him to favour my weapons for his wars." He shrugged. "How many have that honour, eh Willy? You are a military hero but have never asked me to supply you with firearms. I hope you never have to rue the day you find yourself eyeball-to-eyeball with Collado; he armed with my best firer and you with some dud from one of my rivals. Then you'd be wishing you had come to your friend Otto for one that might spare your neck."

Willy Pirkheimer took down Beck's cloak from the door peg and held it for Beck who was storing away a firearm on a shelf behind his bench.

"Albi need know nothing of what happened here, dear Willy. He has enough troubles of his own."

144

"I don't know how you two would get along without me," Pirkheimer said shaking his head.

Otto Beck squinted up at Pirkheimer.

"We labour with our hands. When reviled we bless; when persecuted we endure; I am sure, Willy, we would find a way."

"Fat hock?" Pirkheimer asked with a smack of his lips.

"Lead the way," Beck implored.

Crossing the Hauptmarkt Beck and Pirkheimer happened upon Albrecht Durer approaching from the opposite direction.

"What's this I hear, Albi?" Beck asked. "Willy told me the mystic has been hounding you. I tell you he's the one who's done for Axel, you mark my words. You'll need to keep a close eye on that one for it wouldn't surprise me if he wasn't planning some harm aimed at you Albi."

The bell marking the end of market rang out. Crippled Josef was making his way home when he was stopped by a Quacksalver trying to sell him a potion to strengthen his legs. At the end of his restraining chain, Josef's toothless and clawless elderly bear waited patiently swaying back and fore, outwardly oblivious to the taunts of children shrieking and jumping at him. Traders were packing their unsold merchandise onto barrows and carts but even at this late hour as they rolled up their bolts of brocade patterned with pomegranates and artichokes two foreign merchants were drawing in straggling Nurembergers, dressed in their distinctly sparrow-like browns and greys, seemingly reluctant to leave the colourful attraction offered by the mercers' fabrics vividly dyed in shades of red, blue and gold.

"My dear friend, Otto, and my wise friend, Willy, I think I am fated to have evil days. My French mantle and the doublet wish you both a hearty greeting," Durer quipped as he cast a disparaging glance at Otto Beck's rustic short-cut woollen trousers and patched blue coat missing a button. Then shifting his gaze he whispered, "Well, well."

Beck followed his gaze. "You know them?"

Durer was staring at a tall beanpole of a man and his diminutive post of a companion packing their handcart with rolls of bright textiles while conversing in what sounded to his ear was an Italian dialect.

"I'm not certain," was Durer's hesitant reply.

Beck studied the pair.

"Is that them? Are they the ones who took our bunny? Italians, aren't they? You are certain it was them? Just look at them both! ... their cunning countenances. Tell me, Albi, is it them?" he demanded.

"There is something familiar ..."

"Is it, Albi? Is it them?" Beck hissed.

Getting no response from Durer Beck launched himself at the closest of the merchants. Pandemonium broke out, a rangy hound belonging to the mercers barked furiously and was only restrained by his tether from getting at his master's assailant. Beck was maintaining a near inaudible monologue as he furiously pummelled the short post. Once over the initial shock of being attacked the little fellow began to defend himself.

"Albi - the other!" Beck wheezed as open palms rained down on him.

Durer gaped open mouthed. The beanpole meantime had sought refuge behind a stack of brocade.

"What are you playing at, Otto?"

Beck ducked a flying fist then dodged an attempted tackle by the post.

"Hey lads, over here," Beck bellowed to a group of barrowmen waiting to be hired.

The barrowmen were delighted to exchange their game of dice for a brawl and with impressive alacrity they got stuck into the skirmish much to the consternation of the mercers.

Hopelessly outnumbered the post tried to finish off Beck with a mighty blow to the bridge of his nose. The sound of a twig cracking preceded a scream from Beck as he cupped his hands around his throbbing nose and blood trickled between his fingers. An astonished Pirkheimer appealed for calm and

146

for a few moments all went quiet with Beck clinging tenaciously to the sleeve of the post while the beanpole lay prostrate on the ground having received a severe beating.

"It might not be them," Durer yelled.

"Get me out of this, Albi," roared Beck, "this buffoon's broken my hooter."

The barrowmen were in no mood to be denied now that their blood was up. Having incapacitated the beanpole their attention turned to the post who had just driven a fist into Beck's jaw. A piercing shriek stopped everyone in their tracks. Beck's name reverberated across the square. As the schlosser looked for its origin a punch landed him smack in the eye.

A furious Maria Kohl elbowed her way to the heart of the tumult and without concern for her own safety positioned herself between Beck and the post. The beanpole pulled himself up and leaned on an elbow.

"Stop!" Maria demanded in her thick Spalt dialect.

Obediently disappointed, the barrowmen slunk away. A macabre leer was fixed on Beck's face; lips and teeth coated in blood. He crept away in Maria's wake. Only when there was sufficient distance between him and the post did he recover his familiar swagger.

***

Beck's fingers repeatedly searched out his tender and swollen nose but he got no more sympathy from Durer and Pirkheimer than he had from Maria Kohl. He banged his fist hard against the table. "At least we showed them, he said defiantly.

Pirkheimer examined Beck's face - black and blue from its beating; a swollen eye, squint nose and coat sleeve caked with dried blood. He shook his head in disgust as he loosened spoon and dagger from his belt and drew the platter in the centre of the table towards him.

"Can we sup our dinner in peace?"

Durer inhaled noisily. "I never said it was them…"

"They were Italians," Beck broke in.

"This town is full of Italians. You can't pick on all of them," Pirkheimer barked back.

Beck turned on him. "They're foreigners. You know what foreigners are like. Why are you picking on me? I'm the injured one."

Durer glared at Beck. "Your Maria is also a foreigner but you have no problems associating with her."

"She's from Spat. That's hardly foreign," Beck complained, "anyway I haven't married her so that tells you something."

Willy Pirkheimer leaned forward, his elbows on the table and addressed Beck as if he were a child. "The guard at the gates were alerted that a group of strangers suspected of terrible crimes in Nördlingen, Rothenburg ob der Tauber and at Augsburg might be making for Nuremberg."

"What sort of terrible crimes?" asked Beck.

Kidnap of a child they are suspected of having eaten, to conceal all traces of her. What looked like a boiled human head was fished out of the river Lech. There is no record those Italian merchants were anywhere near any of those towns and their permits were all in order when they were admitted. There's no reason to think they are anything other than what they claim to be, genuine traders, that the good people of Nuremberg are delighted to have here," Pirkheimer explained.

Beck scowled at Pirkheimer. "Those two have just come from Augsburg," he hissed, "Maria told me so."

"And how would Maria know?" Durer demanded. "I've heard far too much about Maria and what she knows. It strikes me she knows a little too much or thinks she does. Between what goes on at Wolgemut's place and my house, in tow with you I may say, she's well-informed. And talking about you," he wagged his finger at Beck, "lately you have been hiding away. What is it you are up to behind our backs?"

Ignoring Durer's question Otto Beck rubbed at the stubble on his chin. "Having the right papers doesn't excuse them breaking my nose. And where is the thanks that's my due for coming to your assistance? Oh, don't mention it, Albi." Beck balled his fists in frustration, hoping to draw an apology from

Durer. He subjected his artist friend to a resentful glare out of his good eye but no contrition was forthcoming. "I have been severely injured in the course of protecting you and this is the thanks I get? This is the thanks!" A podgy fist banged down again on the table.

"Blockhead," Durer muttered under his breath.

"Alright," Willy Pirkheimer roared, "this is unseemly. I happen to know the Italians were carrying invitations to the Kaiserburg on their arrival. There's nothing to suggest they had anything to do with stolen paintings or any crime, come to that." He pulled a plug of gristle from his mouth. "What we have is a coincidence. Two pictures, two very similar pictures it appears, stolen; one belonging to Albi and the other to Herr Wolgemut. Herr Wolgemut was asked to pay a ransom but Albi has not. The question is, why not? Why has nothing been demanded for the return of his *Field Hare*? … that is assuming the thefts are related. Herr Wolgemut has been cheated out of his money, although it never was his in the first place but Frau Wolgemut's uncle's, and Wolgemut blames Albi who tried to help but failed. The question is - one of the questions - why was Albi dragged into Wolgemut's affair when they have not been acquainted for years? That's right isn't it, Albi?"

Durer nodded.

"Why not just use his creepy lackey?" Pirkheimer continued, " is what's been puzzling me. And why hasn't Wolgemut demanded Albi repay the lost guldens?"

"He said I should help recover the picture because I was mentioned in the ransom letter," Durer said.

"Did you see it?" Pirkheimer asked.

Durer shook his head. "Only instructions that Schmeichler gave me but that wasn't the actual ransom."

"And there's the coincidence of the two stolen pictures being the same." Beck piped up.

"What's on your mind, Otto?" Pirkheimer asked.

"Well … you know … the rabbit thing," Beck replied between mouthfuls of pork.

"Hare," Durer said.

Beck rolled his good eye. "The way I see it Wolgemut's getting on in years. His income's drying up. He pretends he's lost a picture and ..." Beck's voice drifted away.

"And?" Pirkheimer prompted. "Where does that get us? He's lost the gold so he's not gained from any pretence - Kläuschen over here," he shouted to Ana's grandson again kicking his heels next to Müller.

The boy slapped a hand over one eye and staggered like a drunken man towards the three friends, staring in fascination at Beck's battered face.

"Gone blind, Kläuschen?" Pirkheimer asked.

"I'm Herr Müller ... or Herr Beck," the boy replied matter-of-factly.

"Well little Cyclops fix your orb on this." Pirkheimer slackened off his purse strings and fetched out a coin which he plied between his fat fingers before making it disappear. "Now where has it got to?" he asked, making great play of looking under the bench and table before producing the coin from behind the lad's ear. "Ah, here it is however did you manage that young Kläus?"

The child giggled grabbing the coin out of Pirkheimer's outstretched hand. Then with a final glance at Beck he ran off to show his grandmother. From his chair by the door Müller watched the child before bellowing across the inn.

"Hoy, Councillor - have you hunted down Axel's murderers yet? That mystic, Hut, will have to take care of that scrawny neck of his. He might find he's in for a close shave of his beard with a very sharp razor in a clumsy hand." He ran a finger across his throat in a slitting motion. "It's come to something when innocent town folk can't go about their business in peace without being accosted by foreign devils." His eye slid in the direction of Collado and his companions sitting in half-shadows at a far corner. "If our magistrates refuse to protect us we'll have to take matters into our own hands." He wiped spittle off his chin with his dirty red skullcap.

Pirkheimer was tempted to respond to the grain merchant or Red Cap as he was sometimes called but thought better of it.

The Councillor was by nature a conciliator but his run-in with Collado left him unable to speak out in his defence. Further, he knew him to be less of the hero Beck claimed than a soldier of fortune whose loyalty was secured by payment. As for the pilgrims he had given consideration to Hut's sermonising and while the man's ideas were unsophisticated and confused he suspected there was more right than not at the back of them.

On the other hand, Otto Beck had been nodding in agreement with Müller over their antipathies towards strangers despite the schlosser cultivating a number of them as customers whereas Müller's income came entirely from within the city which might account for his willingness to give full vent to his intolerances.

There were barrowmen, too, in Brauer's eating and drinking with their usual abandon. They talked none-too-quietly about various Nuremberg folk, including Müller, who one called a brute, a dog and the devil who was long overdue a lesson for what he did to people in the town. The grain merchant was used to being the subject of scorn and feigned deafness against their barbs.

"Suppose Wolgemut has not lost his money?" Beck asked. "Suppose it was a trick - or that sneak, Schmeichler, has it? Who's to say it wasn't him who set upon Albi in that alley? In the dark it could have been anyone."

Durer looked at Pirkheimer.

"Then what accounts for his anger?" Pirkheimer asked.

Beck considered the question. "Well … stands to reason … he has to show anger. He claims a thief has made away with a picture. He's hardly going to turn round and say, thanks for being so stupid as to let me get the money back without a fight, Albi, is he?" Beck asked.

Durer was up making a grab at Beck but Pirkheimer was quicker and pulled him down into his seat imploring them both to stop their bickering. Durer's face was crimson with rage and his breathing rapid as Willy Pirkheimer demanded calm with an emphatic motion of his great paw.

"What has got into everyone tonight?" he demanded.

Beck stared at Durer. "Wolgemut was given that money to buy back the picture - by his wife's uncle. What's easier than making up a story of a loss and appealing to a rich uncle to cover the loss? After all it's no secret Gudrun spends two stivers for every one her husband earns. That's why she and old man Wolgemut are forever quarrelling over money."

"What uncle?" Pirkheimer demanded impatiently.

"His uncle …her uncle? … I don't know which uncle, the one that provided the purse. It doesn't matter does it? Maria tells me there is a wealthy uncle." A smug smile splayed over Beck's face.

Pirkheimer tilted his great head. "Let us just suppose that Otto is onto something, for the sake of argument, Albi, before you take to your high horse again. Wolgemut sees Albi as a rival." His words came hesitatingly as he assembled his thoughts. "He is in a way … and it might be conceivable he would seize an opportunity to damage Albi's reputation … let's say by questioning his integrity. I think it unlikely but let us consider it could be so." He stroked his chin then shook his head. "No, it's not satisfactory, Otto, after all he has not dented Albi's reputation for few know of the theft so all he could have gained from such a scheme is money."

"Which is perhaps all he was ever after, as I said," Beck held up his hands in triumph. Money is what we all seek, is it not?"

"It is not," Pirkheimer rounded on his companion. "Some of us have finer ideals."

"And those who say that are the ones who have most money," Beck muttered. "Not everyone can survive on that silver-lined cloud of yours, Willy. Some of us have to dirty our fingernails to fill our bellies." To make his point Beck brandished a pair of calloused hands; blackened from their years working metal and fingernails split and broken. "The hands you are quick to ridicule produce the wealth that Nuremberg's Burghers love to reflect in. Let's face it old man Wolgemut's output is drying up and he wouldn't be the first man to want to put down a rival."

Pirkheimer groaned. "I grant it is a puzzle. Perhaps those Italians are behind this mischief. They can be tricky fellows but how would they know about Wolgemut or Albi come to that? And why the hare, or the rabbit or whatever's involved? I can't see reason behind any of it."

"Because it is a rabbit - sorry a hare, Albi ... anyone could get rid of something like that easily enough without raising too many questions ... we might have hare worshippers in our midst," Beck mused.

"You said that before," Durer said, breaking his silence "when the fleshers were going on about strange ceremonies at the palace."

"Ana brought it up but, yes, it could be what's behind Nuremberg's picture crime," Beck agreed, "we've all heard the rumours."

"And they thought they would make do with Wolgemut's rabbit?" Pirkheimer snorted.

"It might have been so poorly drawn it was taken for a hare," Beck chuckled, then warming to his reasoning, "and when they discovered it wasn't but that Albi had the very thing at home they went in search of his picture."

"So, we are looking for hare worshippers now?" Pirkheimer asked.

"It might have been stolen by command of someone ... someone who has a reputation for strange behaviour." Beck winked with his good eye.

"You have someone in mind, Otto?" Pirkheimer enquired.

"There is no need to utter a name for we all know of mysterious goings-on up there." Beck nodded in the direction of the Imperial palace.

"I would stop right there, Otto," Pirkheimer counselled.

Rumours of eccentric rituals at the Kaiserburg involving men in hare pelt hoods fashioned in imitation of the creatures and drinking the animal's blood had long circulated throughout Franconia. Nevertheless, it was a foolhardy soul who gave voice to such gossip within earshot of others.

"Still, there is nothing to tie in the Italians," Pirkheimer insisted in an effort to steer the conversation onto safer ground. "They may be entirely innocent - as innocent as - any other poor maligned persons ..." he was treading warily to avoid mention of any prince at the Kaiserburg. "If I were to suspect anyone it would be Wolgemut's man, Schmeichler. A slimy toad is that one."

Beck laughed. "That's not like you, Willy."

"I'm indulging you, Otto, my friend," Pirkheimer winked at him. "And cheer up, Albi, we'll work this one out and get your picture back in no time."

"Your big bunny," Beck added mischievously, "oh, I didn't say, Albi, – you remember that hound of Wolgemut's ... the poor beast ... he dropped dead. Maria said she saw a hawk hovering above the meadow and when someone from Wolgemut's workshop went to investigate they found the brute - cold and well pecked. Old man Wolgemut isn't having the best of luck. Oh ... and it was Maria's brother."

"What was Maria's brother?" Pirkheimer asked.

"Those Italians - she heard by letter from her brother in Augsburg that a pair of Italians were involved in some trickery or another."

At that moment a great commotion erupted. Someone had looked in to tell that the little Schutzen princess was missing from home. Immediately men started running out of the inn to join the search for the child. Durer and Pirkheimer got to their feet intending to follow when a stool flew through the air just missing the big man. About twenty revellers began shoving, jostling and insulting one another in the foulest of terms. Pirkheimer tried to intervene. His giant presence often proved a soothing influence on the intoxicated and hot-headed but no-one paid him heed, if anything the melee grew more frenzied until a rush of bodies, including Herr Müller and the Spanish gentlemen, ran after two men accused of being mystics. Otto Beck, too, ran out but returned quickly informing Durer and Pirkheimer he saw the alleged mystics running along Königstrasse towards Marthakirche pursued by Müller and four barrowmen.

***

Later that same evening Willy Pirkheimer was reading in his library when he lifted his eyes from his book and thought back over the meeting of Burghers and gild leaders that had only just finished at the Rathaus to further discuss the presence of Thomas Hut and his band camped outside the Laurenzer Forst. With feelings running high the Council felt obliged to act to contain mounting unrest over their failure to charge anyone for the horrific killing of Axel Marx. Hut's interrogation came to nothing and the longer the murderer was on the loose the more the Council came in for criticism. Hut had confirmed he had grown up in the tiny settlement of Spat but no longer lived there instead he devoted his life to *helping people understand the true meaning of holy worship.* Nuremberg's Burghers and master craftsmen mainly rejected this as nonsense and a cover for his real intention to instil terror and cause confusion and mistrust among the good people of the town. They drew up a statement condemning his release and laid out a plan to remove the menace from Nuremberg's environs.

Chapter 16

He found the strength of Hercules yet the more he fought to loosen the straps that bound his wrists and ankles the tighter they gripped. Bindings wound around his head prevented him seeing his tormentor or tormentors, he could not tell their number, for none uttered so much as a sigh. As for his own tongue it was stopped fast by a filthy rag tasting of lubricating grease and mould that was stuffed into his mouth preventing the roar of fear and frustration that tried to escape from deep within his being.

Manhandled, he was slung across the back of a short-legged animal that groaned with shock at its sudden burden. In this manner he was taken, belly down and jolted this way and that with the beast straining under his bulk. The route was at first familiar for he smelled the places where manufacturing was done; where by day smiths fired and shaped metal for animal shoes and locks and trinkets and weapons that brought strangers to Nuremberg from every quarter: east and west and north and south. Animals roused from sleep snorted at being disturbed convincing him they neared the Frauentor port. He heard voices but they were too indistinct to decipher what was said above the tap, tap of animal hooves on flagstones as he was borne along. Out in the open wind tugged at his clothing causing him to shiver; from cold but fear, too. There was the reek of the great midden heaps where night scavengers emptied their wagons piled high with human excrement before the terrain grew rough and uneven, joggling him so that blood rushed through his ears like the sound of a river in spate. He considered using the movement to topple off the beast and make his escape but his tethers were knotted fast and so he resigned himself to his fate but wept all the same. The tears that welled ran silently for he would not let his assailant see his distress.

The strapping around his head was soon saturated reminding him of another time when he was carried in a similar manner.

156

Then he sat straddling the neck of a pony with his father at his back promising adventure that only men must know of - thrilling him, a mere child that he might be considered a man. The rain fell that evening but his eyes were not covered and he saw other boys there, some familiar faces, riding with men; a nocturnal procession of horses and flaming torches led by his father. They stopped at a clearing by the edge of the forest with all dismounting and mingling briefly before a hat was produced out of which each adult picked a tin token. A second cap full of tokens with numbers written on them was produced and each child told to draw one out, he recalled his number was three. It appeared to be a good game which some of the boys imagined would involve night hunting in the wood and he remembered the excitement he felt and pride that his father was in charge – and laughing at friends with their miserable expressions who he decided were scaredy-cats.

There was to be no hunting that night nor on any of the subsequent nights he and the other boys were taken to the clearing. When each child's number was called, he was paired with a man with the same number token and together they went off in search of privacy, not difficult in the dark, and the children were forced into intimacy with the men. That first time when a stranger took him roughly by his skinny arm he begged his father to intervene but his father had looked away, eager to satisfy his own fiendish desires. He never spoke to any of the other boys about what happened to them on these occasions and none of the other boys ever played with him again.

Townsmen both powerful and humble were united in their wickedness and forever fearful that one day their depravity would be exposed. Sometimes a child died from injuries inflicted by the men's play and at least two he knew of drowned themselves in the Pegnitz. While most lived their lives normally a few boys matured into men of the same mould as their assailants. It could be said he was one of them – having borne every humiliation heaped upon him as a boy and surrounding himself with an emotional wall that none could breach.

The animal drew to a halt and he was dragged off its back and dropped onto wet grass. His heart beat fast and his breath came quick fearing their intent. Hands hauled at him and pulled him to a spot where he felt heat. It pleased him for his limbs were so cold he lost all feeling in them. Soon the heat grew more intense and he wished the blustering wind would cool the extreme temperature that was all on one side but even the wind at its height proved no ally.

Fingers played about his head and then the blindfold was off and he saw a well-stoked brazier, the kind charcoal burners might use, with flames leaping out its gaping mouth and the piercings around its body. The firebox was wedged between two rocks and no more than the width of a man from him; its glowing hellish heat transfixing his eye.

Sweat ran down his face and neck and he was sure his skin was blistering. A foot kicked his back sending him yet closer to the brazier and now his face and chest felt as though they were turned to liquid such was its fiery intensity. Gasping he fought for breath for suffocation was upon him. He imagined his single eyeball was turning to water and running out of its orb and seeing nothing but scarlet darting fireflies.

***

Scarlet was the colour of his pain. Intense its depth. It overwhelmed his wits casting him adrift - out and in of understanding.

A fifteen-year-old youth was fishing in the Pegnitz one evening as night stole along Nuremberg's lanes tumbling over its riverbanks. Two pike, fresh and glistening lay on the grass. He hoped for a third before being compelled homeward and to bed. It was then they came for him. Usually he was left alone for he was as much a victim of his brutish father as any child in Nuremberg but the father was a slippery catch, not easy to land and he proved an easy proxy.

They surrounded him, cat-calling and assailing him with foul words. But when taunts failed to slake their thirst for vengeance, they jabbed at him with sticks and punched him with flying fists till finally they stabbed him with blades so carelessly one sliced through an eye and turned him into a Cyclops. His shouts for his mother to save him were futile for she had long since gone from his life and it surprised him to discover a buried ache from the loss of her.

The father, for years his sole guardian, made no mention of the wayward wife and mother but always it was the two of them against the gossip and tittle-tattle meant to sting - and did. Many Nuremberg folk depended on them, for their grain. Who could survive without bread? So, they had to shut up and come knocking on their door, their gaze averted pleading for corn; the price of them. Always a price. Few could hold out for long against the ravages of starvation and then it was time to strike a bargain - for their womenfolk and children to service the grain merchant's intimate longings in return for the release of a sack of meal. For those unwilling to submit to their evil desires there was the humiliation of scraping bark from birch trees to grind into *flour* boiled up with forest mushrooms to stall gnawing hunger; one degradation traded for another.

Hellish heat suffused his body and his mind. The son created in the image of the father both of them making it their business to know everyone else's business. Knowledge was power and power could be exercised as tyranny. So shame was instilled into husbands who collaborated into cajoling frightened wives to enter the viper's nest that the family might eat. Where a woman was rejected a child might become the means that would fill family stomachs.

His body shook uncontrollably and his eyes were now sightless. He trembled at the touch of a hand on his shoulder. Never as a man had his great strength let him down but the intense heat sapped him entirely so when he tried to stand his legs buckled under him like he was a poor hamstrung horse.

Throughout his suffering some of the rage that defined his life resiled. At last from his throat escaped the bellowing of a

159

tormented soul. He was in his way a simple man; used to being the wielder of authority; a characteristic inherited from his father and the reason for their notoriety throughout Nuremberg. The Müllers were feared in the same measure as they were despised - for the influence they exercised and their wickedness.

There were countless numbers, therefore, in and beyond Nuremberg that might wish Müller dead for news of their evil was carried in mouths and whispered behind hands and spread on the wind far from the city so their disgrace was known in places where they were mere names uttered in horror. And no-one who knew of them wished anything more than the removal of those beastly men from God's earth.

He thought he was in his own bed and could not understand why fellows were dragging him out of it. If this was a dream, he mused, he should soon be free of it. With his head cocked to one side he heard the strike of a hammer on metal and listened to its rhythm until an involuntary spasm of alarm pulsed through his quivering flesh.

If by now he hadn't been blinded he would have recognised the beast that mystic children had played just hours before. An old damaged life-sized bull crafted by the city's smiths for use in pageants and abandoned awaiting repair or melting down no longer felt little feet clambering across its back. A frightful clash of metal upon metal invoked wild panic during a moment of clarity in his head, releasing a series of images of practices he hoped forgotten and he turned his face, unseeing, in the direction of voices. Tables turned.

"*Überraschen*" the word twisted, it landed hard.

Surprised. He had to admit he was surprised. Surprised by all he was being put through. His faith remained strong but he could not tell if he was already dead. He thought it unlikely.

"I thought him you," he heard spoken.

A wave of black horror swept across Müller. It was enough for a man to be held responsible for his own sins - but for another's?

Other voices cursed him - accosted him with profanities. He was grabbed again, not gently like he remembered his mother's hands stroking him but prodded and pushed. He was being pressed into an aperture so roughly that his red cap was dragged off his head.

The grain merchant was never seen without that cap; a kind of talisman that bound him to the mother who made it for him. That was when he had two pretty blue eyes; her looking into them as she arranged the cap over his sweet curls and kissing him and telling him how handsome a boy he was, so when the youths blinded him he wore his red cap pulled down over the unseeing eye so was able to pretend he was still the fine-looking son his mother could smile at with pride. He heard an animal grunt with such deep yearning then realised the sound came from between his own quivering lips.

His girth was such that considerable force was needed to push him in so his legs could follow. His captors succeeded though a shoe was lost during the business and it and the red cap were trampled into the wet mud. Once encased he found he could extend his legs so in an odd way he drew comfort from his predicament.

If his spirits rose at all his sense of relief was brief. The prison shuddered from the impact of heavy strikes of a hammer defying the resistance put up by metal forced together. Strike upon strike. It was at this moment it occurred to him his memories of kindness shown to him by his mother were creations of his imagination for he could not remember a time her hands were comforting. Then his consciousness was all but snuffed out. He scarcely noticed the acrid smoke, though his teeth chattered. By the time flaming horns pricked his fleshy bulk Herr Müller was beyond earthly torment. Tickling and licking that once excited his base desires from the fingers and tongues of Nuremberg's women and children while husbands and fathers wrung their hands in despair for a sack of grain hoist onto their shoulders was lost on him now as greedy flames hungered for his buttocks, his calves, his feet, his strong shoulders and his broad back. His sweat ran free, mixing with the piss and shit that flowed out of him.

When Nuremberg's Red Cap departed this life his body was already a steaming joint of yellow bubbling fat popping and whistling to the amusement of a small audience transfixed by noises escaping from the bull; for the ingenious beast was equipped with a series of pipes which transmitted each and every squeak and groan as if fire had brought the creature to life.

A hand picked up the faded crimson cap from the ground, shook the worst of the mud off it and hung it from one of the bull's horns. Savage justice had been served.

Chapter 17

Those still asleep at the first peep of light on the first Thursday after Michaelmas, the third day of October, missed its rain-soaked beginning for a determined sun shimmered between veins of cloud suspended in an azure sky. In the Knoblauchsland contingents of gardeners bent over planting next season's garlic bulbs chatted amicably, pleased to feel the warm sun on their backs.

Maria Kohl rapped on Otto Beck's workshop door. She was most insistent that he stop what he was doing and accompany her and her mistress out to the wild lands for the weather was promising fair and he had agreed he would do so the first good day after Michaelmas. When she saw his face more bruised and swollen than it had been the previous day she hesitated, for in truth she was ashamed of his appearance but then she had given her word to her mistress who was desperate to be free of the tensions that gripped the Wolgemut's household, even for a short time. The state of Beck's face would have to be tolerated.

Maria was not thinking of her mistress so much as herself. No sooner had Beck opened his door to her than she grumbled how unbearable Gudrun Wolgemut was, listing her many faults and her endless grumbles.

Beck was less than sympathetic. He had concerns of his own and Maria's constant chatter irritated him. She was stubborn and refused to leave until he agreed to escort both her and her mistress into the gardens and pastures outside the city with a promise to help him test out his new hand gun in one of the open spaces.

Over a breakfast of rye bread, hard yellow cheese stuck with caraway seeds chased down by a small cup of black dunkelbier Maria mentioned that Frau Wolgemut's rages were becoming more frequent and her treatment of Maria unbearable – even accusing her of being behind the theft of her husband's picture and was threatening to expose her to him.

Beck advised Maria to ignore Gudrun Wolgemut's temper tantrums but at the same time her charge against his Maria worked its way into his mind, though he was careful not to say anything of the kind to Maria. "We have to look no farther than those Italian traders," he said, "and I was right to teach them a lesson yesterday."

Maria Kohl put down her cup, still half-full of beer, and studied Beck's battered face. "I don't know who came off worse in that dispute but according to Frau Wolgemut they are entirely innocent for they were being entertained by the Wolgemut's when Herr Durer's picture was stolen."

"Were they?" Beck asked, with surprise, "how does she know when his picture was stolen?"

Maria shrugged her shoulders. "I don't know."

"And if they were at Wolgemut's then they had an opportunity to get their hands on Herr Wolgemut's picture. They are more guilty than I supposed," Beck said.

"But what about Herr Durer's picture. I don't suppose he has entertained them ... "Maria began.

Beck interrupted her. "Of course not. The question is, can we believe Frau Wolgemut?"

Maria sighed. "The morning is wearing on, Otto, and she will have more reason to complain if I don't get back soon. Make sure you do something with that bruised eye and broken nose for you are a fearsome sight. Now go and fetch your donkey while I collect my mistress and we'll make a day of it in the Knoblauchsland. You can be the ears for her complaints and I shall get some peace and together we will produce the perfect weapon for that malicious-eyed Spanish devil of yours."

She pressed a finger tenderly against Beck's half-shut eye while he grumbled that he could ill-afford time away from his workbench but his plea fell on deaf ears. If he could but admit it Beck welcomed Maria's help with his hand gun because he could not fathom out the difficulty he was having with it and he could ill afford to lose the patronage of Collado, foreigner that he was. With Maria gone Beck gathered together the bits and pieces he would need to test the weapon before making his way to the stable to saddle up for their bucolic foray.

***

Later that morning three less-than-contented riders passed through the city gates taking the hard-packed earthen track out to the Knoblauchsland and farther on to Laurenzer Forst. Progress proved slow on their short-legged animals but the sun accompanied them, lightening their mood. Gudrun Wolgemut confided to Beck that the theft of her husband's painting made home life difficult and she welcomed the distraction of a leisurely ride into the countryside. Beck nodded though he hardly heard her words for his head resided in his workshop with his hand guns. He had little appetite for the grievances of not one but two women.

The forest reared up before them. Dark and foreboding it was little wonder such places were held in dread by most civilised people. Yet here on its fringe was a scene of much industry - Nuremberg's bee farmers tending the hives that provided the city with honey for its lebkuchen, some of the sweetest gingerbread in the area, beeswax for candles and seals and stiffening for thread for the leather trade. Three foresters were chopping tree branches into logs which they piled onto a cart. A pair of dead-eyed trappers passed on their way into the forest and charcoal burners; hard men by reputation available for hire for any purpose in exchange for a coin or two – turned to stare at the trio on their short-limbed beasts. Each of these men was intimate with the ways of the mysterious woods.

Otto Beck was less repelled by the countryside than most from the town for here he liked to hunt. Occasionally he was accompanied by Durer and Pirkheimer though neither of them was as enthusiastic for the sport as he. Durer preferred to go into Nuremberg's wild hinterland in search not of animals to slaughter but subjects to sketch: clumps of grass, belts of trees, islands amidst the river, streamlets – which he would meticulously record on pieces of raw paper. Having captured a scene; caught impressions of light and shadow through hatching and cross-hatching, he would take these sketches home and integrate them into his formal works. So true to nature were Durer's depictions Beck knew it was possible to pinpoint an exact spot if ever they had to return to it.

Witches' fingers of dangling birch screened the edge of the forest scratching faces of passing riders. Beck went ahead with Frau Wolgemut while Maria trailed behind on an animal that had lost its taste for adventure. Beck warmed to Gudrun Wolgemut for she had become friendly and entertained him with her stories so it occurred to Beck his Maria was exaggerating her mistress's imperfections and he fancied Maria was as much, if not more to blame, for their difficult relationship.

Soon they were close to the mystics' encampment with its rudimentary shelters of threadbare rugs draped over branches surrounding a dead fire of blackened ashes. Leaning against the trunk of a tree was a frame of intertwined willow branches on which hung skinned carcasses of a dozen or so hares. Beck shouted back to Maria to get a move on. She was skirting rather than taking the more direct route through the camp, not once looking at it or Beck.

One or two listless figures crept out from beneath the coarse drapery of their shelters; ill-clad and doubtless grateful for the day's fair weather. They gawped at Beck and Frau Wolgemut on their donkeys. Silence gave way to comment followed by laughter. A boy and a girl stared at Beck with his swollen and blackened face. Beck turned his head away from their scrutiny and was astonished to see young Günter emerge from behind one of the skins in the company of two young females; one of them the pale slight child that hung about Thomas Hut. He froze when he saw Beck.

"Herr Beck," Günter began, rather desperately, "I was on an errand and got distracted by these girls but now I must be off." His face was red as a salmon's gill as he scampered to be on his way. Then he stopped and looked over at Beck as if intending to engage with him but finally simply retreated into a grove of silver-trunked birches.

Looking about her, Gudrun Wolgemut asked about the whereabouts of the sect's master.

"He's probably shitting in the wood."

The anonymous reply drew more laughter from camp-dwellers and an expression of disgust on the face of Frau Wolgemut whose mouth dropped open at the instant she met Beck's eye. Gudrun kicked her donkey's belly till it picked up speed and caught up with Maria who was well ahead.

"Do you think it shallow enough for us to ford?" Gudrun asked when at a fork in a river. She blinked, rubbing at an irritation in her eye.

"I wasn't thinking of crossing. There's a meadow over there I'd like to get to," Beck said.

"I would rather go this way. It looks safe," Gudrun pointed, still blinking.

"Looks can be deceptive," Beck insisted.

"Well, I think it's fine. You two go to your meadow and I'll take this route. We can meet around the time of the ninth bell. Can we hear it out here?" Gudrun thought to ask.

Beck shrugged. "If the wind is with it."

Gudrun Wolgemut heeled her mount's belly urging it to tackle the water but the animal was reluctant. Losing her temper, she kicked it with greater force but still it would not budge. Exasperated, she looked around for an alternative crossing and found herself staring at the head of a boar wedged between two tree trunks in the river shallows which had apparently panicked her donkey. Gudrun looked over at Beck who proposed she come with them but Gudrun Wolgemut was determined to go her own way. She repeated they meet after the bell at the ruined Frauentor and go back into the city together. Then, riding her beast upstream she found a crossing that satisfied her little steed but if it had shaken off the image of the boar's head the woman seated on his back had not. She could not forget the empty globes where its eyes had been and considered herself brave for such a hideous spectacle would

167

have been regarded as an ill-omen by most of her townsfolk, especially given it lay in a river populated by water sprites and within a forest where every imaginable evil creature, goblins and elves existed for mischief. Pushing aside such fears, Gudrun Wolgemut continued on her way.

"Who would throw away a good old cutter's head?" Beck asked, not expecting a reply from Maria.

Maria Kohl shook her head. "Perhaps the rest of him is beneath the water," she said, watching her mistress ride away along the opposite bank.

Beck looked there, too. "Will she be safe on her own?" he asked.

"She will be - who would tackle that one? I'm glad to be free of her for now for she's been more than usually ill-tempered lately, what with this business of that stupid painting then Herr Durer losing their money and now the dog lies dead. She found it; half eaten poor brute. And, Otto, I forgot to tell you about her scheme to sell a painting to Prince Ernest. It was going to make them so much money and on and on she went about it till suddenly she stopped. I tell you, Otto, I am sick fed up of hearing about paintings and hares and rabbits."

"She should know the Prince doesn't pay for anything," Beck said, "if he can get away with it - which he often can. What was the picture she tried to sell to him?"

Maria laughed, "Oh, I don't know - all I do know is he didn't take it – returned it, saying it was no good."

"He sent it back?" Beck asked, pulling a face, "it must have been pretty awful – and it wasn't meant as a gift?"

"He might have kept it if it had been a gift but he probably didn't think it worth spending money on. I don't think she intended me to know about it but one day she was beside herself with rage and it slipped out. Hoping to keep the money herself, I expect. What's more a letter she gave me to pass to the errand boy happened to fall open and – well, who wouldn't read it?"

"What did it say?" Beck asked.

"It promised Herr Wolgemut would paint another - of greater merit. If she had Herr Wolgemut's permission to make such an offer I've no idea or if it was sent, for she then demanded I give it back to her." Maria Kohl chattered on with Otto Beck paying little attention. "Did you hear me, Otto?" she demanded.

Otto Beck smiled vacantly.

"Have you noticed anything strange about her eyes?" Maria asked, "how big and dark they've become. She drops belladonna into them every day. Thinks it makes them more attractive by appearing large and mysterious. Or so I imagine."

***

As for the lady in question she had journeyed but a short way for despite her confident appearance she found herself somewhat wary of the enchanted beings of the forest and their sorcery. She had no wish to enter the woods but to stay at a meadow where one or two pretty flowers still bloomed despite the lateness of the year and where at the perimeter of the forest long tassel-headed grasses swished delicately. Gudrun Wolgemut jumped down from her donkey and arranged her sketching things - a pad of trimmed paper and some charcoal points. She set about drawing the elegant grass heads that her husband would dismiss as commonplace and undeserving of an artist's time - yet she knew from what she had seen of the works of Albrecht Durer that beauty was in the eye of the beholder and she tested her own rudimentary skills against Durer's exquisite executions.

Some quarter of a league beyond the river fork Beck and Maria arrived at an open grassy area surrounded by bushes, large limes and several ghostly white skeletons of dead trees. Only the faint rasp of the foresters' saws reminded them that others laboured while they enjoyed leisure. The grassy plain was home to a row of braziers, one of which contained irons used by the bee farmers to burn out holes in living trees to encourage bees to move into them. Beck and Maria dismounted their small steeds glad to shake off stiffness after their short but bumpy ride and immediately they set about gathering twigs and dry leaves. They lit a fire in one of the braziers and in no time a fine blaze roared into life.

Otto Beck and Maria Kohl lay down in idyllic intimacy disturbed by nothing more than birdsong and an occasional inquisitive roebuck. However, for Otto Beck passion was but a brief indulgence for his mind inevitably strayed to his hand gun and the improvements he must make so Maria found herself drawn into a conversation about how to help him.

Scouring the pasture Beck picked up a long branch, forked at one end and pushed the straight end deep into the soil so that it stood erect and steady. He untied a bundle, the length of his forearm, that was strapped to his saddle and extracted two lengths of iron wrapped in cloth. One iron, a hollow tube, he dropped onto the grass. Gripping the solid rod, he wrapped the cloth over its tip, tying it with a leather thong before plunging the opposite end into the hot fire. Returning to his donkey he removed several other items, including a wooden pole, a small ball of string and a third rod and put them down on the ground along with a dark leather flask and cloth bag. Loosening the bag's drawstring he shook out fragments of material and whistling a simple tune he picked out a piece of metal piping.

"Stop that, Otto. Each time you whistle you summon the Devil closer to you - to us," Maria complained and knocked three times against the wooden pole.

Beck said nothing but stopped his whistling, nonetheless. He ran his hand along the piping, admiring its smoothness and weight then fished a fragment of pyrites out of the pouch and secured it to the instrument. Unscrewing the cap on the flask he tipped it up so that powder trickled into the aperture in the rod and using the thinnest of the metal rods he forced a piece of rag down into the tube after the powder, to prevent its escape. From inside his jacket he extracted a blunt needle and a single length of straw which he broke into pieces and taking up the thin rod he rammed the straw into the tube. Steadying the cylinder between his knees Beck flattened out a scrap of cloth, a bigger piece this time, and tugged open a pouch fastened to his belt, spilling its contents of little lead balls onto the cloth. One of the balls he introduced to the lip of the tube and it rolled in easily. Too easily … when Beck lifted the pipe the ball rolled out so he retrieved it and dropped it back in but this time he pushed a wad of cloth in after it, preventing it escaping. After dusting some of the powder around the cup-like hole on the cylinder's grip end he turned to Maria.

"I thought you'd forgotten about me," she teased, taking the loaded tube from Beck. "Here, my fingers are smaller and can work this more easily than your great fat ones." She adjusted a little spring attached to a tiny wheel. "It's necessary for this part to be perfect so that the wheel can spin and spark the pyrites to ignite the gunpowder thereby setting fire to the main charge in the barrel. It's precision will ensure the weapon's accuracy and prove its superiority to a matchlock, for it will not be so sensitive to the wet - and has another advantage of being easily concealed - for those who want to take a life sneakily."

Beck grabbed the weapon back. "I know," he insisted. He rested it against the 'V' end of the branch post then prodded the wheel into position with the blunt needle. When he heard a click he pulled on the spring-loaded dog and tilted the weapon towards a row of birds perched on a lime branch.

The explosion toppled the stick and sent Maria into gales of laughter. "Best yet," she cried, "but you might have to run after those donkeys."

Beck turned to see the pair of beasts run to the far side of the pasture. "Gave those birds something to think about and that branch looks like it's had it." Beck skipped through the long grass towards the lime tree.

"I had my eyes closed," Maria called out chasing after him.

"Well, I'll be …"

"What is it?" Maria asked when she caught up with him. "Did you do that?" she asked doubtfully.

"I suppose I must have," Beck replied. He held a large bird aloft. "A goose hawk, that's what this is, a goose hawk, Maria. And a good size one."

Maria Kohl rested a hand on the bird's black and white breast.

"It doesn't feel very warm."

"The weather's cold, of course it's not warm. I wouldn't say it's cold exactly. Certainly not rigid." Beck prodded the hawk with his stubby fingers.

"It's very handsome," Maria remarked inspecting the bird more closely. "I can't see where it's been hit."

"I expect it glanced off the body. I'm sure I saw it come down," Beck said.

"Oh well, it's fresh enough. It'll cook up nicely. Do you want it or will I take it back to the Wolgemuts?"

Beck was not listening. "It still isn't firing smoothly … and look what it's done." He bit on a broken fingernail.

Maria peered over his shoulder. "It's the wheel - it should lock - it isn't running as it should. You'll have to re-cut it, Otto. I told you, you must be very exact - and the chain has to be exceptionally fine while strong enough to pull the spring." She jabbed a reproachful finger at Beck's workmanship. "Do you want me to do it?"

Beck edged away from her. "It's too much like a miniature cannon. Cannon weren't designed to be held in the hand," he complained defiantly. "I don't think this wheel lock has any advantage on a matchlock."

"Of course, it has," Maria insisted, "just think, it can be fired whatever the weather without fizzling out – only its parts must run true."

Beck took another step away from her. "You've said that."

"You have to be patient, Otto - to make it nice and neat so it runs easily, like clockwork, and sparks against the pyrites each time." Maria's tone had taken on a note of exasperation.

***

172

That same afternoon an order was issued by Nuremberg Council following a complaint against Thomas Hut that he was reportedly seen in the company of a local woman which was deemed improper therefore meriting investigation; a task which fell to Herr Wolf and the reason for his excursion outwith the city. What he discovered in the course of his duties both surprised and repulsed him, and raised a difficulty in how best to handle the affair, discretely and responsibly, for he had no wish to embarrass the woman named yet was mindful of his obligations to the Council. Nervously, he ran his blue intaglio ring around his finger.

Wolf spoke with the mystic leader, Thomas Hut; a conversation that was uncomfortable not least because the clerk had seen the hilt of a dagger jutting out of the mystic's waistband. In the event no harm came to Wolf who found Hut easy to talk to with only a slight tendency to lapse into sermonising.

"I will give power unto my two witnesses," the mystic quoted from the Book of Revelations. "And they shall prophesy a thousand two hundred and three score days clothed in sackcloth." He had smiled as Wolf read out the charge of his immoral association with a respectable married woman of Nuremberg and readdressed the claim to the clerk. Wolf squirmed and found difficulty maintaining any air of authority over the holy man because it appeared the stranger had intelligence of his own relationship with Frau Wolgemut. This being so Wolf considered the mystic was in league with her and if this was so he was in near as precarious a predicament as Hut.

Hut leaned close in to him so the golden crucifix he wore caught the sun's rays as it dangled from his neck sparking light into the eyes of both men whose faces were all but touching. Hut's spittle sprayed droplets onto Wolf's cheek as he looked deep into Wolf's eyes as if reading all that was in the clerk's head.

Wolf tucked his feather quill behind an ear, stopped up his inkpot and rolled up the paper on which he recorded some of

Hut's responses. Far from succeeding in recording Hut's admission of guilt to the charge of indecent conduct with a married woman it was Wolf who felt exposed. The one saving grace was it had been him sent to interrogate the preacher and not another who might have learned the truth of his own liaison with Frau Wolgemut which came as the result of his overstated account of his influence at the Rathaus rather than their shared passion for each other.

The mystic placed a hand on the clerk's shoulder and proffered a thin smile. This came as no comfort to Wolf who was not a brave man but was determined to make amends for all his misdemeanours. Once away from the mystic camp the clerk was in no haste to return to the Rathaus but instead he ambled along the paths that criss-crossed the Knoblauchsland for his mind was sore troubled and in need of quiet reflection. Imagine his surprise to find himself meet up with the very lady in question and her with no good explanation for being in the vicinity of Hut's camp. Wolf being on foot and her atop a donkey they spoke little before going their separate ways.

The longer he trod the pastures outside Nuremberg the more Adolf Wolf felt the weight of circumstances bearing down on him: his infatuation with Frau Wolgemut, certainly, but then a plague of memories of himself as a child at the mercy of men of the town who lusted after him. Those men were both frightening and frightened creatures for they distrusted one another knowing their unnatural acts were wicked and liable to punishment twice over - once under civic law and again through the judgement of God but so insatiable were their base appetites they persisted, regardless.

As he crossed the gardens of the Knoblauchsland Wolf compared the apparent wrongs of the mystic Hut with the deeds of men from years back who still enjoyed their liberty and positions within Nuremberg society and a part of him understood the mystic's desire to denounce evil and expose hypocrisy. Still, his duty was as a servant to the Council.

***

174

Long shadows were bleeding between the birches surrounding the meadow as Maria strung the goose hawk to her saddle with Beck's twine and the two started for home. They were overtaken on the track by an ox-drawn wagon loaded with cut boughs driven by an old man with two fresh-faced youths trotting alongside. They all waved and greeted each other.

The mystic camp was nearly deserted. A crouching woman tore up bitter herbs which she dropped into a cooking pot suspended over a now well-burning fire. A very small child next to her held a flask containing a liquid. They watched the approaching riders.

Unlike on their outward journey when Maria gave the camp a wide berth she appeared happy to come in close now that it looked almost abandoned and after having a word with Beck he dropped down from his beast untied the goose hawk and offered it to the surprised woman.

"Something more substantial for you to chew on," he said.

***

Gudrun Wolgemut was waiting for Maria and Beck at the old Frauentor gate south east of the city. It appeared that her ride out had agreed with her for she was in good spirits and smiled broadly at their approach. "I had a wonderful time. Can't recall the last time I felt so content."

The trio looked around on hearing a "hallo" to discover Herr Wolf approaching on foot. He doffed his cap to Frau Wolgemut and nodded at Beck and Maria.

"We meet again, Frau Wolgemut. I am honoured. You have been on an expedition and are looking quite pink."

Gudrun Wolgemut examined her reflection in the miniature Venetian glass she took from her pocket and saw her cheeks were flushed and her eyes watering somewhat. "Why, Herr Wolf ..." she began, "I've had an invigorating afternoon, Sir. We went around the forest to watch the animals and birds at play."

It was said as if such places were innocent distractions but something in her mistress's tone had Maria wondering if she was not a little put-out.

"I hope you were careful for there are menacing forces outside the protection of the city walls that no decent woman would be safe to encounter. In addition, there are the mystic nuisances, Frau Wolgemut, dangerous people who are not fit to be around respectable society," said Herr Wolf, his heavy-lidded eyes brimmed with concern.

Frau Wolgemut's pink face flushed and she dropped her gaze. "I met only the swineherd, Wedigo ... in the acorn wood but I fancy those mystics are harmless, Herr Wolf, and I am certain I can take care of myself."

"I hope you can, Frau Wolgemut, for one can never underestimate the cunning of some. The greater the power the greater the cunning."

Beck and Maria exchanges looks, baffled at his meaning. His words appeared to unsettle her mistress whose dark eyes flashed with anger that quickly subsided and yawned, as if bored by the conversation.

Otto Beck took this to be an invitation to speak so he agreed the heretics, as he called them, should be sent packing for there were all kinds of mischief going on inside the city, such as an attack and robbery on Herr Durer.

"Is Herr Durer injured?" Wolf asked.

"Only his pride," Beck sniggered then noticing Frau Wolgemut's reproachful look decided to say no more.

"I did hear that Herr Durer was involved in some failed plot to serve your husband, Frau Wolgemut. And that he lost a small fortune of Herr Wolgemut's gold."

Frau Wolgemut would not meet his eye and with no word of confirmation or denial she tugged on her donkey's rein and looked to nudge his haunches to spur him on when she changed her mind and turning, smiled prettily at Herr Wolf thanking him for his concern and said if it were not for the lateness of the hour she would talk more with him.

Their little encounter at an end the four went to enter the city when a party of eight militia riders led by Herman Kalb cantered out of the port. On enquiring about their urgency, Kalb shouted a reply that Ana Brauer's grandson, Kläuschen, had disappeared and they were going out to search the surrounding area before nightfall.

Chapter 18

Back in the city many Nuremberg folk abandoned work bench and forge to search for Kläuschen. Klara and Ana buried their faces in their aprons; men took to the river in pairs of boats dragging nets between them; some stood on Debtor's and Hay bridges and plunged long poles deep down in the Pegnitz probing for the child's body; young boys threw stones at a matted corpse of what might have been a cat a or large rat; the appearance of a dead dog floating downstream attracted crowds to the riverbank - *look it is Ulf; No, Ulf is so fat he'd sink;* Ulf was reported sleeping on the doorstep of his old home until driven away by boys with stones; cellars were turned upside-down; church crypts explored; people took to tracks and trails, ventured through woods and up by the palace near the Laufer tor where a skinny youth armed with a flaming torch was lowered by rope into a deep well and emerged to declare he had found two dead cats and several birds but no child. The city's inner moats were painstakingly cleared of years of the accumulated rubbish that lured both rats and children in search of hidden treasure. The boy's uncle was roused from his workshop in the Am Ölberg and immediately set-off with his fellow glass-blowers to poke around under bridges, in pig sties, tip-toeing even up into the clerestory and behind the organ of St Sebaldus.

In the lands north of Nuremberg search parties walked as far as Furth and Erlangen. The town's militia spoke to the swineherd, Wedigo, who complained bitterly that his estranged brother, Widukind, had stolen his best boar and vowed to avenge the loss but could tell them nought about young Kläuschen before he and his trusty black hound were sent on their way.

By nightfall a great gloom hung over the fair city of Nuremberg. Not even in Brauer's, especially not in Brauer's, was there a stiver's worth of cheer. Klara and Ana were both there but their regular customers were mostly out searching for the child, including Herr Müller, it was assumed. That possibility struck a chill into the hearts of both women.

Albrecht Durer had been among those out looking for the boy, along with all in his household and workshop, but returned dejected. Retiring to his apartment in despondent mood Durer gazed idly at the flocks of black rooks wheeling above Nuremberg's elegant spires and towers against a portentous pewter-grey sky.

An excited Gudrun Wolgemut did not wait to be admitted into Durer's residence but let herself in. "I've given Maria short leave - she has an assignation," Gudrun whispered conspiratorially.

"Otto?" Durer asked offhandedly.

Gudrun confided it was not Otto Beck but Peter Henlein that her maidservant was meeting. "Though she thinks I don't know," she added with a smile.

Durer was dumfounded. Otto had never mentioned he had a rival for Maria's affections.

Anton shuffled through the passage to discover the identity of the intruder. On recognising Frau Wolgemut he loitered, his hands busy wrapping a smalt-blue rag around engraving knives and burins. Noticing him in the doorway, Durer instructed him to light two of the tall candles that sat on either side of the hearth.

"Please don't go to the expense," Gudrun protested, already slipping out of her heavy unfashionable coat.

"It's no trouble, the day has turned so dreary and a little light enlivens the spirit," Durer declared and together they watched flames dart into life in response to Anton's flint striker.

"Even so, I don't mind. At home we seldom light a candle until we can see nothing at all," she said.

Once alone, Frau Wolgemut huddled up to Albrecht Durer, placing her hands around his face. He pressed his cheek against her cool forehead and with his finger traced the contours of her finely defined lips. They kissed, the lady stroking Durer's fair coiled locks and soft mousy moustache.

"You are an exceedingly pretty man, Albrecht Durer."

Gudrun Wolgemut's opinion did not come as a revelation to him. While not overly vain, Durer recognised his good fortune at being endowed with a very handsome face. Beauty, whether found in wild nature or a human face was, in his opinion, something that should be appreciated for its own sake and the reason he took so much interest in his appearance. This preoccupation with his looks was regarded as conceit by some of his fellow-citizens and inappropriate for a man who was after all a mere artist. Had he become a goldsmith like his father, they whispered, he might have reason to act the peacock; as it was he was no better than a jobbing artisan from one of the lesser trades. Durer was not oblivious to common gossip but neither did he dwell on it. He knew he was gifted with a rare and precious talent and that few in Germany could surpass him in his chosen occupation.

Anton was summoned and two goblets brim-full of a rich red wine were served to Gudrun Wolgemut and Albrecht Durer. They drank and conversed on matters wholly inconsequential with Frau Wolgemut breaking off from time to time to examine the room for she was much obsessed with measuring the comforts of the Durer home against her own, and found it superior in every way.

"For the safe delivery of our lost pictures," the lady raised her glass in a toast. "This has been such a trying time," she confessed.

A blinding flash lit up the dim interior followed by a terrific crack of thunder. Durer and Gudrun Wolgemut peeked out at a storm unleashing its force over Nuremberg.

Durer raised his cup of wine to her. "I promise you with my whole heart I will do my best to see this affair righted. And Frau Wolgemut let us not forget to pray for the safe return of Ana's grandchild and the Schutzen princess."

"Ah, yes the children, I had forgotten. Is there no word of either of them?" She watched the rain pour down, the deluge near drowning her words, "To think they are out in such weather."

"None, I believe. Ana Brauer and the Denck couple must be out of their minds with worry," Durer replied.

A few moments of silence while both reflected on the happenings of past days was broken by Gudrun Wolgemut. "Tell me, Albrecht, have you other works similar to the hare study that was stolen?"

Durer thought it a curious inquiry but he answered, nonetheless, explaining that the lost *Field Hare* was his sole such image worked into a painting but he had several sketches he might consider using for a new picture. Frau Wolgemut looked disappointed - for him and his loss, he assumed, and her words and his thoughts were followed by another silence, more extended than the first. Durer supposed she judged him for failing to secure the return of her husband's picture and their purse of gold. He picked up a square of paper Gudrun Wolgemut scribbled on during her previous visit.

"You have a most capable hand," Durer purred.

Gudrun Wolgemut blushed and dismissed the compliment.

"It is true. You have a real talent," Durer insisted. "Have you taken instruction from your husband?"

Gudrun Wolgemut laughed. "No, my husband doesn't approve of me frittering away my time on such trifles."

"This child - is it yours?" Durer asked artlessly.

Gudrun Wolgemut's mouth sprung open, her eyes fixed on the drawing. Yet another silence imposed itself between them that Durer was compelled to bridge with a change of subject. He had only just begun speaking about his *Adam and Eve* work when his hand was grabbed and squeezed by Gudrun Wolgemut. Unsure how he should act, Durer did nothing but hold his tongue for several moments.

"Might I test your fortitude, fair Gudrun?" Durer asked after a time.

"You intrigue me, Sir."

"Would you indulge me by describing your husband's stolen picture for I have no real sense of it?"

Gudrun Wolgemut released her hand from his, studying Durer intently before replying. "Why, it was a pretty little painting of a hare. But surely you know this?"

"And you've seen it?" Durer asked.

"Of course, I've seen it. What is your meaning?"

"Only that I am intrigued it sounds so cannily like my picture."

"I hope I misunderstand you, Albrecht Durer," Frau Wolgemut said.

Durer persisted. "It's not a subject I've known Herr Wolgemut ever to have tackled." He stood with his back to Gudrun but she was reflected in a tall gilt looking-glass dominating a corner of the room. Their eyes met in the reflection.

"What are you implying, Albrecht?"

"This is not easy for me ..."

"Yet easier for you than it is for my husband." Her words shattered the warmth between them with their cold clarity. "He has been abused twice; first he was robbed of his picture and then the money he entrusted into your care, Albrecht. He has suffered greatly; you cannot deny that."

"My lady, we both find ourselves in difficult predicaments and I have no wish to imply anything but good against the character of Herr Wolgemut but ... if I ..." with that his words extinguished on his tongue.

"That is precisely what you do imply," Gudrun Wolgemut raged. She stood with her hands on her hips confronting Durer. "I came here to put your mind at rest after talking with my husband and advising him not to pursue the matter but it appears my intervention has been rash. I do not understand you, Albrecht. You are all vainglory." With that she hurried to the door. "I must be away." She paused, checking her appearance in the Venetian glass that always dangled from her waist cord.

"Don't be so quick to scold, fair Gudrun. And look how the rain pours down. Wait for a break in the weather, till it's safe to be out and I'll accompany you home."

Gudrun Wolgemut informed Durer she had no need of his companionship and she would battle the tempest on her own. Durer made no reply but collected her much-darned threadbare cloak and holding it out for her observed its inferiority to any his own Agnes would deem to wear. My Agnes, he mused wistfully, would prefer to be a prisoner within their home than be seen out in such a singularly drab and mended garment.

Frau Wolgemut pulled open the door and as if under orders the rain ceased. She smiled back at him but Durer detected little joy in the look. He turned the key in the lock and poured himself another cup of wine. When he looked for the little drawing of the babe he discovered it no longer there.

***

"I smell a woman." Otto Beck stood in the doorway stroking his chin. "Is Agnes returned?"

"Where did you spring from?" Durer demanded. I've already locked up.

"I came in by the side door, it's wide open and the wet was coming in."

"Did you shut it?"

"Of course, I did." Beck followed Durer into the scullery.

"That was Frau Wolgemut you smelled. She perfumes herself highly with rose water and sandal wood."

"Ah, the fair Gudrun … and was my sweet Maria with her?"

"No," Durer replied sharply.

"Ah," Beck sniggered. "Maria has told me of her mistress' many trysts with Nuremberg's virile youth. Not that I place you in that category, Albi. Alas, it seems her husband cannot hold onto her for any time. I'm surprised it's taken you so long to notice her, Albi."

Durer considered mentioning Maria and Peter Henlein but reflected on the rashness of so doing. "So long? I hardly know the lady."

"You met her last year, though you scarcely acknowledged her. You and Agnes were at the Rathaus for the apprentice prize I think it was and I introduced you all. Maria was there with her. Surely you must remember? Agnes would, I'm sure. Ask her when she returns. On second thoughts, maybe it would be best if you didn't. Frau Wolgemut certainly noticed you - Maria told me she couldn't stop talking about you and was asking all sorts of questions till Maria became sore fed up with them."

Durer stared stupidly at Beck.

"You still can't remember? You're getting to be an old man, Albi. But I admit she wasn't so handsomely turned out then. Maria says she's been putting a lot more effort into her appearance lately - and is forever gazing into that Italian looking-glass of hers. According to Maria she's got quite vain … and that … well, she's very jealous of Agnes for your Agnes is always attractively attired. Old man Wolgemut has never given Frau Wolgemut what she says she needs for clothes. Maria wonders why she stays with him but then what would become of her if she left? However, enough of that, there's something I must tell you."

Durer poured out a drink for Beck and they wandered into the workshop where traces of the day's activities were strewn around. Beck picked up a length of framing, admiring its decorative oak leaves. "Nice carving. Three corpses have turned up," he blurted out.

"Kläuschen?" Durer asked with a gasp.

Beck shook his head.

"Not the boy - all the dead are mystics."

Durer's mouth fell open. "How? The mob?" His face an essay in horror.

"No, no," Beck reassured him, "it's claimed they were poisoned."

Durer whistled. "So, they weren't hunted to their deaths?" He searched Beck's face for confirmation. "But what was the nature of the poison?"

Otto Beck stared at his feet and swung the piece of picture framing back and fore. He grimaced.

"What is it, Otto?"

Otto Beck swallowed hard then cleared his throat. "I don't know - but earlier today I shot a bird beyond the garlic lands – Maria and I had gone out there … we gave it to that young mystic girl to cook. She's one of the dead."

"The frail child?" Durer asked.

Beck absentmindedly traced one of the carved oak leaves with a finger.

"Bird? What bird?" Durer asked.

"I was trying out a contraption … for a new type of weapon and when I fired it the shot took down a bird … at least I'm fairly sure it did but Maria wasn't certain. A goose hawk it was - and quite dead. I would have taken it home but then we passed the mystics and … well, they looked more in need of it … we thought to offer kindness." Becks words withered on his tongue.

"And you think your bird poisoned them?" Durer asked.

"I don't suppose so, but those who ate it died. Of course, they don't know the bird came from me, from us, Maria and me. At least I don't think so. It's more likely it was just a coincidence that after eating a bird they fell ill. It's the talk of the town it was a bird they ate and maybe it was a different one altogether. Maybe they harbour the pest."

Durer shuddered. "Poor child," Durer whispered.

Beck dropped the carved frame length, covered his face with his fat hands and echoed, "Poor child indeed."

"You think this goose hawk you shot might have been poisoned?" Durer tried to make sense of what he had heard.

Beck looked at him, his face quite pale. "It might not have been my hawk. When I think about it there was no sign of injury on the bird … I assumed I had killed it."

Durer chewed on his lip. "I saw a goose hawk on Tuesday evening when I left Wolgemut's."

"They are not so unusual," Beck said.

"Nor usual. I cannot recall the last time I saw one - not a goose hawk," Durer said.

"No," Beck reflected, "nor me."

***

Otto Beck was not a man to be confined by bells. The curfew bell had tolled long since but instead of making for home after leaving Albrecht Durer's house he went straightway to his workshop. It was as he approached the Rathaus he recognised another sneaking through the dark and recognised the figure as Schmeichler, one hand held a lantern and the other was cupped over an ear as though it caused him hurt. Curious to know his business at the Rathaus, Beck crept closer listening out for his uneven gait on the stairs. The servant's steps fell silent and fearful he had been discovered the locksmith hung back. Voices from above indicated Schmeichler had reached his destination and Beck tiptoed up to a landing where a thin line of light exposed a door to one of the chambers slightly ajar. Closer still he stole and pressed his ear close to the opening.

"You have no right to question me."

Beck recognised the voice as Herr Wolf's. Their conversation was hard to make out for one spoke so quietly and the words were indistinct. The other was a more powerful speaker.

"The lady and I are nothing to each other. You do both me and your mistress a grave injustice with your false accusations. I am a respectable servant of this city and she is the wife of a much-respected painter. Your loose-tongue can do much damage to upright citizens, Herr Schmeichler, so I appeal to you to desist or I will take this up with Herr Wolgemut."

"I come at Wolgemut's bidding ...," not all Schmeichler's words carried to Beck's ears, "... is that lady to me? ... respect for Herr Wolgemut ... hollow when ... your actions ... "

"Then take yourself off at once," Wolf commanded, "and tell your master that rumours of any intrigue between his wife and me are utterly false. I scarce know his good lady."

"You were observed … intimately … this very chamber not seven days since … Wolf."

Wolf's reply was inaudible to Beck who now stood very close to the open door with an ear to the gap and his thumb jammed into his mouth. Wolf was being careful with his words but piecing together the snippets he overheard Beck deduced Wolf claimed Frau Wolgemut had requested his help to have her husband appointed to paint the oil portraits for the City Chamber and was disappointed to be told the commission had gone to Herr Durer.

Schmeichler's response emerged as nothing more than a grunt and his retreat from the room so brisk Beck was forced to seek cover in a recess at the end of the landing before making his escape from the Rathaus just as Wolf left through the great door.

If Beck had been as capable a thought-reader as eaves-dropper he would have discovered that Wolf vowed to end his association with Frau Wolgemut for he had grown mistrustful of the lady of late; of her motives and conduct and those with whom she associated.

Chapter 19

Adolf Wolf rose early on the first Friday after the Feast of Saint Michael and setting off in a direction entirely different from his usual he did not stop until consumed by the gloom of the tall granary at the entrance to the labyrinth.

Light drizzle, little more than mist, saturated the pink earthen footpath beneath his feet and the heady sweet odour that rose from it caused Wolf to bring his hand to his nose, fleetingly, for it would not do for him to be seen behaving so sensitively; as though he did not belong there. He removed the blue felt hat he absent-mindedly set upon his head before leaving his house - out of respect for the impoverished who dwelled in the labyrinth's mysterious crooked lanes. A hat of such quality, of such extravagance, was a mark of his rise in fortune, however moderate, and evidence of his escape from the labyrinth's burdensome poverty. Removal of the hat had dislodged a quill tucked behind his ear where an inky stain marked him out as a literate man. Wolf bent over and retrieved the feather.

It was less out of shame of his humble beginnings that Wolf acted than a sense of himself and the extent of his ascent in society. Still, Wolf harboured a memory of his former self; miserable and too afraid to dream of escaping the suffocating stench-ridden and corrupt oppression of the labyrinth with its warren of higgledy-piggledy streets lined with tradesmen's hovels, walls stained green with damp and bellies never quite full. His overwhelming emotion was mainly of relief at having broken free from the labyrinth's callous grip; its coarse-tongued women and toothless men leering at pretty young girls and boys. While valuing his own liberty it pained Wolf that his mother still lived in that sinister district because of her own obstinacy which ensured he was never completely liberated from its influence and sinister associations.

Even at this unearthly hour a small child, a boy he thought without certainty, already occupied a step directly opposite the granary, innocently playing with a furry black kitten. Wolf felt a pang of anxiety that the child might suffer torments similar to those inflicted upon him or that he would suspect his intention. The boy, if boy it was, looked up and grinned at Wolf. Bending over the clerk whispered into a dirty little ear and pressed a coin into an equally dirty little hand then passed to the child his handsome velvet hat. Small fingers curled around the coin and held fast to the hat as the waif scampered off towards Wolf's workplace, the Rathaus.

Two nights previously Adolf Wolf had sat opposite his mother, both of them perched on stout three-legged oak stools; their heads bowed so they almost touched ensuring nothing of what passed between them could be heard through the hovel's thin walls and into a neighbour's inquisitive ear.

Herr Wolf wrung his hands while seeking his mother's reassurance. His vulnerability both distressed and pleased her: it pained the elderly woman that her son's agony persisted yet she drew comfort from his continuing dependency upon her. For all that Frau Wolf was not able to reassure her son and they parted in a state of sorrowful unease.

Frau Wolf was proud of her son's achievements but quietly satisfied, too, of her role in his advancement; for without her determination and sacrifice he would have struggled to make his mark, of that she was certain. And for all that Wolf's rise in the world meant to both neither ever spoke of it nor the troubling means by which his elevation came about.

The granary walls soared into the pewter grey sky dwarfing Nuremberg's soberly-clad citizens who stuck their noses out through cracked-open doors to sniff the air before scurrying rat-like along the labyrinth's twisting alleyways to do good and do bad.

Number fourteen grain store with its steep tiled saddleback roof stood third tallest of all of Nuremberg's buildings, after the great church of St Sebaldus and the Imperial Palace, the Kaiserburg, triumphant on its promontory overlooking the town.

The cold stone edifice of the granary chilled the clerk making him shiver. Looking up Herr Wolf's eyes sprang wide open, startled, for he was sure a face stared back down at him from a narrow casement high up in the attics. Wolff attempted to shake off his disquiet. He was resolute. He would succeed where in past times his courage had failed him. Out of their hovels spilled rat-like folk bent over and weighed down by poverty and infirmity, their faces lined as if etched for printing. None stopped at the granary; there would be no witness to his sinful scheme.

The door groaned under Wolf's prodding hand. Specks of grain gyrated on light beams and an odour that was not unpleasant, nevertheless, smelled of fear to Wolf who was consumed by a weakness of spirit or corpus and powerful desire to spew. Yet he did not.

From the doorway Wolf considered the worm-holed stairs lit up as grey shadows and cast a hesitant eye upward. The bottom step quite worn in its middle from the passage of feet both large and dainty. It took Wolf's middling foot in its green leather slipper without complaint. When his second foot rested on the step the street door slammed shut with Wolf marooned in a place of terrifying gloom. He waited, listening, denying his presence to any that was not meant to know of it. Triumph he was sure would come from stealth.

Then there were two Wolfs on those stairs. He knew them both. The bold one, though he was not so very bold, rebuked the other for succumbing to doubt. That weaker self was the more typical of the two but today Wolf hoped it would be the former who succeeded in defeating his demons; he was prepared to clash with his other self - in a battle of wills. At first his weak self was consumed with regret for having introduced the lady to the foreign merchants but what was done was done and could no longer be helped. There was regret, too, for being so beguiled by her he had exaggerated his influence with the Burghers at the Rathaus and shame, too, at misjudging her familiarity with the stranger in their midst as one of intimacy. Mistakes he had made could not be undone and the other Wolf reasoned that the evil perpetrated on him was much worse than any harm he had attached to the lady.

Wolf's fingers searched out the knife tucked into his belt and so his resolve was emboldened for its long, broad blade was reassuring. So, too, were the words from Exodus in the Holy Book that sprung into his mind:

If there is further injury, then you shall appoint as a penalty life for life, eye for eye, tooth for tooth, hand for hand, foot for foot, burn for burn, wound for wound, bruise for bruise.

Well-seasoned oak risers shifted and creaked to Wolf's unhurried ascent through a heady fusion of grain and wood dust; acid as fermented sour dough. Each step was tentative - the sole of his boot; foot explored and hand secured. In this manner he progressed towards that place with its unholy secrets.

Wolf gripped the handrail, smooth beneath his damp palm following the steep raked angle from landing to landing. Ever upwards. The stair treads now so narrow Wolf's toe was his compass. Not a pinprick of light glinted in the oppressive darkness. He was almost there. Herr Wolf lingered, sniffing the air he listened for any sign his presence was exposed. His broad forehead creased like spring furrows as he strained to listen. What he heard was a faint rush of air playing around his ears. But - wait - was it - air?

The weaker Wolf would have turned and retreated to secure anonymity among the rat-people below. The other Wolf prevailed. His fingers curled around the hilt of the dagger that pressed against his thigh. He would not be cowed. Wolf looked down into the darkness of the stairwell knowing that outside the sun would by now be casting light on the lives of Nuremberg's folk going about their everyday business. Within him hope was alive yet ahead he knew lay dread. He reached into his coat for his ivory crucifix and held it for a moment.

Herr Wolf rocked forward, giddy - his boot slipping on a scattering of grain. He swallowed hard for his throat was parched and he thought of the face at the window - if a face it was yet he could not want it otherwise so close was he to banishing the brute he had struggled with most of his life. And at that Wolf smiled.

Adolf Wolf the man of some consequence would no longer live like a child at the mercy of ghosts and spirits, instead he would confront his demons. That being so his hand trembled and dry ashes packed his mouth; the dreadful anticipation of a child sent here by his mother that established a pattern that cursed his life. The perpetrator long dead lived on. Ahead was hewn from the same block.

He was there; not at the very top of the building for there were in all six upper floors. On a landing he turned to face the outline of a door made visible by shreds of daylight seeping out from cracks in the walls. Beneath the weight of his foot a sigh - out of compassion or betrayal? Wolf cast another nervous glance down the stairwell.

In years gone by his mother scolded the child for all his chatter about evil spirits and fiends he'd insisted meant him harm. She chided him that he must suppress such nonsense or else one day what he most dreaded would devour him. Wolf snorted at the recollection and reached for the pitted iron door latch with trembling fingers.

Adolf Wolf found himself in a spacious airy hall half-floored with a gap near as wide as the room that opened into a lower chamber packed with corn. A veil of dust and grain fibres floated lazily in the dazzling brilliance of shards of light penetrating the attic's windows. There in the granary loft amidst the stench of fear the sweet desire for vengeance impelled him onward, drawn by the radiance of goodness. Herr Wolf advanced to the opening and peered over the edge.

***

A bead of perspiration glistened on Adolf Wolf's forehead. Looking down into the void Wolf felt a jab against his back and he felt a rush of air as a stick of a woman flew past him; down into the blackness below. No cry was uttered and Wolf could not think who she was or where she had come from for

192

no woman lived in this place for many a year, not since Frau Müller. As Herr Wolf rocked back and fore, unbalanced by the push on his back and the appearance of the scarecrow figure, his grip tightened on his dagger.

He rarely cried. Not even as a boy, abandoned to the humiliations of the monster - for his own good - his mother claimed, for she saw no other way to fund the learning that would provide his elevation in the world.

Adolf Wolf's childish spirit died that first time yet he did not weep, only biting the knuckle of the thumb he took to sucking to escape from his nightmares. He did not cry at the familiar aroma of cruelty - the sweet sickly stench of the granary that assaulted his senses with every draft escaping from between its joists and boards.

A firm touch, a prod, a jab – was what he had felt of Satan's claw. He supposed it Satan's as the stick figure swept past. But Satan a woman? The shock and the pressure against his back left him rocking to and fro. He uttered no sound as he hurtled downward, behind Satan, towards Hell he imagined, though the desire within him was that he should resist.

As in life Wolf's death was a quiet affair; his frail body landed with the faintest of thuds onto a cushion of grain that did not disturb so much as a wakeful mouse.

Chapter 20

Late that night

Albrecht Durer sat bolt upright. Every bell in every church tower seemed to be tolling news of fresh tragedies. And shouts - all the same.

"Fire! Fire!"

Durer threw back his covers and sprang out of bed. In his drowsy state he fumbled with the window catch before securing the Ladenmännchen to prevent the shutter from swinging back in on him. Leaning out from the window, he called out to moving shadows, "What is it?"

"Fire has consumed the granary at the labyrinth."

Hurriedly dressing Durer then made his way across town, shivering at every droplet of thin mean rain soaking into his jerkin. Günter and Anton followed close behind. Most of Nuremberg, it appeared, had abandoned slumber to follow their noses - for the distinctive reek of charred grain was powerful strong and the air rent by the roaring of a tortured beast.

The great moving phalanx of inquisitive citizens was confronted by the awful sight of greedy tongues of fire licking at the pitch-black night out of a muddled shape that was once a granary. This hellish place with its hisses and explosions attracted and repelled the good people of Nuremberg. They drew in closer then were sent dashing for cover as timbers groaned and crashed to the ground shooting sprays of sparks into the night sky like so many vermillion shooting stars that rained back down onto heads and shoulders, extinguishing as charred debris. And the north wind blowing with all its might revitalised the inferno whenever it showed signs of growing weary.

Shouts, cries, barked orders, warnings, pleading, arguing and weeping; men and women toiled shoulder to shoulder passing pails of water from hand to hand; tubs and jugs; vessels of every description pressed into service. Heavy wagons shoved by yet more collective shoulders, drawn by skittery brown oxen and panicking braying donkeys - over-loaded with barrels full of water scooped out of the Pegnitz by soaking-wet volunteers. The night of the fourth of October 1504 would be remembered for its pandemonium: screaming, wailing, barking dogs, whinnying ponies, wild-eyed grunting oxen and crashing of timbers.

"More men! More men! To the river. More water!"

A silhouette of people in single file, their legs near giving way under heavy wooden yokes fastened across aching backs. Fountains and wells drained of every drop of water to quench the thirst of the dreadful fire.

Granaries were so vital to the survival of the good citizens of Nuremberg during the scarcities of winter they were administered by the Council. The loss of a granary full of corn would be a serious blow for with less grain came price increases that would push the poorest in the city deeper into the jaws of hunger. Bad enough to lose grain meant for milling into flour for bread but the granary also stored casks of tallow intended for candles and for greasing tools and every kind of necessary mechanism to be found in craftsmen's workshops, and still more that was to be used in cures for ailments. The fire turned what had been plenty into nought but smoke curling into a carbon sky.

For those living in the vicinity of the granary fear of fire spreading to their homes had them running hither and thither to salvage everything they could of their belongings: stools, chests, cooking pots, bedding, clothing - flung almost carelessly into the surrounding lanes, out of the immediate reach of the flames.

A bed-ridden old woman was carried from her room by youths; one supporting her under her frail arms and another taking her legs. She was wrapped in a blanket and left shivering with cold and shock, precariously balanced on a low stool, a yellow striped cat sitting at her feet.

How hard the men, women and boys of Nuremberg fought to preserve their city from ruin. When one wilted through exhaustion another stepped in to his or her place. Durer spent many arduous hours alongside a night scavenger, a midget of a man, who had to stretch-up his arms to receive pots and pails passed to him by the artist but who never shrank from carrying out his duty.

***

The night tried everyone's faith - worn out from fetching water, applying water, passing pails of water, shovelling earth, tearing thatch hooks out of walls so roofs might be raked off and salvaged. Time ran fast but destruction was faster and deafening: yells, bawling, the roar of flames, groaning and splintering timbers amidst an all-pervading stink of burning. People who had fallen into bed dog-tired after searching for the disappeared children and wakened out of the briefest of sleeps by incessant tolling fire bells scarcely knew which way up they stood. When there was no more they could do they huddled numb with despair and dread thinking about new terrors that lay in store for them - the murder of Axel Marx, the disappearance of little Schutzen princess and Kläuschen, a food store lost – what could be next?

Chapter 21

Acrid smoke clung to Nuremberg like a winding-sheet around a corpse. The drizzle that persisted through the night was reduced to a diaphanous smirr clinging to the blackened remains of Nuremberg's labyrinth granary. Throughout the dreadful night bells tolled; as a fire alarm at first and then to mark a day of sorrow for the town.

Albrecht Durer had gone home, bathed and changed into fresh garments but despite his fatigue he took himself back to the scene of the inferno where he found others were of like mind.

There had been no question of sleep for the women, men and children who lived next to the granary who spent an anxious night praying their homes would be spared. They were a forlorn-looking company waiting for official permission to return home once the danger of fire rekindling had passed. Out in the open they sat or stood guarding their few possessions now thoroughly soaked. A local baker was distributing pieces of rye bread from a wicker basket to grateful frozen souls and a cheese maker sliced up rounds of sheep's milk cheese for them to eat with the bread. When word came that the danger was over this sorry-looking assembly mutely carried drenched possessions back into their homes but some fared less well for buildings nearest to the grain hall had been demolished to stall the fire's progress and their residents found themselves homeless. A few, a very few, passed judgement on Müller's granary, now reduced to a timber skeleton, deeming it purified of the wickedness associated with it.

Thick-headed from lack of sleep Durer jumped at the touch of a hand on his shoulder. "Willy - how is the greatest man in the world this dismal morning?"

"All the better for seeing you, my insignificant friend." Willy Pirkheimer tugged at Durer's neatly darned blue mantle.

"I pulled this on in a rush," Durer explained, glancing at his coat. "My French brown coat sends you a hearty greeting but it was in no fit state to meet with your fur-trimmed wool so remains confined within my oak chest and my old blue must suffice."

Pirkheimer gave Durer an affectionate smile but his eyes took on a sombre appearance. "These are unsettling times," he said, "I told you before of the misfortunes that affected Augsburg."

"A granary fire, there too?"

Pirkheimer shook his great head. "No - those violent deaths we spoke of," he shifted his weight, "I've since learned that Hut and his followers were in that district when that happened."

Durer nodded as he absorbed Pirkheimer's meaning.

"But," Pirkheimer added, "so were all sorts of other folk. Like here in Nuremberg, Augsburg has large numbers of strangers travelling there every year. Most carry papers that give them passage and come and leave peaceably. We should not suspect they are all in league with the Devil. Talking of him I hear it said in Augsburg that their misfortunes are being blamed on witchcraft and demonic practices. I have to tell you, Albi my friend, my head will not admit to such far-fetched notions, for I think men of flesh and blood are at the heart of it all," Pirkheimer confided.

"I share your scepticism of sorcery, Willy, for it is certain devious men are behind these barbarous acts," Durer said.

"Of that we can be certain, Albi, and we cannot eliminate strangers from suspicion though I will not fix on them whenever there is a calamity. We should not despise them and not let others aim their wrath at them before they look closer to home for the ones responsible."

"Do you have anyone in mind?"

"No."

"But we cannot discount outsiders."

"No, I don't discount anyone, including a certain party of Spanish gentlemen who also arrived hot foot from Augsburg and whose appearance coincides with their and our misfortunes. From my dealings with them I fear they are ruthless at heart for all their professed religious fervour," Pirkheimer said.

"What is your opinion of the Italian cloth traders? Are they innocent in your view?"

Pirkheimer drew in his breath. "I think it unlikely the blood of your Italian peddlers is stirred by violence and menace. Whoever is behind all these terrible events – fire-raising, murdering our poor Axel and the abduction and possible killing of two infants – have succeeded in creating a state of terror in our city."

"Whoever is to blame must be punished but in my heart I cannot condone all that is done to those who are guilty for it's not twelve months since a fire-raiser was smoked to death in the Hauptmarkt. Do you recall it, Willy. That is a sight I never wish again to witness - to see a man bound to a plank of wood with his head held inside a barrow of tallow and it filled up with smoke from lighted damp straw. The cries of the fellow from such a drawn-out death live on in my head. Surely it is better to dispatch a guilty man quickly and not take pleasure from his ordeal? Even murderers have been let-off with a branding and banishment from the city on occasions."

"On not many occasions, Albi."

"No, on not many occasions - depending on the importance of the unfortunate victim."

The pair withdrew from the burned-out building when a gust of wind reignited an area of smouldering timbers causing consternation and the city guard was once again called in to relieve fire-battle-weary townspeople.

Fresh dry earth was dug and carted in by heavy-eyed men who threw shovel loads of it over still warm timbers in the hope of smothering fresh outbreaks of fire. Street gutters slippery from rainwater and the run-off from river water used to extinguish the blaze made it treacherous underfoot. Willy Pirkheimer would have tumbled had it not been for Durer catching hold of his arm but there was something else, beyond his difficulty with balancing, that troubled Pirkheimer.

"Albi, there is talk of the Council reviewing your commission for the portraits, Pirkheimer said."

Albrecht Durer frowned. "But why? I thought it settled."

Pirkheimer looked kindly at Durer. "Rumours concerning Herr Wolgemut's stolen picture are circulating in the town and have taken on a life of their own, my dear Albi, raising a question within the Rathaus - a question over your suitability "

"But it had nothing to do with me," Durer protested.

"I know. I know. And naturally, I have spoken up for you but my opinion has failed to staunch their suspicion that you've played some part in his loss. That is how it is."

The friends stood marooned in their own thoughts until a Burgher and acquaintance of Pirkheimer's approached and whispered into Pirkheimer's ear.

Pirkheimer turned to Durer. Pointing into the shell of the granary he said, "Bones have been discovered in there. Remains of a man, or men."

"Someone is dead in there?" Durer asked.

"Workmen have uncovered two heads, two arms and three legs, it's said." Pirkheimer wrinkled his brow, "Think you know him?"

Durer nodded. "Who doesn't know the three-legged two-headed man of Nuremberg? One-eyed certainly. Is there any news of Müller? I didn't see him helping put out the fire. It's likely it's him, isn't it?"

"Could be," Pirkheimer replied. "Probably."

"Mother would never let me come here on my own," Durer mused.

Pirkheimer slowly nodded his head. He did know. "Most of us avoided this place and now it looks like fate has taken its own revenge."

Durer nodded towards the granary. "Does fate start fires, Willy? Does she come in human guise or is it a punishment commanded by God?"

Durer and Pirkheimer went back into the ruin of the granary where many others were congregated, staring at a carpet of blackened ashes. Another skull had been dug out and it lay between burnt timbers, stark and pale with a slight greasy layer of what might have once been skin.

Durer leaned over it, fascinated. He poked a finger through an orb where once a man had observed the world. Pirkheimer nudged him, pointing him towards a spot farther in, and when they drew in closer they saw more bones - most of them smashed to smithereens. Durer crouched down and picked up a delicate golden chain with a crucifix attached.

With a shake of his head, Pirkheimer said, "The fire wasn't hot enough to melt it." He took it from Durer and examined it. "Look, Albi, at its unusual form, a woman's I would say." He fell silent, searching his memory. "You know, I'm certain I know who wore this – but it was a long time ago. I am sure this necklace belonged to Frau Müller."

Durer shrugged his shoulders. "Why should it not be, this was once her home."

"You're right. My mind is flying off in a strange direction." Willy Pirkheimer looked preoccupied as he closed his great fleshy fingers around the delicate piece.

The friends spent several minutes searching the burned out building before Pirkheimer spoke again.

"She was never without it. Her golden necklace, Albi. Frau Müller came from a poor family. No, she would not have willingly parted with it, of that I'm certain." He went over to the unearthed skull and examining it said, "You know what this could mean?"

"Do you mean, Willy, that Müller killed her?" Durer asked directly.

Pirkheimer inhaled slowly. "It would be far-fetched to decide so but worth considering."

"But which one?" Durer asked.

Pirkheimer took his time in answering. "Not the son, I fancy. He was too young when she disappeared. Her husband was a brute of a man." His voice trailed away.

"Will you share your suspicions?"

Pirkheimer cleared his throat. "I think it my duty. And I expect others will be of similar mind."

"Little good ever came out of this building so perhaps it's as well it is no more," Pirkheimer muttered. "The Müllers never showed a glimmer of mercy even when hunger tapped its bony knuckle against the doors of the poor." He shook his great head, "They were content to hoard supplies until shortage pushed up their price. And what good was their wealth in the end? It turned nearly everyone into their enemy. But for all that, I cannot condone anyone taking matters into their own hands despite provocation and the depth of loathing they aroused.

"You think the blaze was started deliberately?" Durer asked.

Pirkheimer pulled a face, "I don't know, my friend."

The blackened remains of the granary resembled a human anthill crawling with folk scouring its sorry relics; several young boys raking through the warm ashes with sticks uncovered several more fragments of bone; some quite large that might once have been part of a leg or arm and lots of tiny fragments that appeared to be fingers and toes. Eventually an official forager dispatched from the Rathaus came forward to claim all of the remains. Willy Pirkheimer dropped the chain and crucifix into the forager's basket.

As Durer and Pirkheimer were leaving, a cousin of Müller's, a man who ran one of the other granaries, attempted to assert his authority and restrict access to a part of the building that had largely escaped destruction, for he was hopeful of laying claim to any recovered valuables belonging to the miller and preferred to take on that task unhindered by any who were not kin. But the people were not to be moved.

From out the swarming mass came a shout, "Where's Red Cap?" The question was picked up by others and turned into a chorus. The cousin growled and scowled and shrank away before a fine dark ivory cross on a chain was retrieved by a small girl probing debris with a stick carved with tiny oak leaves. She was about to hand over the cross to the town scavenger when Otto Beck sauntered up.

"What's that you've got?" Beck demanded of the child.

"Doesn't matter what she's got, it's city property and I'm taking it," the scavenger said grabbing hold of the cross and walking away with it.

The girl sniggered and went to look for more treasure but Otto Beck followed her.

"What's that you've got there?" Beck repeated.

The girl pulled a face, "I gave it to him."

"That, in your hand." Beck took the broken stick from her.

The child tried to snatch it back but Beck held the piece out of her reach.

"It was mine, give it back to me," she cried.

"And now it's mine." Beck shoved the child aside.

***

When Willy Pirkheimer stepped out of St Sebaldus church and into the path of Prince Ernest and his Chamberlain, the latter doffed his hat, for everyone in Nuremberg knew the Councillor to be a great man deserving of respect. Pirkheimer, likewise, removed his own black felt bonnet and bowed to both men but primarily to the Prince who gave no indication of recognising him and avoided his eye; as was his habit with nearly everyone he encountered. Willy Pirkheimer ignored the Prince's slight and he and the Chamberlain briefly discussed the granary fire and other recent calamities, including a mention of the stolen pictures by the Councillor. The whole while the Prince's reptilian gaze settled somewhere in the vicinity of Pirkheimer's left ear but Pirkheimer's reference to the pictures moved the Prince to join the debate, against the urging of his Chamberlain not to do so.

Prince Ernest explained to Pirkheimer that he had recently been offered a painting purporting to be of a hare but which turned out was nothing of the kind and he had rejected it. When Pirkheimer inquired as to the identity of the artist the Chamberlain succeeded in ushering the Prince away before he could answer.

For all his idiosyncrasies Prince Ernest was regarded as a harmless presence in Franconia - or had been until word leaked out over his habit of worshipping heathen gods in all manner of peculiar ways. His attachment to the hare began in boyhood when he was compelled to participate in the royal pursuit of hunting; a practice he abhorred and shrank away from. When the harried animal was surrounded and finally killed by ferocious snarling men and hounds he would weep. The older he got the stronger his bond with animals became until it appears he adopted their attributes: reptilian eyes; head drooping towards a shoulder, bird-like; long, talon-like fingernails - like on hare's toes it was said. In any case, if truth were told, which it was not safe to do in Nuremberg, there were Christians there whose habits and indulgences owed much to their pagan forefathers - but it was easier to condemn one's own weaknesses when exhibited in others.

Chests full of learned books were carried overland from far and wide to the Kaiserburg to be translated by scribes so that Prince Ernest might read of the Ancients' veneration of animals, especially their intrigue with the hare, for it of all creatures held a special fascination for him. When word spread to the palace that some of the rich brocades taken to Nuremberg by Italian mercers included beautifully stitched likenesses of boxing lapis the traders were summoned to the palace by the Prince's Chamberlain, Slobberer. The Italian mercers were amused by Prince Ernest's childish enthusiasm, clapping hands and jumping up and down when they unrolled their exotic-looking material. It was they who were delighted when it was explained to them by a Steward into whose ear the Prince whispered that they should leave behind the whole bale containing the fighting hares design. And when they were being escorted from the palace that same Steward informed them that the Prince was eager to find an artist who could paint a realistic likeness of a hare to hang over the royal bed and be forever his companion; for all the live ones trapped for him were short-lived.

It happened that those same Italians became acquainted with Frau Wolgemut when she was introduced to them by Herr Wolf when in the town centre. She, too, was much taken by the striking designs and colours of their cloth and it was then she learnt of the Prince's purchase of a whole bolt of the peddlers' brocade and his wish to purchase a good likeness of a hare of any type. Frau Wolgemut let the merchants know she was the wife of an accomplished painter and on hearing this the Italians enquired if he might happen to have a picture - a painting or drawing of a hare that could please the Prince. At this the lady shook her head but instead of leaving the matter there she willingly conspired with them to provide the Prince with just such a picture and share whatever princely sum he should pay for it - which they imagined might be a tidy amount of goldgulden coin.

Now Gudrun Wolgemut was fairly clear in her mind that her husband possessed no such painting but she harboured a hope she might persuade him to create one. She also recalled hearing from Maria Kohl and her husband's apprentice, Joachim, that Albrecht Durer possessed a fine study of a field hare and from such unlikely foundations a plan emerged to make money, one way or another.

Whatever ambition Frau Wolgemut had to persuade her husband to paint the picture of a hare fit for a prince were dashed when he refused to apply himself to drawing any likeness to what he dismissed as a base subject unworthy of his talent. Herr Wolgemut's wife was bitterly disappointed and not having the courage to tell her husband she meant to sell his picture, mainly because she had no intention of sharing the payment with him, only the Italians, she was driven to devise another solution to her problem. First, she looked at every one of the pictures and prints stored in her husband's workshop but there was no work that resembled a hare in any form but when she turned out an old press in a lobby just off the workshop she discovered a small oil painted on board of a rabbit, stuck at the back of a drawer. The work looked old and was not in great condition. In fact, it had the appearance of an apprentice piece for the hand which made it was immature though creditable and great attention had been paid to the representation of hair and muscle. The picture could be said to be of reasonable quality but not excellent and it was not of a hare. She was lost in thought looking at the picture when her husband who had come into the workshop shook her out of her reverie. Demanding to know what fascinated her so Frau Wolgemut had no choice but to show the picture to him. He claimed no recollection of it and she played a game with him, pressing him to think he might have painted it and forgotten it till eventually he believed it was his painting but urged her to return it to the cupboard.

Of course, Gudrun Wolgemut did no such thing. It was this painting that was offered to Prince Ernest, with the Italian gentlemen acting as intermediaries. It was this same picture that was rejected by the Prince, less on grounds of its quality than on the subject being not a hare but a rabbit.

It did occur to Gudrun Wolgemut that she, herself, should attempt to create a hare painting, for her talent as an artist had drawn praise when she was younger, but in her heart she knew she would be unsuccessful in convincing the Prince to accept a second piece that failed to match his expectations. So, it was she came up with yet another plan to make money, by making the picture disappear and convincing her ailing husband whose mind was easily confused he had been robbed of one of his more valuable paintings.

The next step was to concoct a ransom demand for the 'stolen' work and this was crafted by an Italian hand; the picture would be returned in exchange for a considerable sum of goldgulden. As Herr Wolgemut was not himself in possession of a great deal of gold and in any case Frau Wolgemut had no desire to reduce her own household's capital so she persuaded her uncle to provide the ransom purse. At that stage it would have been possible for Gudrun Wolgemut to put a stop to the deception and share her uncle's gold with her Italian accomplices but then her husband began to ask questions about his lost painting and he spoke to Schmeichler about the alleged robbery. This complication led to Frau Wolgemut and the Italians devising yet another scheme to keep hold of the uncle's gold and trick Herr Wolgemut whose interest in his picture that never was had become a difficulty for them. Getting their hands on Albrecht Durer's picture was the next step for Gudrun Wolgemut was in no doubt it would be acceptable to the Prince. This scheme also offered the conspirators the chance to profit twice over, keeping the goldgulden purse and selling Durer's painting to Prince Earnest. In light of this development the Italians insisted on an additional sum to hold their tongues and bargain with the Prince.

Chapter 22

Johannes Brauer's was the proverbial rumour mill when later in the day Albrecht Durer slipped along the bench next to Otto Beck.

"You here already?" Durer remarked.

"You are particularly observant today, Albi,"

"You're usually late, where's Willy?"

Beck yawned.

"Am I boring you, Otto?"

Beck shrugged.

"Out with it, tell me what's wrong."

"My Maria didn't turn up as we arranged, that's all."

Durer made sympathetic noises. "She's avoiding you now, as well."

"What do you mean?"

"Only that lately whenever she sees me, she rushes away as though I've offended her. Have I, Otto?"

Beck pulled a face. "Not as far as I know. She'll come round."

Albrecht Durer picked a loose hair off his coat and blew it away. "Where's Willy?"

Beck glanced towards the inn door as if to summon up the Councillor then from his leather satchel he produced a short piece of singed wood that he placed on the table. "You recognise this?" he asked.

Durer furrowed his brow. "It's similar to some framing I have. Where did you find it?"

"I got it at the burned-out granary."

"Then it isn't mine," Durer replied, leaning back from the table. "Why are you showing it to me?"

"I recognised it from your workshop. Looks identical. Thought it strange it should turn up in a fire where people died."

Durer's mouth gaped open and with the back of his hand he swept the stick off the table. Otto Beck stroked his chin, avoiding Durer's eye. Neither man spoke.

Into the silence wandered Willy Pirkheimer. Putting down his krug of beer he made himself comfortable alongside Durer. "Albi - Otto - how are you both?" His enquiry was acknowledged by nods from both men. "Not drinking?"

Beck shook his empty krug and Durer tried to catch the eye of a pretty, dark-haired girl dispensing beer from two jugs.

"Who's that?" Willy Pirkheimer asked.

"Expect she's covering for Klara and Ana. Still no sign of Kläuschen," Beck answered. "Did you hear Müller was killed in the blaze at his granary?"

Pirkheimer's attention lingered on the serving girl.

"She's but a child Willy, let her be," Durer chided, a touch of annoyance perceptible in his tone.

Pirkheimer paid no heed to Durer's scolding but in response to Beck he remarked it would not be surprising that Müller had been caught up in the fire since it was his granary, "… and with everything else."

"Everything else?" Beck frowned.

Pirkheimer rolled his eyes. "Yes blockhead, everything else. Müller we're talking about - do I have to spell out my meaning? I don't pardon violence - never - but Müller. Tell me though, what goes on between you two?"

Beck snorted.

"Sorry for losing my temper, Otto." Pirkheimer rubbed Beck's stubbled head. "Anger cripples the mind, causes hair to go white - and harms the heart and displeases God."

"What?" Beck asked.

"Anger. I shouldn't have snapped your head off," Pirkheimer said.

Lust and sodomy." Durer leaned his head in his hands. "You mean Müller. Do you think it was him the mystic meant during his rant in the Hauptmarkt? Müller fits that niche."

Pirkheimer was on his feet, relieving the slight serving girl of one of the beer pitchers and dispensing the contents into their krugs.

"Thank you, Herr Pirkheimer." Ana appeared at the table and took the empty jug from him. She handed it to the girl, telling her to refill it and take it around the tables.

"Is there news of young Kläuschen?" Pirkheimer asked her.

Ana Brauer's tears and shake of her head told its own story and the three friends sympathised with the distraught woman. Once she was gone Pirkheimer sunk his face into his hands.

Looking at him, Durer asked "Willy, my most learned and wise friend, master of many languages, detector of all uttered lies, this is one of the worst of times for our city, will it ever end?"

Pirkheimer sat up and squinted in Durer's direction. "Into this maelstrom, Albi, comes yet another mystery. Adolf Wolf did not report for his duties yesterday and nothing has been heard from him. His bed is undisturbed and no-one has admitted to seeing him. But curiously his hat which he habitually wears is at his house without its owner."

"I met him on Thursday, returning from the Knoblauchsland," Beck said.

"Then you are one of the last people to have seen him," Pirkheimer said. He thought for a moment before adding, "It's assumed Müller died in the granary fire but who's to say it wasn't Wolf, also? There were more bones found there than belong to one man."

"But what business would Wolf have at the granary at night?" Durer asked.

Pirkheimer took a long draught of beer. "Who's to say he didn't go there earlier in the day. As I say, he was not at his work yesterday. Today is Saturday and I think I would have heard if he's been spotted, for it isn't like him to shirk from his duties so his absence caused quite a stir at the Rathaus. Remember that Adolf Wolf, like many others in the city, was embroiled in that murky world of the Müllers. Who knows what dark dealings they may have had - or secrets shared? He might have gone there to speak with Müller or confront him, I don't know."

"As you say Müller had many enemies but do you think it possible it was Wolf who began the blaze at the granary - to murder Müller?" Durer asked.

Willy Pirkheimer shut his eyes and considered the proposal. His city was one of the most liberal and cultivated in Europe but as in all municipals it fostered its own seedy underworld.

There were very few families in Nuremberg whose lives were untainted by the wickedness of the Müllers and others like them. Some, as in the case of Wolf, were traded by a parent for favours. They were victims of a culture of bestiality. It was long assumed that when the wife of the elder Müller disappeared without trace she ran away because she could no longer face living with her debauched husband. That she had abandoned her child to his father's tender mercies condemned her in the eyes of the good people of the city who watched as the boy came to repeat the sins of the father.

For long the Müllers were protected by a conspiracy of silence among the most powerful in Nuremberg who connived with them, participated in degenerate practices and lived their lives in fear of exposure. That it was possible one or other of them might remove, through brutal assassination, anyone suspected of exposing their wickedness would surprise few in that city. The trouble was the list of Müller's enemies ran to a very long one, from the highest in the city to the lowest. Wolf's name would undoubtedly be included on that list.

***

Otto Beck was in his shop under the Rathaus making alterations to the wheel lock in the gun he used to shoot the goose hawk when his concentration was disturbed by a sharp rap against his window. Willy Pirkheimer's great moon of a face pressed up against the glass. Beck clucked his irritation as he unlocked the door.

211

"Willy – oh, here let me help you." Beck removed the topmost volume of an armful of books and objects carried by Pirkheimer. "What have you here?' Beck asked, screwing up his eyes a fraction and sounding out the words, "*Dante's Inferno.*" The locksmith turned the book over and running his thumb down its scuff marked leather binding remarked, "I'd have expected you to keep a finer copy than this, Willy."

"None of these belongs to me, they are Wolf's – from his room at the Rathaus. These," Pirkheimer fished an ivory cross and ring set with a blue stone from his pocket, "were found at the scene of the fire and are certainly Herr Wolf's. I'm taking them to his mother."

"He perished in the fire?" Beck asked.

"It looks that way. The scavenger found Wolf's badge of office at the fire - melted but still identifiable. So, there's no doubt we've lost poor Wolf. Other remains found there are believed to have belonged to Frau Müller, God bless her soul - both their souls." Pirkheimer used his foot to drag a stool closer to him and dropped Wolf's things onto it.

"Frau Müller?" Beck's mouth dropped open. "But she's been gone for years ... how?"

"It doesn't look like she did leave, after all, Otto."

Beck inspected the items that included a broken bone comb and a clear glass scent amphora. "I don't think his mother will find much use for most of that rubbish. This is pretty though," he said, holding up an embroidered handkerchief. "Shame it's marked." Beck smoothed out the linen square to better examine its intricate lacework and flower motif. With a none-too-clean finger he traced the lines of a brown stain which spoilt it. "And this was among Wolf's things? Interesting."

Pirkheimer removed his hat and scratched his head. "It's a tragedy and puzzle." He toyed with a tiny pierced brass drum that was lying on Beck's workbench. "I'd better pass on his things though I'm loath to do it. Hopefully they'll prove a comfort to Frau Wolf."

Beck fetched a leather satchel from the back of his shop and together with Pirkheimer they packed it with Wolf's belongings.

"You can hold onto this and return it to its owner," Pirkheimer passed the handkerchief to Beck.

***

Willy Pirkheimer was forced to bend down low on entering the cottage. Once inside he saw himself like a giant in a folk story; unable to stand upright and so was grateful to accept the old woman's invitation to be seated. The room contained two seats: a three-legged wooden stool and a four-legged stool with struts forming a rudimentary back-rest. Pirkheimer chose the backless stool so that the woman might have the better chair but there was a moment of confusion when she insisted on taking the tripod so Pirkheimer balanced his bulk, precariously, on the rickety chair. These two sticks of furniture comprised almost half of all there was in the hovel; the remainder being a coarse bed, small table and a rustic open press containing a few domestic items including two cups and two dishes, cracked and chipped but clean, which Pirkheimer recognised were the same as crockery used at the Rathaus. On the floor was the cumbersome willow basket Frau Wolf used to carry her customer's linen. With her son dead, old Frau Wolf would have more need than ever to continue as a laundress.

Pirkheimer put down Adolf's books and trinkets on the table, watched by the widow without comment. He felt ill at ease. Realising he still wore his hat he snatched it off his head and worked it between his fingers, nervously. Presently Wolf's mother offered him refreshment which he declined for he knew she was a poor woman with little to spare. Pirkheimer studied Frau Wolf, her head bent with her hands piously folded in her lap, and pondered whether her independence from her son was chosen or a consequence of him abandoning her when he moved up through society.

213

"Frau Wolf I deeply regret your loss," he began, "the Council is indebted to the conscientious service Adolf gave to the City and we intend providing you with a small pension in recognition of this."

The face opposite creased by time and ill-fortune revealed no hint of emotion.

Clearing his throat, Pirkheimer repeated his offer for he thought the widow might be deaf. "Frau Wolf,' he said louder this time, "we trust a small stipend will help make your life a trifle easier ..." he broke off when a pair of clear grey eyes set within two muddied circles fixed on him.

"I have no need of charity." The woman's words were barely audible but their meaning was crystal clear.

"It is not charity, Frau Wolf," Pirkheimer protested, "only recognition of the terrible tragedy that has befallen you and our esteem for your son." He waited.

The old woman plucked at her threadbare apron. "My son has provided for me. Your assistance is not necessary."

Pirkheimer was careful not to let his eyes stray around the room lest Frau Wolf feel the inadequacy of her existence; the scant furnishings and single narrow window - evidence of all Herr Wolf would have needed to fire his ambition to flee the clamp of poverty. Pirkheimer insisted the offer was not unusual for the Council rewarded loyalty and there was no shame in taking what was due to her. Still, Frau Wolf remained unmoved so Pirkheimer got to his feet and from his stooped position he bowed one last time to the diminutive widow. "Frau Wolf, I beg you to reconsider. The shock of your son's untimely death will have affected you much. There is no urgency for you to make your decision now. Take your time." He patted the back of her hand; its flesh soft and wine-red.

Frau Wolf looked down at her feet and said nothing.

Pirkheimer waited. He had come with a question in mind, aside from delivering Herr Wolf's possessions and the offer of a Council pension. He cleared his throat. "Frau Wolf may I enquire if you know why your son was at the granary?" He perceived her stiffen but still she uttered no sound. Taking a deep breath Pirkheimer then said, "I'll leave you in peace." As he spoke his gaze strayed to the glass scent jar, the ivory crucifix and blue-stone ring he had brought her - they looked so out of place in a space so bare of comforts. His eyes swept the room, at the short wooden bed with its darned quilt, the mean shelves with their coarse crockery and if he had any expectation of finding a picture of a hare lurking in the impoverished interior he left disappointed. Pirkheimer was closing Frau Wolf's door when she addressed him.

"He was afraid his sins would catch up with him. That jezebel cast her spell on my son." Frau Wolf's words were so quietly spoken it was as though they squeezed from between her lips, involuntarily.

Pirkheimer was not sure he heard correctly and stuck his head back into the room where their eyes met.

"After hearing that pilgrim fanatic speak on Michaelmas my son lost his senses and confessed to me he was minded to leave Nuremberg. It was because he was ashamed. So, you see I cannot accept money from you on his behalf."

Chapter 23

Gudrun Wolgemut gave a start when Albrecht Durer crept up on her as she walked in her garden on Saturday afternoon.

"Hallo, Frau Wolgemut," he said.

"Why Albrecht have you come to see me?" she asked, surprised to see him there so soon after their recent argument.

Albrecht Durer explained he was there to speak with her husband and for some moments Frau Wolgemut eyed him suspiciously before telling him her husband was not in the mood to receive guests.

"Has something else happened?" Durer asked.

Gudrun Wolgemut shrugged her shoulders and swallowing back any reply she might have been tempted to make only dabbed her eyes with the corner of a handkerchief.

Albrecht Durer reached out and took her hand. "Have I made you weep, fair Gudrun?"

She withdrew her hand. Her eyes were red and sore-looking.

"What is this that afflicts you, Gudrun? I have offended you."

Gudrun Wolgemut twisted the plain white handkerchief between her fingers. "It is nothing - but I have a raging thirst and my head aches."

Durer expressed his sympathies to her but then they ran out of anything to say to each other and parted somewhat self-consciously, Gudrun remaining in the shrubbery and Durer heading towards the Wolgemut cottage.

***

In response to Durer's knock, Schmeichler opened the door a crack. "I will let Herr Wolgemut know you are here," he cackled; his focus over Durer's shoulder to where Frau Wolgemut loitered. "Wait here. What is that you have there?"

"What remains of a frame I had around my missing picture," Durer said.

Schmeichler's eyebrow shot up as if seeking refuge under his grubby turban. "Oh dear."

"My proof that Herr Wolgemut and I are in the same predicament. If I could only have a word ..."

"Proof? What kind of proof is a burned piece of wood? It proves only that you have been using kindling to start a fire," Schmeichler cooed. A branding iron of a smile turned into a sneer that stretched from coiled snail ear to coiled snail ear. "You have impugned my master. Those are his very words. Now I doubt he will want to see you about this affair anymore. Be off." He flapped his gnarled hand as if brushing aside a mongrel cur.

"I was sorry to hear about Herr Wolgemut's hound," Durer blurted out.

Schmeichler dropped his head to the side, scrutinising the artist.

Having come to his home Durer was keen to speak with Herr Wolgemut. "Are you quite certain Herr Wolgemut won't see me?"

"Herr Wolgemut is not well disposed towards you, can you think why? He no longer trusts you, Herr Durer, for your conduct has been painful to him. You forget my master is a highly respected man in Nuremberg. He bears no ill-will towards anyone, least of all a person who once sat at his feet as an ignorant novice, and I advise you to desist from pestering him." Schmeichler emphasised this last point with a defiant nod of his head. At the same time the wide mouth gave an involuntary twitch and Schmeichler winced with pain, his hand reaching for his ear. "I don't think I will inform Herr Wolgemut you are here and please do not be tempted to return unless it is to repay my master for the loss you've caused him." He rubbed his fingers together to indicate coin. "Now be off." He half-closed the door but then pulled it open again. "Yes, it was a fine animal - the dog - a great pity." And with that he slammed the door shut.

***

217

There was yet one other visitor to Herr Wolgemut's cottage that day. Otto Beck turned up to see Maria Kohl who received him coolly, only brightening up when he produced the pretty handkerchief Pirkheimer had left with him.

"Frau Wolgemut's been looking for that - and me needless to say. How did you get it?"

Beck shook his head, mumbling something about Willy Pirkheimer having found it. He lied badly but Maria was not curious about where the handkerchief had been found instead she inspected Beck's misshapen nose and sore eye and sighed loudly before disappearing into the garden where she picked a bunch of leafy giersch growing there in profusion.

"What are you going to do with that?" Beck asked when she returned.

Maria took a wooden pastry roller out of a drawer and used it to bruise the goutweed. She poured honey onto the herb and once it was thoroughly coated she plastered the lot over Beck's black and blue eye, for goutwort had remarkable qualities for relieving bruising. While waiting for the herb to do its work Beck asked Maria if Gudrun Wolgemut hired Frau Wolf as their laundress, for he was curious to know how the handkerchief came into Wolf's possession.

Why do you want to know?" Maria demanded.

Beck shrugged off her question as if the matter was of no importance. Maria eyed him for a moment or two then said Frau Wolf was not nor was she likely to be as her mistress and Her Wolf had quarrelled over the Council's commission for the Schopper oil portraits which went to Albrecht Durer.

"They are in need of the income," Maria whispered. "My mistress flew into a fury with Herr Wolf ... gave him his character. Of course, she didn't know I was within earshot. Not that she would have been inhibited... not in the black humour she was in." Maria smirked. "It was the most lively I've seen her in a long while for that mistress of mine is a shallow and lazy woman but don't you go repeating that Otto, do you hear? No, they use a young widow who doesn't charge much for handling their large items and I take care of the small."

"Have you heard Adolf Wolf is dead?" Beck asked.

"I heard he was," Maria replied, "but I don't think that will move my mistress. I don't suppose you want to go home with this over your face." She pulled the sticky green herb away from Beck's eye. "You'll need to apply this again when you go to bed but be off with you now for I have chores waiting; we don't all have time to stroll about the countryside delivering handkerchiefs." She looked at it properly for the first time since he gave it to her. "And what mark is this you've left on it?"

"That's not of my doing. It was like that when it came into my possession," Beck said.

***

Beck was nearing the Laufer tor where he ran into none other than Peter Henlein, a fellow locksmith and clockmaker who was approaching at a jaunty pace from the opposite direction. Beck tapped his hat by way of a *good afternoon* and Henlein raised the brim of his felt cap. Farther on Beck thought he spied young Günter and called out to him but the boy appeared not to hear, instead he skipped on ahead a little swifter. Beck decided to call in on Durer. Anton showed him through to the workshop where he found his friend inspecting a version of his *Adam and Eve* drawing.

"Nice looking girl," Beck said.

"What's that you have there?" Durer asked.

Otto Beck held up Maria's green herb poultice, explaining it would reduce the swelling of his eye. He told Durer about Willy Pirkheimer's visit to him earlier and the appearance of the pretty handkerchief. Durer occasionally nodded as though listening but was more preoccupied with his Garden of Eden picture than any mislaid handkerchief. His interest was sparked, however, on hearing that Günter was seen on the hill for it had been some time since he sent the boy on an errand

and in quite another direction. But what made him really pay attention was Beck's mention of Wolf's death.

"News of it is all through the city." Durer crossed to a bookcase and selected a grey vellum volume of *Dante*'s *Inferno*.

"Second time today," Beck said.

Durer looked at him, quizzically.

"Wolf had a copy in his office. Funny thing to have at your work, don't you think? Not easy to keep your mind on the job with something like that looking over your shoulder," Beck said.

The book lay open in Durer's hands and he invited Beck to come closer.

"Albi it's late - too late for reading such material. We'll be here all night if I try to get my tongue around this tome. Just give me the bare bones of what's on your mind."

"It was something the mystic Hut said that got me looking at it again. That and what happened to poor Axel and the lost children – now Müller and Wolf - and my *Field Hare*. Something malevolent stalks our city Otto. These are dangerous times."

"What has this to do with Dante?" Beck asked.

"Nothing except all of this horror began with the mystics spouting on about sin and retribution." He shook the book, "Their charges and consequences are straight out of these pages and it got me thinking - that wickedness is always with us. Men are made malevolent – sometimes by action and sometimes only in thought, thank goodness – but it's part of being human. What is my *Adam and Eve* picture if not that? But now it is not the perpetrators of evil who are made to suffer, or not entirely, but innocents such as Kläuschen, the Denck child, Axel and the clerk, Wolf. Axel decapitated and de-limbed in a dung heap! Imagine! Where are the children? How many more of us will the finger of death point at? Is the guilt we all carry to lead each of us to vengeance, as set out in this book? Wolf consumed by fire - was he guilty of lust, Otto? I had not heard that of him. And what were Kläuschen and the

Denck girl guilty of that they were made to suffer? And, Otto, which of us will be next?"

Beck gazed back at him with a worried expression on his battered face. "You think these happenings can be laid at the door of an Italian poet?" he asked.

"A long dead Italian poet, Otto. Precisely," Durer replied, "someone may be using his words as his *vade vecum* - selecting a victim to suffer for each of the Deadly Sins as a warning to the rest of us. And here am I creating a picture of the very source of the world's sinfulness." He held up the drawing of Eve that was still awaiting Adam.

"How does he choose his victims - this assassin?" Beck asked. "If it is that man, Hut, he's a stranger and cannot know about us here in Nuremberg. Is it not more likely the assassin kills his victims at random - which makes him more of a sinner than any he is punishing?"

"If that is the case he'll see himself not a sinner but someone who is teaching us all a lesson … a threat, perhaps, or collective punishment by the book," Durer suggested.

"I don't claim to understand it but I fear for our city. More immediately, I fear for myself."

Durer slammed shut Dante's volume and placed it back on the shelf.

***

Otto Beck spent some time with Durer and when eventually he came to leave he decided that instead of going home he would return to the Wolgemut's to see his Maria. Once again that day he trudged up Kaiserburg hill, this time with the aid of a sturdy branch. It was early evening and with heavy cloud cover dark settled in early to Nuremberg on that Saturday so when Beck tripped over a pair of legs sticking out across the path he let out a yell and his stick flew out of his grasp.

"What the …!" he roared, grabbing at the truncated limbs. "Günter! You again! Why are you abroad at this hour and lying down in wait to waylay innocent pedestrians?"

Günter stared up at Beck, wide-eyed and dumbstruck. He rubbed the knee that had taken Beck's weight when he tumbled and looked back towards Wolgemut's workshop, a shadow in the distance.

Beck tutted. "I understand," he said, calm at last, "just don't let Herr Durer know you've been seeing Joachim or he might clip your ear out of envy." He tousled the boy's hair. "Get yourself home and we'll say no more about this. Go on, away with you."

Having dispatched Günter, Beck retrieved his stick and continued to the Wolgemut's but instead of going to the house entrance he crossed over to the print workshop. Noiselessly lifting the latch he let himself in. The interior was in darkness save for a darkling glimmer in an adjoining chamber where men could be heard talking.

The pervading smell in the place was of linseed oil and iron-gall ink. Cautiously, Beck crept across the floor. He had been in the workshop many times and knew its layout - several bows in length with Wolgemut's bulky printing press in a corner. There it was, piled high with layers of parchments, loose copies of engravings and woodcuts. As his eyes grew accustomed to the murk Beck's attention was drawn to a cumbersome oak cupboard carved with coiling ivy and dancing bears on the opposite side of the room from the printing press. It was a piece he had previously admired for its craftsmanship although it was much spoilt with deep blade scourings and ingrained with inks. The ivy reminded him of Durer's broken picture frame and as he ran his hand along its pitted surface he realised the voices from the inner room had fallen silent.

At approaching footsteps Otto Beck ducked out of sight behind a tapestry suspended on ceiling hooks. The space between tapestry and wall was narrow and Beck shared it with drawings, oil boards and prints, compelling him to position his feet sideways to prevent them protruding into the room. He dared not breathe. Someone was in the print room. He waited, tense and cramped. As he turned his foot he heard a loud crack. Lifting the heel of his boot Beck thought he recognised in fragments of green jasper the remains of a little carved dog's head that Herr Durer bought from a sailor in Antwerp as an amulet. How it came to be in Wolgemut's workshop mystified Beck but his ruminations were cut short at the sound of a cough. Cautiously he drew aside an edge of the tapestry and peeked out. There, not two arms' lengths away stood a man looking straight at him. A gagging sound that might have indicated guilt emanated from Beck's throat as he emerged from his hideaway. He bent down to retrieve the broken dog head and in his clumsiness collided with the stacked pictures. Grabbing at them to prevent them from toppling Beck spotted what looked like a Durer work – a study of a hare. He was staring at it, open-mouthed, when he was addressed sharply.

"Who are you and what mischief are you up to?"

The shadowy man was more visible to Beck now; dressed in an ankle-length leather apron with his arms supporting several rolls of paper he appeared to be one of Wolgemut's printers. Beck did not recognise the fellow and was grateful it had not been the apprentice, Joachim, who had discovered him for he would have been able to identify him.

"I...I ...," the locksmith laboured for an explanation, "was looking to place an order for prints ... I called out but no-one replied then I heard footsteps and thought I should not be found having been so bold as to enter these premises at this hour," his deceitful tongue lied, "so I hid when I heard voices."

The printer weighed up the short, stocky man and his eyes looked down at the smashed trifle in Beck's hand.

"It is a strange time and manner to call on business. What have you there?"

"It is nothing," Beck replied.

"Let me see. Hold it up."

Beck opened up his fingers revealing the broken curiosity.

"Put it down," the man demanded.

"But it belongs to Herr Durer," Beck spluttered.

"Herr Durer? Herr Durer? What impertinence is this? Put it back."

223

"As does that picture," Beck nodded towards the dislodged boards and papers at his feet.

"Are you quite mad?"

"What kind of place is this that conceals the property of another?" Beck insisted.

The man took a step forward. He had the advantage of height and build over Beck so the locksmith lunged towards the door his mouth drooped open with fright.

Despite having claimed the picture as Durer's Beck was in truth not now certain it was for he could not recall having seen the study but the style was similar to that of his friend. As for the trinket he now thought it only resembled one in Durer's possession and neither uncertainty was worth a beating.

"What is the real reason for you being here?" the printer shouted. He had put down his load of paper and approached Beck.

A cough escaped Beck's throat in his anxiety. "I was hoping to purchase a ... a townscape of Nuremberg, but I'll return at a more opportune time."

The printer took hold of the door and blocked Beck's escape.

"Might I inform Herr Wolgemut the name of the gentleman interested in a purchase?" he asked, emphasising the word *gentleman.*

"Er, tell him it's Herr Wolf," Beck found himself uttering.

"And can I also say that you are interested in purchasing a painting - Herr Wolf?" The man pointed his thumb towards the upset pictures on the floor.

"I thought the study of the hare looked much like one belonging to Herr Durer," Beck squawked.

"Herr Durer, again." the printer smiled. "And what is the foundation of such a belief, Herr Wolf?"

"It has his monogram ... take a look," Beck replied without thinking, for instantly he remembered Durer told him he had not signed the picture.

The printer went over to the picture and inspected it. "I see no monogram. You are mistaken."

A second fellow emerged from the inner chamber and this one Beck recognised as a woodblock cutter who had been in Wolgemut's employ since Durer's time. The woodblock cutter screwed up his eyes when he saw Beck as if trying to recall him then directed his attention to the hare picture held up by the printer.

Seeing his opportunity Beck fled through the door and picking up the stick he had abandoned there jammed it through the stout ring-pull preventing the door being opened from the inside. Then he took off like the wind. Only when he was well clear of the premises did Beck pull up to catch his breath and reflect on whether it was Durer's picture he had seen and how he had once doubted Durer's claim of a stolen painting. Beck smiled at the thought of Durer's gratitude to him for discovering the *Field Hare*, if it was the actual one, in Wolgemut's workshop of all places. His only regret was that it had been within his grasp for the briefest of moments. This conflux of thoughts sent the locksmith's head into a spin as he tramped homewards.

Beck's return to the town was delayed when he noticed a faint flicker of light through a copse of birches. A blanket spread before a well-stacked fire, the remains of a meal and discarded wooden bowl and grey bone spoon he recognised belonged to the shepherd Widukind. Beck sat down and was warming his hands when a crack from a breaking twig alerted him to the shepherd's return. Widukind, his robe flapping about his feet and face all but hidden behind a long hood that draped down to his chest was accompanied by his old black and white dog. Beck noticed the shepherd's hands were dark and dripping with what looked like blood.

"Herr Widukind are you hurt?" Beck jumped up, full of concern.

Widukind snorted. In one hand he held a dagger while the other cradled something round and bloody.

"She was wounded by an arrow and dying. I could not bear to listen to her pathetic cries so put her out of her misery," he said. "Here, Otto Beck, take this - she was brave and if you eat her heart her bravery will come to you." He proffered the bloody mess to the locksmith.

Beck shook his head. "You have it Widukind."

"I have what is left. Here take it," Widukind insisted.

Beck accepted the gift of the still warm heart holding it close to his own which seemed appropriate. He sat back down and he and Widukind talked and talked. The fire made him sleepy so he did not hear the shepherd tell of seeing two men, one short the other long accompanied by a large dog and carrying a bundle wrapped in cloth entering the castle grounds and shortly after returning with the same bundle. Nor did he hear Widukind comment on the nocturnal practises of Nuremberg's people, including Gudrun Wolgemut whom he claimed received gentlemen after her husband was bedded. Laughing, Widukind poked Beck in the ribs which woke up the locksmith.

When Beck knocked at Durer's door for the second time that day, he was turned away by a sullen Anton who informed him that Durer was not at home. Only when Beck reached Am Ölberg did he realise he was still carrying the bloody heart Widukind had given to him.

By good fortune Beck came upon Durer walking ahead of him in the company of Willy Pirkheimer. As he caught up with them Beck overheard them discuss Durer's commission for the Schopper House oils and how he might lose it because of his suspected involvement in the theft of Wolgemut's picture. The conversation ended abruptly when Beck called out his *good evenings* to their backs. Durer and Pirkheimer turned round all smiles and joviality but this conviviality melted away on observing Beck's bloodied hand. With an uncomfortable laugh Beck hurriedly explained how he came to be in possession of a hart's heart and went on to tell of the incident at Wolgemut's workshop and finding a hare picture behind a screen.

"Oh, and I found this." From his pocket he produced a fragment of what he thought was Durer's green jasper dog head carving.

226

Durer examined the piece, muttering a complaint about Günter and how he would have a word with him over making free with his possessions but his interest lay chiefly with Beck's report that his *Field Hare* may lurk in Wolgemut's workshop. Durer grew more certain that Maria Kohl was behind the missing painting. She had ample opportunity, being a frequent visitor to his home and workshop in the company of Beck. He did not suspect his good companion, Otto, of any involvement, yet there was a niggle, just that, of Otto's perpetual state of hardship, always scrounging drinks from him and Willy. Durer took a deep breath. Would Beck tell him about the picture at Wolgemut's if he had played a part in its disappearance? What? Durer asked himself would be the reason for that – other than play a bluff by being the one to find it. He could hardly conceive of Otto Beck deceiving him yet recent events sorely tested his faith in men and he scarcely knew what to believe anymore. And here was Beck flaunting a bloody deer's heart and in possession of his broken jasper dog head. If his *Hare* picture was at Wolgemut's then he had to get it back. Might it be possible Herr Wolgemut was in on the theft, after all? He decided he would go and tackle Wolgemut again but when Pirkheimer heard his intention the Councillor clapped a restraining hand on Durer's arm, urging him not to act rashly but to hold off till the next day.

***

Having plotted to obtain Albrecht Durer's picture of a field hare Gudrun Wolgemut had the problem of how to get her hands on it. Unwilling to trust anyone outside her foreign accomplices it was the Italians who gained entry to Durer's house with the intention of stealing it and were almost discovered when Durer arrived back drunk from Brauer's. The next evening Gudrun Wolgemut then contrived her own way into Durer's home following his unsuccessful attempt to exchange the gold purse for the missing picture that never was. She had come away empty-handed and later interrogated Maria on the precise whereabouts of his *Field Hare*. The purse with the goldgulden was safe in her possession but the prospect of being able to sell Durer's picture to the Prince encouraged the lady to continue her deception. There was also a matter of social standing or its decline that partly drove her for she resented Durer's growing popularity in the face of her husband's decline. If Albrecht Durer's reputation was damaged in the process of her getting rich that was all to the good. What turned her nearly insane was news that Durer's hare picture was missing, and she wasn't its recipient.

Gudrun Wolgemut prayed in St Sebaldus for life's complications to be resolved so it was both startling and gratifying to then walk into her husband's workshop and discover a beautiful painting of a hare lying there, on the flagstones. Where had it come from? Why was it abandoned there? Could it belong to her husband? Why had she never seen it before? None of this mattered for her prayers had been answered. Gudrun Wolgemut wept in gratitude for her change in fortune. The picture looked like the one described by Albrecht Durer and Maria but then one field hare looked very much like another, so who was to say she asked herself? It was, certainly, a very accomplished work and there was no question but the Prince would pay her well for it. All that remained was to get it to the palace. Until that could be arranged she decided to hide it behind the black oak press with the coiling leaves carved into it in her husband's print room – the same cupboard she had found the little rabbit painting. As the bulky furniture was never moved she had no fear of the picture being discovered.

Close to completing her deception Frau Wolgemut was overcome by a feeling of guilt. Shaking and with her mind on edge she needed someone to blame for her predicament and applied that honour to Herr Wolf. Persuading herself she was content with her life until Wolf encouraged her betrayal of her husband she overlooked Wolf's flattering attentions and the little trifles he brought her that were never provided by her husband because of his grip on his purse and his indifference towards her. Frau Wolgemut would not remember Wolf's acts of kindness only that he was a jealous man who criticised her friendship with the Italian mercers, although it was he who had introduced her to them.

When he lived, Adolf Wolf, had become bewitched by Gudrun Wolgemut. He pitied the woman who insisted her life was unbearable and spoke of her desperation to escape the tedium of her existence. Wolf had not recognised wickedness in her, only a weakness of character that made her susceptible to the trickery of others.

As for the lady herself, Gudrun Wolgemut, it worried her that Herr Wolf knew so much about her innermost secrets and after the first heady months of their relationship she became increasingly agitated that he might betray her one day. Her disquiet over trusting him became greater on hearing out of the twisted mouth of the Prince's Chamberlain that the clerk's name was associated in the Kaiserburg with talking ill of the royal family.

Chapter 24

Albrecht Durer's patience held till dawn broke; taciturn and pearl-grey, reluctant to give up the night. He, Pirkheimer and Beck met at Wolgemut's cottage. Durer's loud knock was answered by a dishevelled looking Schmeichler shivering in a long unbleached linen shirt and a coarse claret woollen blanket across his shoulders. He held a poultice cloth to his ear.

"Herr Wolgemut is unwell and taken to his bed. I will not disturb him," he snarled and no amount of pleading could persuade the servant to inform his master of their presence. When Pirkheimer suggested they have a word with the good lady Gudrun instead they were informed she had gone away, suddenly, in the company of two Italian gentlemen.

"Gudrun has gone?" Durer asked, astonished.

Schmeichler's fat lips moistened by saliva quivered and his eyes settled coldly on Albrecht Durer. "Frau Wolgemut has abandoned the marital home and will not be returning."

Durer, Pirkheimer and Beck looked at one another scarcely able to believe what they were hearing.

"My Maria, where is she?" Beck demanded.

"She was engaged by Frau Wolgemut. Since the one has gone so, too, has the other. I know nothing of her whereabouts." Schmeichler threw the poultice onto the grass.

"My picture ... the *Hare* ... I believe it is here." Durer's claim lacked conviction.

Schmeichler arched an eyebrow which Durer interpreted as meaning this was news to him. "You have put Herr Wolgemut through enough emotional turmoil. I suggest you leave and return, if you must, another time when he is well." As he spoke his eyes were trained on Beck's swollen, squint nose and bruised face.

The statuesque figure of Willy Pirkheimer stepped closer to Schmeichler. "We believe Herr Durer's missing picture to be in Herr Wolgemut's print-shop," Pirkheimer insisted.

Schmeichler looked from Beck to Pirkheimer. A thin sceptical smile hovered about his thick mouth, as if gauging the Burgher's meaning. "Wait here," he growled and shut the door against them.

The sound of his heavy gait along the flagstone passage was audible to the three outside. They waited and shortly the same footfall was heard returning.

"Take yourselves around to the workshop," Schmeichler ordered curtly.

Outside the printshop, leaning against the wall, was Beck's walking-stick. A rattle of a key turning in the lock was followed by the appearance of Schmeichler.

"There is no need to disturb Herr Wolgemut. Come this way," he said.

The three followed him in with Beck taking up the rear, nervous of encountering the two printmen from the previous evening. The room was still dark for its windows were small so Schmeichler proceeded to light a lamp. Not seeing the picture on the floor, Otto Beck looked straightway behind the tapestry, stepping on several loose volumes of prints in his haste. The picture was not there. "Someone has moved everything," he insisted.

Durer caught Pirkheimer's eye. Schmeichler smirked. Albrecht Durer picked up a sheaf of prints and thumbing through them quickly calculated the value of the loose pages at one florin each - twelve stivers the half-sheet and six each quarter - affirmation that print production was a quick way to make a decent living and, despite the matter in question, he could not help but contemplate the future of his *Adam and Eve* engraving.

Willy Pirkheimer cleared his throat. He was uncomfortable at his involvement in the affair which called Herr Wolgemut character into question. He looked at his feet and then at Schmeichler who was hanging the lamp from one of the heavy beams that crossed the ceiling. The lamp swung on its nail sending rays of light in every direction.

"Is there anything else I can help you with, gentlemen?" Schmeichler asked.

Pirkheimer signalled to Durer and Beck that it was time to go but at that very moment a large grey mouse scurried across the floor and slipped behind the dark press with its carvings of ivy and cavorting bears. That was the moment Herr Wolgemut chose to walk in.

"Is that another mouse, Schmeichler?" Wolgemut demanded.

Schmeichler replied it was. Ignoring Durer, Beck and Pirkheimer, Herr Wolgemut complained to Schmeichler that he was sick of mice forever eating his papers and so his manservant got down on all fours, reaching behind the dresser to try to capture the animal which unseen by the company had scampered out the other side and scuttled from the room. Meanwhile Schmeichler dragged a small oil painting on boards out from behind the dresser, holding it up to look at.

"Not another hare?" Beck asked stepping up behind Schmeichler.

Pirkheimer screwed up his eyes to view it better, for it was dirty and its colours dull. "Isn't it a rabbit?"

Albrecht Durer went close up to the picture. After examining it for a moment he looked up, his face beaming. Crossing the floor he showed the little picture to Wolgemut, "Look, it's a rabbit," he said. "Do you remember, Herr Wolgemut I painted this when apprenticed here? You had been teaching me to paint fur. I thought it good then but less so now - though it shows promise, I'd say." He laughed. "Look," he pointed to his initials in the bottom right corner, "I signed it because your other apprentice tried to claim it as his and you punished him for doing so. And you kept it," he added proudly.

Herr Wolgemut stared intently at the picture as if trying to recall a time long ago when he taught the man who stood before him; now master painter in his own right. He shifted his old eyes to meet Durer's then lowered them back to the picture. It was too long ago and he closed his eyelids for that way it was easier to imagine the world as it might have been.

"There's something else in here," Schmeichler said, forcing his arm farther along the back of the dresser and pulling out another picture, not much larger than the first.

Albrecht Durer went over and took the picture from Schmeichler's hands. "My *Field Hare*"! he announced.

Herr Wolgemut released a noise not unlike a child's cry.

Schmeichler looked embarrassed and hurried to his master's side, supporting the old man who had fallen against the cupboard. He explained to him that Herr Durer had got his lost picture back.

Eyes doleful as a frightened dog's gazed up at him, hardly understanding, "I can see from here that it's a fine painting, is it not mine, Schmeichler?" Wolgemut asked in a small voice.

"No, it is Herr Durer's, master."

Old Herr Wolgemut nodded. "It is such a pretty likeness, is it not? I am certain I did it." His observations might have been meant for no-one but himself.

"All your pictures are safe, Herr Wolgemut, but it's likely you have been the victim of mischief. This painting is by Herr Durer's hand, surely you know it well, and he has come to take it back." Schmeichler spoke softly and kindly.

"I have not lost any of my fine pictures?" Herr Wolgemut asked.

Schmeichler spoke again to reassure him but when Wolgemut asked why Albrecht Durer's picture came to be in his workshop Schmeichler could offer no explanation beyond laying blame on some wretch for hiding it in there.

***

The Italian merchants were so eager to return to their homeland they became impatient with Frau Wolgemut for she habitually tripped over tree roots and stepped ankle deep into water-filled swards in her thin-soled town shoes. The leather purse containing her uncle's gold they took from a guileless

Albrecht Durer in the labyrinth was considerably lighter in weight since it had been shared out between the three of them.

A little late, too late to matter, Gudrun Wolgemut regretted paying so little heed to Herr Wolf's warning about her becoming enmeshed with the cloth merchants. The lady's shoulders shook as she shed a tear for Wolf but no sooner had it rolled off her cheek than she sighed for she had more pressing concerns - Nuremberg's militia would undoubtedly be hunting her down, or so she believed, to drag her back to the city and to the Löch to be broken on the wheel for her deceptions.

The party of three plus one hound that had stolen away from Nuremberg while honest folk were going about their lawful business covered a good number of meadows and forests by the time night fell and at last they found themselves in a town called Oberstaufen where they ate a well-seasoned fat cock served up with plenty of mushrooms. There they planned the next stage of their journey which would take them towards the mountain village of Oberstdorf.

***

The bath house favoured by Albrecht Durer was Nuremberg's tenth and located along one of the less fetid areas of the Pegnitz riverbank; somewhat distant from where dyers and fleshers dumped their foul-smelling waste and thankfully away from the constant pounding of the river's water-powered hammer forges. That first Sunday after Michaelmas so many men flocked to use the bath house Willy Pirkheimer pledged to raise the necessity of providing another to cope with demand with the city Council

Durer and Pirkheimer were straightway admitted into the bathhouse but the supervisor took Otto Beck aside to remind him he was in arrears from the last session. Beck was defiant that he was not, despite possessing a duplicate of the tally stick at home that proved the superintendent to be correct. Pirkheimer persuaded the supervisor to issue Beck with a second tally stick which he promised to pay off in full when he next attended.

In the undressing area Durer, Pirkheimer and Beck handed their folded clothes to the wardrobe attendant.

"You look thoughtful, Willy," Beck commented.

The big man grunted by way of reply.

"Something wrong, Willy?" Durer asked.

"What could possibly be wrong? People, including two children have disappeared. Herr Wolgemut has lost his senses. There is an art thief here in Nuremburg. The town's been infested by a blight of mystics and we're so late in getting here all the attendants are occupied. What is there to complain about?"

"I have my picture back at least. Two pictures returned; my childish daub of a rabbit and my fine *Field Hare* - which now proudly boasts my monogram, so it is even more recognisable as mine. The rabbit I don't care to be associated with but my mother wants to hold onto it." Durer chuckled.

"So, will you be looking to the palace as a home for the nomadic hare?" Pirkheimer asked.

"Neither I nor the hare has contemplated that situation at present; we are just content to be reunited. " Durer's eyes twinkled. "But look, Willy, the barber's finished that other fellow, why don't you go and get that stubble scraped from your face. See if that improves your temper," he teased.

Willy Pirkheimer grunted. "At least I don't defile my good looks by letting my chin grow like a billy goat's."

"Would only be an improvement, dear Willy. Hair around the face is manly or so I'm reliably informed by half of Nuremberg's women." Durer grinned.

Pirkheimer shuffled off in the direction of the barber leaving Beck and Durer stretched out on benches next to the bathing pool.

"What's biting him?" Beck asked.

Durer shook his head. "Townsfolk are afraid and asking our Councillors awkward questions. They're being criticised for being too lenient in handling those mystics who they think should have been locked up in the Löch."

As they waited for the party in front of them to finish having their feet washed before being scourged and thrashed in preparation for the steam room Beck picked at his toe nails and Durer tugged thoughtfully on his beard. They were beckoned forward as Pirkheimer returned and a bugle sounded for additional hot water for the foot bath.

"Make some room for a small one," Pirkheimer said as he squeezed in between Beck and Durer.

"That's what the other half of the women are saying," Durer muttered.

"Envy is a sin unworthy of you, Albi." Pirkheimer slapped Durer hard on his naked thigh.

Albrecht Durer unwound a red and white striped turban protecting his hair from being snagged on the attendant's twig switch as he prepared to be thrashed until his skin flushed bright red and stung like the blazes.

"Your hair is particularly lovely, Herr Durer," the assistant purred.

Durer took the compliment with a wide smile. He enjoyed his weekly session at the bathhouse under the washer's gentle hands, kneading and squeezing.

"Finer altogether than those rat-tails Müller keeps under his skullcap," the washer continued, "he rarely washes his head. But you, Herr Durer, it is a joy to assist you. And talking of the Devil, where is he? Normally we see him here for Sunday bathing. I'm not complaining that he hasn't appeared yet, he's so demanding and likes me to help him, just to annoy me, I'm certain. So, he can keep away as long as he likes. Close your eyes Herr Durer while I apply a warm rinse then we'll soon have you all clean and smelling sweet."

The washer tipped a jug filled with soapy suds over Durer's head - plying his fingers about the artist's skull till he produced a rich lather. He rinsed the soap out with copious amounts of lavender-scented water before dragging a horn comb through Durer's long hair and trimmed the ends with scissors he kept

236

tucked into his waist band. Durer made no reference to Müller having likely perished in the granary.

Beck and Pirkheimer were already in the steam room having their fat naked bodies briskly smacked with wet strips of cloth, and were glowing bright pink.

"More at ease now, Willy?" Durer asked.

Willy Pirkheimer ran his great paws up and down his upper arms. "Moderately contented, my young companion - my preference would be to have access to the women's bath house but, alas, I must put up with the pair of you while undergoing my ablutions. You would think one of our bath houses might be mixed."

Beck used a finger to slick sweat away from his eyes as Durer settled himself on a bench alongside Pirkheimer.

"Here suits me well, dutiful master."

"Each to his own, Albi, but you must admit it would be far more civilised in here if we didn't have every common craftsman squeezing in amongst us," Pirkheimer winked, making room for Beck.

"Why don't you use your influence at the Rathaus to have the regulations altered," Durer joined in the play.

"Unfortunately, not all of my fellow Councillors share my delicate nature. I can only ensure these places are regularly inspected," then seeing Otto Beck was at last taking notice, Pirkheimer added, "present company excluded, Otto. Don't take offence."

Otto Beck lay on his back and whistled away Willy Pirkheimer's jocular slight until someone shouted on the whistler to shut up or take his bad-luck outside.

Their joviality was shattered by the sudden appearance of Herman, a leatherman, proclaiming the discovery of a child's body. Pressed for details, he could only say that a party of hunters stumbled on a corpse partly hidden in a thicket near the palace; bloodied, naked and cut open with the lights and vitals missing in what was assumed was an act of witchcraft. The fellow confirmed he knew nothing of the identity of the body for its condition was most horrible; cut about and gnawed by animals. The man ran off to spread his news to other parts of the town.

Beck's stomach heaved. He drew up his knees and rocked himself into near-frenzy for his mind was on the warm heart he had accepted from Widukind and later boiled with a good dash of allspice before eating it with two fat gherkins. He squeezed his eyes tight shut.

***

Durer, Pirkheimer and Beck left the bathhouse soon after learning of the child's murder for it affected them greatly. As they neared the Rathaus they were approached by two members of the town's militia.

"You are Otto Beck, aren't you?" the first demanded of the locksmith.

Otto Beck bridled. "What if I am?"

The officer moved in close up to Beck breathing hard; his breath, warm and sour. Towering over the shorter man the officer fixed a brutal eye on him and would not unlock it.

"They tell me this child's heart was ripped from its body and you were seen carrying a bloody piece of meat last evening," he growled. "You are being arrested for the murder of a child."

Ashen-faced Beck babbled incoherently to the amusement of the soldiers. Willy Pirkheimer tried to intervene on his friend's behalf but his pleas fell on deaf ears for the officer would listen only to what was said out of Beck's own mouth. Beck insisted he was given the heart of a deer by the shepherd Widukind and knew nothing of a lost and murdered child. The officer eyed him coldly, squeezing his hand into a tight fist he pressed it to the locksmith's own racing heart. Turning to his fellow militiaman he ordered that Beck be taken off to the gaol. Albrecht Durer and Willy Pirkheimer vigorously protested but their pleas were ignored and they were left to follow on behind the arresting party in the hope of being more successful with the prison Hausemeister. Their concern for Beck was great since few of those who entered the Green Frog, as the Löch was known, made it out again, alive.

The Frog's Hausemeister held open the heavy door to admit Beck. They all squeezed into the guard room where the atmosphere was thick with smoke from a charcoal brazier. Beck's eyes began to water and his chest grew tight, making him cough. Immediately he was relieved of a small sum of money he had on him along with keys to his house and workshop. As he laid his belongings down on the Hausemeister's table a black fly settled on the back of his hand. He shook it off. Beck's dagger was confiscated lest he used it to kill himself before justice could take its course and as Beck was being confined in shackles, Pirkheimer and Durer were ordered to leave without the Councillor's plea for his friend being heard. Glancing nervously towards the prison door as it shut out his companions, Beck was led away in his heavy chains down a murky corridor with doors to the left and right, their spy hatches pulled shut. Some of the doors were marked with symbols, designating the nature of the prisoner's crime. One of these was in the form of a cat, scratched and flaking, and here the gaoler stopped. Beck's heart sank. The cat cell, he knew, was reserved for sorcerers and Beck realised he must add sorcery to the murder charge against him.

The cell door slammed shut, completing Beck's feeling of isolation and lost hope. He was alone as far as he could make out for no-one spoke to him and as there was neither window nor lamp the blackness around him was entire. While both his hands and feet were chained he was not shackled to a wall. Warily, he explored his cage with arms outstretched, like a child playing *blindekuh*, though he made no mooing noises. And no-one mooed back at him in the Löch.

The dungeon, he estimated, was square - not much beyond his own body span both in width and length. Once his eyes grew more accustomed to the darkness Beck could discern the ceiling stretched high above which meant the air was less fetid than it would have been in a more confined space, though far from sweet. He looked for somewhere to rest for he had no desire to sit on the foul-smelling earthen floor, thick coated with the accumulated waste of previously incarcerated souls. By touch he identified the cell's timber door, two smaller iron doors and a narrow ledge in the wall. The iron doors hung open with a space in behind. Cautiously he ventured in and discovered a slab long enough for him to stretch out, though not capable of holding a man larger than himself, and for a few moments he dared lie down and close his eyes. This relief did not last long for he was afraid that if he slept he would awake to discover the doors shut against him and him a double prisoner. His stomach was all churned up and loud rushing noises inside his head played into his overwhelming sense of dread.

Beck gave a start on seeing the gaoler silhouetted before him. He must have fallen asleep after all and not heard the man enter the cell, but there he was holding a bulky iron-spiked collar. Beck crawled out of the recess and stood obediently while the collar was locked in place around his neck. He knew now there would be no more sleep for the spikes were designed to prevent him from lying down, if ever he dared creep back inside that dreadful hole and that was the point of the instrument, for it was acknowledged that a man deprived of sleep was quick to admit his guilt. Shivering with the cold he increasingly felt damp seep in through his clothing and for all he knew his very skin and he could only assume he still possessed feet for he could feel none. A second gaoler entered and handed Beck a bowl containing victuals of some description though Beck could not say what they were for they tasted of nothing but salt. He picked up a crock left for him on the floor and lifted it to his lips. It was chipped around its rim and instead of the water he expected it contained a liquid that might have been vinegar or herring pickle that further increased his thirst.

A shudder ran down Beck's spine at each groan and shout he heard echo through the Löch. He was terrified in his seclusion beneath the Rathaus while knowing just above him polite and wise government was being carried out by men of learning and breeding. Beck felt a tickle on his face; the fly had entered the cell with him. When next the gaoler appeared, it was to usher Beck out. Wordlessly and with pitiless indifference the little locksmith was led deeper into the Löch through its warren of passages to a chamber considerably larger than his cell. There two Löchschöffen, prison officials, and a clerk sat behind a long oak table chatting to one another. At Beck's appearance they fell silent.

Beck's eyes stared wide with terror which was a normal reaction for those who got as far as this chamber in the Löch's inner sanctum, for here were machines designed for torture. Beck stood stupefied at what he imagined were thumbscrews but which on closer inspection he realised were ink pots.

The spiked collar around his neck was removed before Beck's interrogation. He was asked to explain how it was he was seen in Nuremberg brandishing a bloody piece of meat suspected to have come from a murdered child. Beck re-iterated his innocence; blaming Widukind the shepherd for any wicked act perpetrated against a child. Every word spoken was meticulously recorded by the clerk and the whole account, Beck was informed, would be passed to a civic committee for scrutiny. Beck's examiners were rigorous but civil and they advised him that there were several witnesses to his strange and frightening behaviour and cautioned him his situation was grave for, by his own admission, he displayed the heart and then ate it.

At this point in the proceedings Beck vomited liberally to the disgust of the three men behind the table and the gaoler was ordered to return him to his cell until such time he had recovered his manners.

***

Willibald Pirkheimer vigorously defended his friend, Otto Beck, to a fellow magistrate but was told Beck had failed to convince his inquisitors of his innocence and that his actions were in keeping with witchcraft which it was suspected was behind the child's death and mutilation. Pirkheimer was informed that Beck's attempts to shift blame to Widukind the shepherd strengthened their suspicions that Otto Beck was a mischievous and duplicitous wretch.

Willy Pirkheimer listened politely to the magistrate but his dogged character would not allow him to abandon Otto Beck for he was certain of his innocence. Pirkheimer's entreaties must have impressed the Löchhüter for eventually he agreed to look more closely at the charge against the shepherd.

Chapter 25

The route grew steep and more arduous underfoot with hazardous rocky ascents and near vertical drops at every turn. Frau Wolgemut welcomed the beanpole's offer to carry her bag, for out of the three of them she struggled greatest with the wild landscape. On and on they travelled, through that day and even part of the night in torrential rain that turned the terrain muddy and slippery.

Gudrun implored her companions to tarry awhile for her breath came quick and her feet were painful and bleeding. The Italians did wait but with growing impatience; their eyes forever searching the skies for ill-omens and the land for Nuremberg's militia. They were keen to be home and cajoled the young woman to get back up onto her feet - urging her onwards in their strange foreign lilt.

***

Nuremberg's Council was eager to see peace restored to the city and under their captain, Herman Kalb, a company of militia was prepared to apprehend the shepherd, Widukind.

Herman Kalb enthusiastically took up his role. "The shepherd, Widukind, you say? His own brother, the swineherd Wedigo, already accuses him of stealing his best boar and now he is suspected of murder - of ripping the heart out of an innocent child! Widukind that lives among us is a thief and a murderer!"

Not everyone in Nuremberg was quick to condemn a man without a hearing among them Willy Pirkheimer who despite his insistence Widukind should be questioned about the heart he gave to Otto Beck did not immediately conclude the shepherd guilty of slaying a child.

"Violence is not in Widukind's character. I'm certain he would never harm a living soul and I refuse to believe he had anything to do with stealing Wedigo's old boar, either. I fear, however, he is in grave jeopardy," Pirkheimer insisted to all who would listen.

***

The shepherd was not where Beck had last seen him but traces of a fire were discovered and nearby snagged on a willow branch hung a strip of pale blue ribbon. The search party split up to cover the ground more quickly for it was feared the shepherd would claim a new victim before being apprehended.

The clanging of his flock's bells exposed the shepherd's whereabouts and he was apprehended close to the very place the child's mutilated corpse was discovered. No remains of a slaughtered hart were found.

As the seized Widukind had his wrists secured with cord his black and white hound barked excitedly until subdued by a kick from a boot. The shepherd spoke to the animal and it slunk away.

The strapping around Widukind's hands was attached to Kalb's saddle and so they set off with the shepherd half-dragged and half-running down into the city at a pace set by the horse and rider. The hound obeyed its master and stayed to guard the flock.

Widukind was taken along the same dreaded corridors of the Löch as Otto Beck. It took Widukind's old eyes longer to grow accustomed to the gloom, so used to daylight were they, which was a scarce commodity in a dungeon with only a few oil lamps set into wall niches and wax tapers to produce scant illumination.

The Löchwirt who received Widukind's purse told him he would deduct what was due for his keep and confiscated his dagger and spoon for he said the latter was of such thin metal it might be employed to inflict injury on himself or another. Other possessions Widukind kept in a bag such as a pair of sheep bells, a wooden comb with many of its teeth missing, and a small crucifix were likewise impounded.

244

Little was explained to the shepherd about his situation and neither was he informed it was on the word of Otto Beck, the locksmith, that he found himself in goal and that he would take Beck's place in the cat cell. Widukind shuffled along the gaol's musty, cold corridors - shackled waist and foot with a spiked collar around his neck and then pushed into the cold comfort of the cat cell.

A man's good reputation and his many kindnesses could quickly evaporate once rumours of his supposed wickedness spread. Every doubt anyone ever had about Widukind was exposed to scrutiny and imaginations were fed with wild speculation over his solitary habits removed from civilised folk. Within a short time Widukind was being cursed not only for putting a child to death but horribly mutilating the child's body and in support of his presumed guilt he became the main suspect for many other unexplained atrocities committed in the city of Nuremberg over a long span of years.

Aside from Pirkheimer, and Albrecht Durer who carried no influence at the Rathaus, few were willing to speak out in Widukind's defence although some folk still held to the belief that the visiting mystics had a hand in one or all of recent mysterious deaths in the city *for wasn't it they who accused the folk of Nuremberg of all kinds of evil?* However, only one man faced the sword and scales of justice in Nuremberg that Saturday in October 1504 and that man was Widukind the shepherd.

Widukind, longer in leg and body than Beck, was ordered into the cramped wall recess and the iron gates locked. The short space but most of all the spike neck ring prevented him from lying out flat and he was forced to lean on an elbow while staring out into the darkness. And in this manner, covered by a piece of stinking matted pelt he found in there to stave off the freezing damp cold, he thought about his flock and his hound. Despite his discomfort Widukind drifted into semi-slumber till wakened by a tickle on his foot for he shared his confined space with a small brown rat that scuttled along his leg and out through a metal grating where it found a second rat that it chased, biting on its tail and ears, both of them squealing - from delight or injury Widukind could not tell. Widukind's consolation was there was no eating in him, yet, and the rats would find their own escape routes out of the miserable Frog to find better pickings.

***

Gudrun Wolgemut's departure from her home and from Nuremberg meant Maria Kohl was now homeless. In a strange way, having to rely on herself after being released from Gudrun Wolgemut's employment Maria Kohl re-discovered the confidence she had as a very young woman. She did not find Otto Beck at home and so tried his workshop at the Rathaus. She rapped on the door several times and loudly on the window before Otto Beck's button-like face appeared.

If Otto Beck expected the urgency of her coming was to comfort or show him pity, he was mistaken. Maria made no reference to his confinement in gaol and appeared to be unaware of it. There was something in Maria Kohl's demeanour that had him hold his tongue.

Once admitted Maria took time to cast her eye around the familiar workshop with its callipers, tiny hammers, die plates, files, pincers and awls till at last she found courage to say what she came to say. When she began Maria scarcely stopped to the astonishment of Otto Beck whom she accused of stealing her ideas for his inventions. Beck denied Maria's charge. It was absurd for her to claim, he insisted, that she a mere woman understood the complexities involved in the manufacture of mechanisms whether they be locks, hand guns or timepieces. Further, he protested, her constant prattling was more of a burden to him than any enlightenment she proffered. He laughed away her pretension that she was in any way an inventor insisting it was he, Otto Beck, who was open to experimenting to make him a better smith. As if to underline his position Beck pulled open a drawer and taking out a wheel mechanism brandished it before Maria, insisting that what she laid claim to was no more than a modified version of timepiece escapements he had been working on for years. Growing more angry Beck indignantly informed Maria he worked hard six days a week, and on occasions seven, while she by virtue of her womanly labour enjoyed the luxury of excessive free time and he would no longer listen to her wounding words and lies.

Maria, laughing off his attack looked deep into his eyes then landed a mighty kick on his knee which caused the locksmith's leg to buckle. Looking up from his humiliating position on the floor Otto Beck watched Maria sweep out of his workshop and his life.

Chapter 26

Exhausted and frantic with worry Widukind released from his cage in the wall was pushed and prodded along the prison corridor still clutching the fetid pelt covering. Descending a short flight of steps he found himself in a lofty room and there his fear was total for before him was an Aufziehen set into a beam in the barrel roof.

The prisoner was released from his shackles then stripped of shoes, hooded cloak, shirt and leggings before his hands were secured by a rope that was passed over a pulley. Widukind was hoist aloft and dangled with his arms pulled high and awkwardly behind him. He was left like this to consider his plea and suffer pain he never thought possible. Distressed and humiliated and in total dread he looked down at three men conversing convivially. From time to time a question was barked up at him relating to the death of an unnamed child.

When the torture failed to elicit any admission of guilt Widukind was lowered just short of the floor only to be immediately hoisted up again, making his stomach dance and somersault. Several times Widukind's torturers repeated this procedure without getting him to admit guilt. A stout basket filled with heavy stones was brought in and tied with ropes to the shepherd's ankles and again he was lifted up, the weight dragging on his limbs causing him to gag and cry out for the pain in his ankles, knees and the tops of his legs was excruciating and the area around his girdle felt under terrific strain. Widukind believed he would be split asunder. And yet he would admit to no crime and so he was lowered to regain some strength, for they were not of a mind to execute him but to hear his admission of guilt, for none at the Löch would take justice into their own hands for fear of being themselves condemned by man and God.

Of course, it occurred to Widukind that confession would end his torture followed by the blessed relief of death. But for all that he would not give them the verdict they demanded.

There was nothing for Widukind to eat when he was returned to his cell but he drank every drop of the sour water though it took all his strength to lift the filthy vessel to his lips for his arms did not feel as though they belonged to his body. The gaoler waited until Widukind finished his draught before re-shackling him in irons so heavy they more or less pinned him down.

Cocooned in his rat-infested dungeon Widukind was cut-off from the outcry in the streets of Nuremberg that its city Burghers were failing to protect them from the horrors inflicted upon them. The uplifting kinship that marked Michaelmas had all but crumbled. In a remarkable manoeuvre, Nuremberg's magistrates decided to share responsibility for the city's predicament with the Imperial family, for none of the Burghers could forget their authority rested with the people and there was no appetite for shouldering the entire blame for the current state of fear. In consultation with the Kaiserburg, it was agreed that Widukind's trial should be conducted in public with Prince Ernest in attendance to witness what was expected would be Widukind's confession and subsequent execution, so ending the panic afflicting all of their lives.

Chapter 27

The good people of Nuremberg opened their heavy sleepless eyes somewhat warily that Tuesday in October. Not since the black pestilence ravaged families and threatened trade had the town felt itself so hostage to the Devil.

News of Widukind's trial spread like wildfire and the curious and the wrathful made their way to the Hauptmarkt to witness the application of justice. Prince Ernest arrived along with his slit-eyed Chamberlain and his Steward; each man splendidly attired for the occasion in Turkish blood red and fiery gold. Beneath a magnificent red velvet canopy the royal party took their places alongside city luminaries. Prince Ernest's herald fussed over the proximity of the Prince to the place where the accused would stand but in the end nothing was altered.

Adelina and Alba Denck, the diminutive parents of the Schutzen Princess, clung to one another in dignified silence at the edge of the crowd. Adelina recalled only days since, near that very spot, she bought a short length of silk ribbon to dress Hanna's hair - the same blue ribbon found hanging from a willow branch close to Widukind's camp.

Ana Brauer stood in the thick of the crowd, nervously plucking at her apron and the blue woollen shawl she pulled around her shoulders as the man accused of murdering an unidentified child from the city was brought unsteadily and blinking into the daylight all bound about with heavy chains.

The shepherd was given no right to defend himself except through a lawyer appointed that morning by the chairman of the court and without Widukind having spoken with him. Widukind's name was written into Nuremberg's legal ledger and the charge of murdering a child and practising witchcraft, against God's law, was entered. No mention was made of the theft of Wedigo's best boar. A summary of the answers Widukind gave under interrogation in the prison were read out and he was asked how he pleaded. In a thin uncertain voice he denied both charges and his words were repeated to the dignitaries and crowd of commoners by his lawyer in a booming voice.

A fretful and pallid-faced Otto Beck when summoned to give evidence was listened to in silence and allowed to go largely unchallenged by Widukind's representative. Proceedings drew to a close without any summing up from the chairman of the court and only the briefest of consultations between him and the Prince. Then the verdict was announced.

***

Having rested overnight Gudrun Wolgemut and her companions continued their journey; the distance between her and the Italians increasing with every step, despite the Italians now carrying Gudrun's bag of money and her personal items so she might walk more unencumbered and soon they became quite separated from the lady.

Gudrun Wolgemut stuck to the arranged path - or what she believed to be the way. Exhausted and frequently overcome by dizziness Gudrun Wolgemut finally slumped down onto the cold turf thinking constantly of her husband, Nuremberg and implausibly, Albrecht Durer, whom she pictured as she first set eyes on him, resplendently dressed in his plush green earth and red velvet tunic over an ivory silk blouse. He appeared to her as if he stood before her; his intelligent almond eyes searching her out. That pleasant interlude lasted no more than a moment for Gudrun Wolgemut could not forget he was then in the company of his wife and later when they were introduced he showed no recollection of them having met previously. It was painful for Frau Wolgemut to grasp how little she meant to Durer and how he failed to look upon her as a potential rival to *his Agnes,* as he hurtfully and habitually referred to his wife. Gudrun Wolgemut's breath came slow and laboured as she pictured Agnes Durer attired from head to toe in the best finery that Venice could supply and tears trickled down her cheeks. And even though Gudrun Wolgemut had set out to trap Albrecht Durer and convince herself she was not attracted to him, she could not quite persuade herself this was true. She cried aloud remembering at the very instant the hare picture came into her hands, just like the rabbit one when her husband caught her in his workshop, it was cruelly snatched away by Schmeichler's approaching footsteps obliging her to hurriedly conceal it behind the oak cupboard. Her husband had confronted her, accusing her of such terrible things such as plotting to destroy him and his reputation and of consorting with men, to his enduring shame.

Gudrun Wolgemut looked at a scrap of greyish paper in her hand and uncurled it with her frozen fingers, tracing the outline of a baby pictured on it. Alone, forlorn and miserable her salty tears soaking through the paper blurring the sketch lines and washing away all trace of the child Gudrun Wolgemut sobbed loudly in a manner she had never permitted herself to do since the death of her infant daughter. Despite her exhaustion she dragged herself once more to her feet, hitched up her skirts and set off for Italy, her thin calfskin shoes squelching through the soft yielding turf. Never once did she apply her conscience to the poor dead soul of Adolf Wolf whose adoration of her led to her taking advantage of him to promote her husband to the Burghers of Nuremberg ahead of Albrecht Durer, and in consequence herself as well.

At long last Gudrun Wolgemut dragged herself to the highest point where she looked down over the descent that would take her onto more solid ground. Numbed with cold and soaked to the skin she clenched her raw hands into fists of sheer determination to survive. Her fatigue was nearly entire with her legs loathe to move and she sank to her knees, dejected. Scouring the mountain side for sight of her companions she called out, beseeching them to slow up and wait for her but no sound came back save for the whistle of the wind.

**

At the trial of the shepherd, Widukind, the evidence against him was found to be persuasive although there was disappointment that the accused refused to admit to his guilt. It was decided, therefore, in the tradition of dispassionate justice in the city of Nuremberg his execution would be carried out at dusk. It was customary in Nuremberg that punishments were administered swiftly, for it was desirable to have murderers and sorcerers removed from decent society without further ado.

With daylight fading Nuremberg's citizens gathered once more to witness the discharge of the court's ruling. The occasion lacked the usual excitement in anticipation of an execution because many of those gathered in the square were familiar with Widukind and although they had been initially certain of his guilt doubts were emerging and people had no wish to have him suffer without certainty he was a murderer. However, they also recognised that evil must be purged. Lit torches were strung from trees and posts and any unaware of what was happening might imagine themselves strayed into the jaws of Hell for the night was all aflame, choking smoke and fright.

The arrival of Josef and his bear attracted children, more impatient than their parents for the shepherd's execution. In the meantime they contented themselves by tormenting the old bear. Hans, the Abtrittanbieter, turned up, offering the services of his bucket and taking time to chatter with his many acquaintances. Ana Brauer looked on, her eyes filled with despair and sadness. On the other side of the square their arms so tightly wrapped around each other they might have been one person stood Alba and Adelina Denck, parents of the missing Schutzen princess. Durer and Beck were in the crowd. Beck had to be persuaded to attend because his own brush with death at the hands of Nuremberg justice left him troubled and fearful.

It was Beck who noticed that one of the children teasing Joseph's bear was riding a cockhorse made from a short stick jammed into a hart's head - one eye dull and lifeless the other pierced with the shaft of an arrow which the child used to steer the toy. Abandoning Durer he pressed through the crowd and went across to where the children were playing and tugging on the arrow he pulled it free of the head. There on its metal point was Prince Ernest's mark. The child told Beck that he and his friends found the remains of a deer in a meadow near the Imperial Palace and took home what they were able to carry; the head they used to make a cockhorse and each of them got the beast's four hooves to wear around their necks like necklaces, and Beck saw that they did.

A beating drum had the crowd surge forward like excited hens at the sight of corn. The execution of Widukind the shepherd for the murder of an unknown child and for practising witchcraft was about to get underway. Beck looked around for Durer. He wanted to tell him about the cockhorse. The crowd pressed forward, roaring like a wild beast. Beck could not see any sign of Durer so making his way through the throng he approached the chief magistrate, distinguished by the finery reserved for such solemn occasions but was prevented from speaking to him by a militia guard. Beck looked for Willy Pirkheimer and spotted him about to take his seat alongside his fellow Burghers. He shouted out to him but his voice was drowned out by a woman's screams. There was a flurry of excitement deeper into the crowd followed by more shouting then more screaming and laughter. The city guard was ordered to discover the cause of the outburst.

"The child is safe!"

"The woodchopper's widow has rescued the child!"

Everyone was talking at once, looking around and pointing - *The child was safe? But which child?*

Alba and Adelina Denck strained their necks to see and hear what others had seen and heard. Adelina Denck crossed herself and mouthed a silent prayer and let herself be led by her husband to the source of the excitement.

Ana Brauer, her mouth pinched as though she dare not breathe, was carried along by a sea of hands.

An officer of the guard yelled out an order for people to stop pushing but so great was the noise that few could hear him. And still the identity of the child remained a mystery and with so many crowded into the square and with all the pushing it was impossible to see any sign of a rescued child.

Another scream and a hollow cry of anguish brought silence to the hundreds assembled in the Hauptmarkt. Ana Brauer and the Dencks stood side-by-side as a channel opened up to admit the found child.

***

As if freeing herself from her past Gudrun Wolgemut dragged off the combs securing her long raven hair so that it tumbled down her back, as though she were a maiden not yet wed. From her eyrie high up on the mountain she looked down the hillside lit up by a huge moon and a counterpane of glittering stars. Narrowing her eyes to their limit Gudrun Wolgemut imagined she could make out footprints belonging to the Italians and their hound sunk into a patch of snow far below. They had safely navigated the perilous side of the mountain.

Exhausted, her eyes heavy-lidded, Gudrun committed to memory the route she should follow and despite the lateness of the hour began her descent towards the snow field, concentrating on each painful step, for the rocks were perilous and slippery. Step after step after step. The going was treacherous but with the ascent behind her Gudrun permitted herself a glimmer of optimism for the downhill leg of the journey. She was certain she heard the Italians not so far below and drew courage from the sound of their voices although she still had no sight of them.

Gudrun Wolgemut came at last to the field of powdery white snow which was larger than it looked from above. She made it there almost bare-foot for the stitching in her shoes was broken and the soles partly detached. Unable to cross the snow in them she worked her way around the edge. The route being tricky Gudrun Wolgemut took her time and when she arrived at a field of ice-covered boulders could only cross it crawling on her hands and knees. She succeeded, however, but at a cost of more damage to her shoes and feet and her fine elegant fingers were blooded and bruised, their fingernails entirely broken.

The perilous boulder field had sapped Gudrun's strength and her progress grew ever slower. The cold was such she dared not sit down to rest and shivering almost uncontrollably forced herself onward. The moon that lit her path then vanished plunging her into near total darkness. It came as a surprise, therefore, to Gudrun Wolgemut to find her way impeded by a broad waterfall that might have been a curtain of glass, for in the freezing temperatures most of the cascade was frozen leaving only a trickle of two hat-strings spilling over the craggy wall. Gingerly working her way across the cataract was like walking on slippery eels and she needed all the concentration she could muster. Gudrun Wolgemut willed her hands and feet to perform in unison but they became disobedient and in her frustration she tore at her hair and would have wept but for her resolve not to give up. The moon showed its face once more to the mountain and Frau Wolgemut gasped on seeing her reflection in a large shard of frozen water. Just as she reached out to touch her faintly illuminated face an angel spread its wings and Gudrun Wolgemut's ice-trapped eyes gazed into inky darkness.

She did not hear the crack, the cascade splinter. A monstrous blade sheared off and sliced through Gudrun Wolgemut's beautiful milky-white neck and she dropped like a bird struck by slingshot, down the long and staggering heights that finally delivered her into Italy.

The two Italian gentlemen were disturbed from their sleep by a sudden noise and looking up they saw what they assumed to be a large bird swooping down the mountainside but so drowsy were they neither paid it much heed and they settled back down to rest knowing the tricky mountainous crossing was behind them and they were almost home.

***

"The boy lives!"

Ana Brauer hugged and squeezed her grandson so tightly the boy complained he could not breathe. She shook her head and laughed as tears streamed down her old lined face and she caressed the boy's own poor face much scratched by thorns. Well-wishers besieged them, relieved and joyful that the child had come to no harm and then a dog wriggled its way in; barking and jumping up at Ana, as if to protect the child from her.

"Ulf is here," someone shouted.

The boy was speaking. His quiet voice difficult to hear except by those closest to him who spread his words to other ears and yet more ears - *the boy ran after Axel's terrified dog that was being harried by hunters and found he was lost deep within the forest. He crawled through thickets of thorny bushes tearing at his clothes, his face, his hands and bare legs. He found the dog asleep near the dead woodchopper's house. The cottage door opened and a bent-over old woman invited them inside. She washed his cuts and fed him on stewed leaves and roots that tasted both sweet and bitter and he fell asleep. Next day they all set off for Nuremberg but the woman being so old and cripple could only walk very slowly.*

"Where is the woodchopper's widow?" someone shouted - but she had been swallowed up by the heaving mass of well-wishers.

Axel Marx's hound, Ulf, Anna and Kläuschen set off in the direction of Am Ölberg, cheered by the joyful crowd.

People shrank away from Alba Denck as he picked up his sobbing wife Adelina who had collapsed on the ground, for now it was certain the child horribly murdered was their own sweet Hanna. Adelina gasped and clutched at her chest thinking of the torment her little daughter had suffered. Now that they knew for certain the victim was their child and not Kläuschen they could not bear to remain for the trial of the man who took her from them but longed only to be home with their memories of the girl as she lived. And those gathered there in the square were relieved by the Dencks' departure because they had no words to offer them and the couple's presence was painful for them to endure.

The relentless drum beat stopped and a trumpet blared. The execution was about to begin.

Widukind walked as upright and dignified as the iron fetters around his ankles and hands allowed. In place of his familiar long brown cloak he wore the white robe of felons about to be executed. The spike collar had been taken from his neck but the shepherd's shoulders sagged, his arms dangling idly, as if detached from those same shoulders, as they almost had been through his torture. Widukind would be spared the customary final torment; there would be no red-hot tongs pinching his flesh in one final humiliation. Whether or not Widukind was aware of this privilege was not obvious; his mud-brown eyes stared out vacantly, as was normal for those who consumed the Stärkenden Trunk - the strong draught given to men and women before being taken from the Löch to their final tribulation on God's earth.

The white mantle was dragged off Widukind's lean shoulders and he stood before his fellow-townsfolk in a threadbare blue woollen shift; a slight shiver running down his body, most visibly along his pale hairless arms. Widukind raised his head and looked across the huge crowd anticipating his death. He appeared to be searching out a familiar face and his eye settled upon Otto Beck whose mouth was open, as if shouting.

The Löchschöffen read out the charges against Widukind followed by the court's verdict to Nuremberg's forty-two Councillors and Prince Ernest. Some of them looked agitated. Unusually, muttering was heard from the ranks of the Burghers, God fearing men, expressing doubt over the judgement. A messenger was summoned and sent away.

Beck had found Durer and together they desperately tried to attract Willy Pirkheimer's attention but the militia barred their way. They shouted Pirkheimer's name but the noise of the crowd was too great for them to be heard. Then, Otto Beck let out a terrible guttural scream. The dignitaries in their cushioned chairs turned their heads. Willy Pirkheimer stood up. To his left and right his fellow-Burghers murmured and shook their heads. With his eyes fixed on Beck, Pirkheimer worked his way past the city's luminaries out into the assembled mass of townsfolk to where Beck and Durer were pushing against the city guard. He listened to them and turning around he went up to the chief magistrate who spoke to the next man and so it went on through the rows of dignitaries and heads came together.

The citizens of Nuremberg were growing impatient. The curfew bells would be ringing soon and still the guilty breathed God's pure air. They were hungry and tired and wanted to be home but they deserved to witness justice carried out in their name. What on earth could the city's chief magistrate have to talk about at this late hour? Had not the guilty verdict been proclaimed?

Eyes turned at the arrival of a city messenger and the solid line of guard opened up to permit him entry. In his hands where a scroll bearing some vital message might have been expected was a loaf of bread.

Durer and Beck exchanged looks, knowing what was coming.

"They've brought in stale bread because they don't want to appear weak but cannot prove he is the miscreant and are nervous of putting to death a man who has not admitted his crime," Durer whispered, playing anxiously with his carnelian beads.

Hundreds of pairs of eyes; large and small, dark and light, intelligent and stupid watched the chief magistrate tear the loaf apart. It was so dry it crumbled between his fingers. He approached the prisoner, Widukind, and crammed a large handful into the shepherd's mouth, parched from the dread of what awaited him. Widukind tried hard to chew - his face creased with the effort but his mouth was as dry as blown sand. Tears welled up in his weary dark eyes for his terror was great, and he prayed to God to let him eat. All was hopeless. The shepherd's remaining teeth would not grind down the bread.

Behind Widukind's closed eyes he pictured his faithful black and white dog protecting his flock of sheep.

The chief magistrate watched the prisoner's struggle with a sense of growing relief. Justice takes various forms, he knew, and he would not have to bear the guilt of putting to death an innocent man. The people had their verdict, finally.

Excitement rippled through a section of the crowd. Albrecht Durer was waving his arms and pointing at something. The chief magistrate followed the gesture, seeing what everyone else saw - Widukind's mouth gaped wide open. The bread was swallowed.

"By the grace of God an innocent and gentle man has been saved from a terrible wrong," whispered a relieved Albrecht Durer to Beck.

Nuremberg's dispassionate justice had delivered its verdict on an appeal against sentence by a person unnamed. Widukind the shepherd was proclaimed innocent of the charge of murder and mutilation of a child and on suspicion of witchcraft. The bread test proved that.

The royal party were quick off their seats, slinking away before even the chief magistrate ascended the execution platform to proclaim to the hushed gathering that a pardon had been granted to Widukind because of severe doubts surrounding his guilt. Then a cheer rang out and Widukind's name chanted again and again, dissipating the shame hitherto attached to him; for surely the hand that caused a child to die so horribly was none of their own but a foreigner's?

In exchange for his freedom Widukind was obliged to swear that he would seek no retribution from man or authority within that area governed by Nuremberg for his confinement or for injury he had suffered while held in the Löch. He was also obliged to agree to banishment for his natural life for it was deemed essential for the great city of Nuremberg and its citizens that it suffered no taint to its reputation.

***

Albrecht Durer arrived home in low spirits thinking how close it was Otto and Widukind were to execution and lashed out at the furniture with his foot.

In his attic chamber Günter listened to his master's outpouring of anguish with mounting unease, for he had no idea of its cause. He wondered how long it would take before suspicion fell on him for the picture theft since there had been no talk of Joachim being the thief, which had been his intention. Surely he thought he could no longer risk living at Herr Durer's home but he delayed his departure long enough to attempt to write a note to the master he had so ill-served and heavy of heart and brimmed-full of shame he blew his nose on his shirt, dressed quickly and frightened and embarrassed by his foolishness he slipped out of Herr Durer's house.

On a night colder than many of late with winter a step closer, a hunched-up figure stole through Nuremberg's streets absent of the noise and crowds of earlier. Günter knew one day his sins would catch up with him and he would have to face his demons but he was not ready for that. Instead, he cursed his misfortune at having run into Herr Beck or rather Herr Beck running into him near Wolgemut's cottage before he could retrieve Durer's *Field Hare* from where he had hidden it at Wolgemut's workshop in an effort to blame the theft on Joachim. The picture was not where he left it, behind a tapestry, and as he began to search the place he was discovered by a printer who chased him away. Günter cried out in his wretchedness - for he so wanted his master Durer to be indebted to him for recovering his *Field Hare* and so appreciate him in the same way he did Joachim.

In search of salvation Günter visited the mystic's camp on Thursday last, for he had been struck by Thomas Hut's words at the Hauptmarkt on Michaelmas about discovering God in himself. He was beguiled by the handsome preacher who spoke kindly to him and was intending going to him again but by the time he reached the Hay Bridge Günter changed his mind and turning around he hurried northwards, taking his leave of the city entirely on his own.

Chapter 28

"Albi! Open up!"

Albrecht Durer put down his paintbrush on hearing a familiar voice.

"Why are you locked in, Albi?" Willy Pirkheimer demanded.

Durer unlocked the door to his workshop. "My dear master Pirkheimer I have decided I will no more take chances with thieves and murderers abroad. You don't bring me more bad news I trust my most worthy companion? I don't think I can cope with any more misery and suspicion."

"A call has gone out for citizen volunteers to hunt down those mystics for the people are afraid, Albi. They're rising up against the Burghers."

"Then why are they chasing mystics? Shouldn't they be attacking the Rathaus? - and if you don't mind me saying so, dear Willy, that would mean you."

"Cut out the nonsense, Albi. None of this violence is anything to do with me, you know that. People are angry that those fanatics were let in here in the first place."

"My faithful friend as one of our principal magistrates you do have responsibility for what happens here in Nuremberg. I speak as the common man might, you understand, and not as your devoted admirer. It's surely not right that any mystic might have his or her head bashed in without good cause."

"Plenty believe there is good cause though I am not among them for I'm not unsympathetic to their teachings but suspicious of them, nonetheless. I fear more violence with them fomenting trouble in the district. We mean to do them no injury if they prove themselves innocent of charges laid against them. Will you join us?"

"With reluctance, Willy, for I suspect them blameless, though I didn't always believe so. If they are guilty then they deserve punishment but we've seen how close the city was to carrying out a great wrong against Otto and the shepherd. Let's not repeat that mistake."

"I'm of the same mind but I've a responsibility as a magistrate to be there and I'd like you by my side, Albi."

"Have you asked Otto?"

"Otto has refused. Not from any scruples only that he is too busy but I suspect the time he spent in the Löch has much to do with his reticence to become more involved."

Durer looked past Pirkheimer into the dark of the night. "Surely any search should wait till daybreak?"

"The mood is that what must be done should happen quickly. The guard is already raised. I thought you might wish to witness the pursuit not as a spectacle but as a moderating influence alongside me. If you're coming, you'll have to hurry for I want to see all is done fairly," Pirkheimer said.

"Heigho!" Durer called on Günter to fetch him his mantel but when the boy did not appear he went and found it himself.

Durer and Pirkheimer rode quickly through Nuremberg's dark deserted streets, mounted on a pair of the finest of the city's home-bred horses, from Willy Pirkheimer's own stable. They met up with around thirty men and hounds; all but Pirkheimer and Durer were armed - several carried halberds, one with a zweihander, others had long-barrelled arquebuses similar to those Otto Beck produced. Flaming torches were distributed among riders for while the sky was clear and the moon bright the forest would be dark and darker still for the day had been windless and smoke from smouldering charcoal domes would have settled at the Forst.

Across open country they rode - past smiths' braziers and fire pits, past gardens cultivated by farmers and farther on towards the Laurenzius Forst. Also riding in that direction was Collado and his men, swathed in thick furs, astride their magnificent white chargers. They had tracked the mystics from Augsburg, toyed with them and relished another opportunity for yet more sport with ones they condemned as false Christians - angels of the Devil - before turning their backs on the Bavarian winter and returning to Spain.

Archers and cross-bowmen were still some distance from the camp when a horn blast ripped through the comfortless blackness of night. Despite rumours of the mystics fleeing their camp most of them were waiting for daybreak before moving, including their leader and there was panic at the sight of approaching flaming torches. Skins and fleeces were stripped from branches and quickly rolled and bound with leather. Hut shouted to his followers to run for their lives, then waited alone to face Nuremberg's envoys.

***

"We are ordered to remove you and your followers from this place and confine you in prison until you can be tried for sorcery and acts of violence perpetrated against the citizens of this town," the chief prosecutor proclaimed from the saddle of his fine stallion.

"We have a right to be here," Hut replied, his voice calm. "We've hurt no-one only implored each one of you to obey God's teaching. Our family welcomes every man, woman and child seeking God."

Thomas Hut was happy to engage with the militia officer knowing each moment's delay assisted the escape of his family of followers - several barefoot and inadequately clad to spend a night outwith shelter.

"You do not belong here and, therefore, have no rights within the demesne of the City of Nuremberg," the commander began, "you and your fellow zealots are charged with spreading fear and alarm among our citizens and bringing cruelty and death. It is, therefore, the will of the people that you are held to answer these charges.

Herman Kalb jumped down from his horse and stamped out the campfire's glowing embers signalling a change in mood. Whatever scraps of Christian charity stayed the hands of the search party till now were dispelled. A rock was hurled at Thomas Hut then another. From bushes behind Hut a stone was returned, for it appeared not all his followers had obeyed his order to flee. A coppersmith called Georg running with the company of foot screamed and grabbed at his face before collapsing. Willy Pirkheimer and Albi Durer rushed to his aid amidst a great tumult of noisy shouts and threats against the mystics. Hut shouted towards the forest, urging his followers to stop throwing rocks and in the same instance the militia commander roared out, "Put down your weapons and come with us now."

Hut studied the faces of the angry men confronting him, their features contorted by the light of their burning torches. He looked at their dogs; alert and snarling – anticipating the chase and he turned and ran, grabbing a bow and quiver of arrows as he went and was quickly swallowed up by the thicket of trees and shrubs.

Herman Kalb was quickly back up on the back of his charger ready to run down Hut. As he raised his arm signalling to his men to follow an arrow plunged deep into his chest. Kalb fell from his horse and the animal took fright, bolting into the forest, reins hanging loose about its neck. They were grabbed by the fugitive Hut who tugged at them to slow the beast until he was able to spring up into the saddle before kicking its belly into a fast canter.

Leaving Durer tending to the coppersmith, Pirkheimer took control of Kalb's care, barking out an order for six men on foot to convey their leader back to the city. The coppersmith who was by now sitting up assured Durer his injuries were not serious so the artist followed the rest of the search party in pursuit of the mystics. But Kalb's injury meant no-one was in charge of the search and men scattered at will. Durer found himself alone, armed only with a smoking torch to illuminate his way through the forest. He had not gone far when a moving shadow caught his eye. On closer investigation he discovered a woman hiding under her shawl and struggling to free her skirt held fast on a thorn bush. Durer jumped down from his stallion to assist her.

Els stared back at Albrecht Durer; each dumbfounded at the sight of the other.

"What are you doing here," Durer shouted.

Els looked afraid, her eyes wide with terror. "After hearing Thomas Hut say all those things when I was at your house I was so frightened for my soul I had to speak with him, seeking salvation," she explained.

"But why are you running?"

"I decided to join them and then the men came from the city and I had no choice but to flee," she said. "But I should not have taken this." She took a book out from under her shawl. "I'm sorry, Herr Durer, it was wrong of me to take it. Please have it back."

"The Nicholas de Cusa book – why do you want it?" Durer asked.

"Listening to you," she sighed, "you are so knowledgeable about the world … I want so much to learn …"

His Eva, Durer thought, and lowered his head so their foreheads touched.

"It doesn't belong to me, Els, but to Herr Pirkheimer. Still … his house in the Herrenmarkt is filled with books – it's his boast that he possesses every Greek book ever printed in Italy. When he isn't with me and Otto in Brauer's or running Nuremberg his nose will be this far from the pages of a book." He separated his thumb and forefinger a fraction to illustrate the distance. Just then several men and dogs rushed past, barely glancing at the two of them.

"Why don't you come back to Nuremberg with me and I'll get him to show you around his impressive library? He's a fine fellow and will allow you to borrow as many volumes as you wish, for he is kindness itself."

Els succeeded in untangling her skirt and separated herself from Durer.

"You are very kind Herr Durer but I long to explore places far away from here – as you have done. Those tales you told me when I was playing Eve - about Italy and other places you've seen … made me realise I could end up a seed and nut seller all my life until I grow into a wrinkled walnut like my grandmother. I want to improve myself and have heard great things of Heidelberg and so it's there I mean to go first, if I can."

"By stealing?" Durer asked unkindly.

Els lowered her eyes. "Herr Durer you have not paid me for being your Eva," she said defiantly, "so you might say I took this book as payment."

Durer smiled. He fished three pennies out of his purse and closed Els's fingers over the coins. "Your grandmother will miss you. We will all miss you, Els."

"Yes, she will for a start and I'll miss her for she's been very generous to me but I hope one day to return - perhaps with a trade behind me. Wouldn't that be worthwhile?" She gave a half-smile, loosened the cord on her velvet purse and dropped the pennies in one by one.

"If you are after a skill you might learn one here in Nuremberg. Whatever you want - I'm sure a master could be found ... "

Els's finger pressed his lips into silence.

"Hold onto the book, Els," Durer said. "One day when you're sufficiently proficient to be able to read and understand what it says come back here and we'll discuss it together. Then we can return it to Herr Pirkheimer." He gently tugged a lock of her flaxen hair and kissed her lightly on the cheek. "Don't be tempted to go through the forest, it's too dangerous. Take my mount and go back towards the town then out onto the main road."

With hardly a moment's delay Els covered her head with the shawl and tucking the book under the waistband of her skirt she let Durer help her up onto the tall animal. With his *farewell Eva* ringing in her ears she rode away in the direction he advised.

***

Four barrowmen were among the foot militia volunteering to defend the city from wickedness and heresy. Their enthusiasm for the cause was tempered by apprehension of parts of the

268

Knoblauchsland, for its reputation as a place frequented by coarse men seeking pleasure with children and so they slackened their pace to lessen the distance between them and the city. The reputation of the Knoblauchsland did not dent the courage of two crossbow-men but having come straight from an inn where they consumed much beer they were quite out of wind and their laggardly progress provided plenty opportunities to discuss other possible lurking dangers and agreeing they were ill-disposed to subject themselves to the perils of the forest in daytime it would be folly to risk its malevolent influences after dark. As they skulked back to town by a circuitous route, hoping to avoid awkward questions over their allegiance to the city they were distracted by an obnoxious odour.

"It doesn't have the usual charcoal smell," one remarked.

Guided by the reek they found themselves in a patch of open ground a good distance from the menace of trees and where they might have expected to see smouldering heaps of wood attended by a fire-watchman the area was deserted. With one torch between them the pair kept close as they followed their noses. It wasn't until one stepped into horse dung they held the torch lower. There was a lot of dung, as if several horses had spent time there. But dung was not the cause of the reek. The fellow with the torch swept it back and fore, illuminating the spot. That was when they saw it.

The stench was powerful, causing one of the men to spew up his beer. Silhouetted in the moonlight was a bull, its breath coiling out of its distended nostrils or so they later reported. Nearer they crept as one body for neither was brave enough to approach alone, reassuring each other with nervous glances. The beast never moved. They knew it then. They had clambered over it as children when it stood in the town. Huge, made of metal, this animal was all rivets, testifying it was neither flesh nor blood. Not a word was exchanged between them; they communicated with nods and grunts. One dragged a foot over fire-scorched turf under and around the monster.

His companion whose name was Griswald took hold of the torch and venturing closer to the creature he peered at it.

Griswald's eyes sprung open as if on springs and the guttural sound that leaked from his throat sent a ripple of terror along his companion's backbone. Their first instincts were to flee but curiosity got the better of them and they set about tugging at a hammered-in seal until a mess of bubbled fat and bone stuck with fragments of cloth was exposed. Then they turned and ran, fast, as though the Devil himself was on their tails and they did not stop until the city gates were slammed shut behind them.

***

Thomas Hut had a head start on his pursuers and being familiar with the layout of the wood, its corridors and impenetrable thickets, he was making reasonable progress. Those chasing him, especially the mounted militia, did not feel any great urgency in hunting down their main quarry knowing their horses were more than capable of overtaking a man on foot. What they did not realise was Hut was escaping on Herman Kalb's swift stallion.

The tangled thickets of the forest frustrated the man-hunters from the city, with no knowledge of the twists and turns of tracks through the wood their progress was often blocked by low branches and thorn bushes that snagged their clothing and tore at skin until both they and their animals bled. The deeper they advanced into Laurenzer Forst the slower was their progress. One group led by a single torchbearer halted at a riverbank to ascertain the water's depth and current before crossing in the pitch dark. The torchbearer dismounted and straightway tripped on a tree root. As he fell forward his torch was flung into the water where it extinguished. With just scant moonlight able to penetrate the tangle of trees and undergrowth the party were wholly reliant on their dogs to guide them through precarious undergrowth.

The search was noisy with horns constantly sounding but the only one they welcomed was three-blasts signalling another fleeing mystic had been captured.

Two brothers, beekeepers who were familiar with the forest, searched an area sparse of trees. One raised the alarm and they halted their ponies to listen for any movement of people. Stealthily they walked their ponies forward and found themselves surrounded by a herd of squealing, frightened pigs darting in every direction, their neck bells clanking urgently. A swineherd brandished his staff, making angry noises for having had his beasts disturbed and scattered. He hurried after them, holding up his mantel to prevent it from tripping him up. One of the brothers called out, "Hey, Wedigo – have you seen strangers go by?" From under the long cowl of his faded blue coat, the swineherd gave a slight nod and pointed in the direction the brothers were already heading, away from him.

The pair had gone but a short way when one brother pulled on his pony's rein to slow him then shouted to the other.

"That swineherd, he was holding up his coat, did you see?"

"What of it?" asked his brother, taking the lead.

"Why would a man whose life is spent walking over rough ground and in and out of woods not cut his coat to a practical length?"

"You think that wasn't Wedigo?"

"That's what I'm thinking. There's only one way to find out. Let's turn and take a closer look at him."

He called to their hounds but they failed to return so they set off, the one with the torch struggled to keep it aloft for he was not adept at riding and the going was very uneven and precarious with overhanging branches. His brother relied on his own and his pony's eyes to navigate and went on ahead. Having gone some distance without finding the herdsman he widened the search area until his beast threw back its head, halted and started pawing the ground. Jumping off the beast the rider disturbed a number of hogs jostling with each other next to a pool of dark liquid. They fled and he crouched down, sniffing the substance. Turning to address his brother at the approach of a rider he was dazzled by the fierceness of the flame in his hand.

"Looks to be blood," he shouted to him and receiving no response he repeated his observation but the rider rode away, abandoning him to the dark. Cursing his brother he investigated further and found himself looking down at the body of a man whose lifeless eyes stared back at him; the corpse's overshirt saturated with blood. Peering closely at a weather-beaten face, he reached out and closed the dead man's eyelids for the corpse's intense blue stare troubled him. A tug on his sleeve had him spin round ready to ward off an attack only to discover a ferocious thorn hooked onto his coat. Tearing himself free its barb ripped into the skin of his arm.

Meanwhile the second brother had become hopelessly lost and finding the going treacherous he was virtually bent over his saddle - a perfect position to spot the dog. His brother's large black hound lay dead on a tussock of grasses. It had been shot through by an arrow. Slipping down from his pony he stared at the beast's body. Then he noticed his own dog. Alive – fixed by arrows to the trunk of a stout tree, one that was familiar to him for it was used by bees and so a source of honey. The animal's foot was stuck fast in a trap that had all but severed the limb and it looked to him that the dog had been struggling to free itself using the tree trunk for leverage when it was shot. He knelt down and stroked his dog's head, speaking kindly to it but when he tried pulling out an arrow he found it was stuck fast causing the animal to howl with pain. He sat on beside his faithful hound for he had not the heart to slit its throat with his dagger.

It was while waiting for the dog to expire this brother saw what might have drawn his hound to this spot - tree branches above where he rested bore a crop of wretched fruit: corpses of cats, dogs and foxes in varying states of decay dangling at the end of short ropes. These sacrifices to heathen gods were left by men and women who lived and cropped the land around Nuremberg and whose ties to the past held fast. When from under his hand he felt life expire from his poor beast he got up mounted his pony and rode off to find his brother. Neither brother realised they were being watched, although one suspected it, for the forest was just the sort of place where dark forces dwelled.

When three Spanish men of war rode away on their fine chargers they did so from a conviction that the two men they observed in Laurenzer Forst were innocent townsmen hunting mystics and were not heretics, unlike the person they found surrounded by emblems of paganism in defiance of God and who they dispatched in his name.

When at last the brothers were reunited the accounts of their exploits in the wood were followed by as swift a retreat as they were capable of from the forest's dangers. The injured one held his torn arm across his chest from where a stain the colour of burgundy wine saturated his sleeve.

Elsewhere the parties and individuals who had gone into Laurenzer Forst on the trail of mystics headed homeward. None of them, including Albrecht Durer and Willy Pirkheimer, tracked down Hut although several of his followers were rounded up, secured with ropes and dragged back to Nuremberg.

Chapter 29

The strange tale of the town's discarded bull effigy made flesh and bone was dismissed as fanciful by those who heard it nevertheless a delegation from the Council was dispatched so that Burghers might reassert their authority for townsfolk were angry that Hut had evaded capture.

A new militia commander had been appointed for Kalb died of his wounds before arriving back in the city. This new man went with the delegation of officials to investigate the claim and put an end to the cock-and-bull story sweeping through Nuremberg. However, when they arrived at the place, they discovered the report had not in fact been far-fetched and did not express the true horror of the scene.

Stuck to and protruding from apertures on the beast were what appeared to be flesh and pieces of bone - whether they were human or animal was impossible for any in the delegation to say. One envoy picked up a stick from the ground using it to prod the melted mess but while pieces of congealed flesh and blood attached to it he was made none-the-wiser. Neither the militia commander nor any from the Council had ever heard of the bull previously coming to life and none was keen to remove more of the metal casing for fear the phenomenon was either the result of witchcraft or a divine message connected to the mystics which they were at a loss to decipher.

Careful scrutiny of the area found fire was responsible for causing flesh within the beast to melt but the significance of its meaning was too much for anyone there to explain. The militia commander picked up a shoe and showed it to the others. What a shoe had to do with a metal bull they could only wonder at. Another found a spoon, its handle bent out of shape. He held it up to his eyes and thought he detected something inscribed on it, initials of its owner perhaps but it was too dark to decipher them. The commander suggested the flesh that oozed from the monster belonged to a man pressed inside it. This proposition was met with nervous laughter from the rest of the official body who decided they would return to the city forthwith and so they did with the militia commander given charge of the abandoned shoe so it might be examined more carefully.

***

Willy Pirkheimer greeted Durer as the painter emerged from the kirk of St Sebaldus, his face tilted upwards towards the glimmering sun.

"Gratitude has enhanced your piety, Albrecht."

" Gratitude?"

"Aye, for disposing of one of my finest stallions."

"Ah, yes, Willy. I regret my rash action – in a way. I could only think that Els was in such danger she would fare better on four legs. I will endeavour to repay your philanthropy."

"I'm sure you will, my friend, and I wish Els only good fortune. I believe she is a young woman of character. Whether or not that is good or bad depends in the company I wager."

"You catch me not in the best of spirits my great and noble friend but in need of confirmation of my devotion to God. And what of you, Willy?"

Pirkheimer pulled a face. "I am more well than you my handsome rogue of a companion. You are too sensitive a soul to engage with this wicked world I fear."

"As ever I am your most willing servant and slave and my spirits are raised in your company." Durer smiled broadly, poking his elbow into Pirkheimer's considerable paunch. "But Günter has run away - has cleared his things and gone."

"Young Günter? When? Why?"

"It is entirely my fault. I fear he's been gone a full day and a night for I've been so caught up with my *Adam and Eve* picture I gave no consideration to the boy. If I thought of him at all it was that he was off visiting his parents but it appears not to be so for they have not seen him."

"A strange business for I understood he was making good progress under your instruction? He was so determined to make a success of becoming a painter," Pirkheimer mused.

Durer stroked his dead fox, again draped around his shoulders. "He was under my roof and I failed him. It would have been better if I'd kept him under lock and key as any careful master should but I allowed him his liberty.

The two companions stood and stared at St Sebaldus before heading for Brauer's inn.

"I was thinking, Willy, when I discovered my *Field Hare* missing Joachim was in my workshop. You know how thick he and Günter are - were - do you think he might have taken the picture to Herr Wolgemut's?"

Pirkheimer took Durer by the arm before replying to him. "I'd say that likely but he'll only deny it for he is brazen. I've lost count of the times that youth has appeared before the Council for fighting but I wouldn't like to think of him facing an interrogation for he's but a lad who will outgrow his foolishness. But have you stumbled on the reason for Günter's disappearance, I wonder?"

"You suspect Günter? Or that harm has been done to him? Could it be he is hurt?"

"We can pray he is not. No, I don't suspect Günter for why would he hide your picture at Herr Wolgemut's? Yet it is strange he has left with no word of explanation for his disappearance. He might have suspected Joachim and blamed himself for befriending the lad, that's all. If either of them has any blame in this affair I would think it Joachim."

"Even you, Willy, my most honourable and greatest friend on earth doubted my word over the missing picture, did you not?"

Willy Pirkheimer smirked and placing his great fat paws on Durer's shoulders shook the very thought out of him; although it was true.

"But what of Otto? Have you seen him this morning?"

"Neither hide nor hair of him since yesterday."

"What is he up to, Willy? We two stars in the firmament have been deserted by all who know us," Durer joked. "Otto has become very secretive of late."

"He doesn't confide in me, either, and it's a strange thing but I have sometimes caught him staring up at St Sebaldus tower, as you were doing."

Albrecht Durer and Willy Pirkheimer turned around and looked skyward, above St Sebaldus' spires, imagining what it was there that captivated Beck.

"Perhaps he's been looking for an escape from Maria, fine woman though she is. Women are such fickle creatures, not to be trusted with our emotions." Pirkheimer shrugged his broad shoulders.

Durer's face took on a pained expression. "You constantly insult my Agnes. She does not deserve your endless clucking."

"I made no mention of Agnes, my handsome companion, but I have noticed that for a married couple you and she spend an unusual amount of time apart. I'd say that state of affairs speaks for itself."

"Then you'd be mistaken, dear Willy. I have nothing but love and regard for my fair Agnes so kindly turn your vinegary tongue on some other creature more deserving of your disdain."

"I was not really setting out a case against Agnes as much as Maria Kohl. It's being rumoured she has taken up with Peter Henlein."

"Hmm, that will not please Otto."

"If he ever emerges from whatever furtive activity keeps him away from our company so that the rumour might settle on his cloth ears."

"Henlein the locksmith of all people!" Durer said, "Those two are rivals of long-standing. I foresee trouble, Willy."

As for the locksmith himself, he was in a black mood that would not have benefited from gazing up past the steeples of St Sebaldus with their celestial backdrop. His fascination, alluded to by Durer and Pirkheimer, was more prosaic for his interest lay with the tower clock. He was a clockmaker after all – as well as inventor of all kinds of clever devices.

***

Townspeople cleared a way for Collado and his companions astride their pale stallions and if these men who spilled blood for God and power were ever concerned they would be suspected of harming a single hair on the head of anyone within the vicinity of Nuremberg they were pleasantly reassured for no savage dogs bared their teeth as they took their stately departure, unless a token growl from Ulf counted.

The trio of Spanish gentlemen were keen to be on their way, having suffered disappointment at failing to track down the principal heretic, Hut. They were confident there would be other opportunities to make an example of that gentleman for his audacity at questioning the hierarchy and ways of the church.

Once out of the city they pulled up their white chargers and turned to view the pretty town of Nuremberg one last time before returning next spring. They exchanged dark-eyed glances and half-smiles and one of them unbuttoned his vestment and pulled out a filthy and scorched piece of scarlet cloth which he flung into the air. It caught on a branch of a birch tree and there it settled. His companion slipped off his steed and re-knotted the stiffened corpse of a boar to the back of his saddle. He ran his hand along his stallion's rump, bloodied from the slaughtered animal. The mark, he reassured himself, would wash clean and the porker fill their bellies during their long journey to the southern lands. Collado's hand felt behind for the weapon he'd purchased from Otto Beck; several more were wrapped in velveteen brocade and secured to his saddle. They would make do with them until Beck finished his improved design in a few months' time. The three acknowledged each other, hauled on their reins, kicked their steeds to a canter and then a gallop.

Widukind waited for them to leave then stole out of the birch wood. Reaching up he retrieved Müller's singed red cap. He wondered if he should risk reporting the incident to the Council but thought better of it, for he was already near to the city and risked becoming under suspicion again so he scraped out a hollow in the soft earth with the spoon returned to him following his release and buried the cap and placed a heavy square boulder on top to prevent wild beasts digging it up. He stood, his head bowed, for quite some time, thinking not of Müller but his brother, Wedigo, whose body he identified; slaughtered by a mystic he was told.

***

The departure of the Spanish mercenaries was also observed from high up on the berg's battlements by Prince Ernest. He, too, was about to embark on a journey, farther than the plains of Spain, over land and over all the seas. The acquittal of Widukind the shepherd had proven awkward for the Prince for there were risks that stories of human sacrifice would leak out of the mouths of palace servants. The death of the man called Wolf also pained him for he was sure it would bring nought but calamity upon Nuremberg as any deliberate slaughter of wolves unleashed terrible anger among the gods.

Slobberer, the Chamberlain, slunk up to the prince. With one hand he led his own chestnut steed and with the other Prince Earnest's ebony mount, the swiftest in Franconia it was said.

"Time we were leaving, Highness."

Prince Ernest looked down on his city contemplating whether this might be the last time he would stand at the Kaiserburg for while a royal prince, child sacrifice - albeit one as beautiful and healthy and deserving as Hanna Denck now enjoying a delightful existence in the afterlife - was liable to attract critical attention from agents of civic justice. The Chamberlain sighed on noticing a small stain on his blue velvet jerkin where blood from sweet Hanna Denck's delicate heart had leaked from his crooked mouth when sharing a morsel of that delicacy with the Prince - a fragment only for the rest was offered to the gods. The Chamberlain fussed over the mark, irritated by it. He blamed the Prince and his insistence they consume unusual flesh in search of the sacred hare which hid in children's hearts - boiled, always, for they were not barbarians. It was not for himself he indulged in such activities for he and his wife were blessed with children but for his prince and his wife who were seven years wed without issue; despite braiding her hair with heads of corn so that the Prince was compelled to consult the ancient writings which all advocated the sacrifice of an innocent heart in tenure of the hare as a certain cure for infertility.

***

Anyone eavesdropping in Brauer's late on the afternoon of the second Thursday after Michaelmas would be led to believe nothing of ill had recently occurred for the inn echoed with jolly laughter and teasing. Life came with whatever it offered, habitually hard for the good folk of Nuremberg; though no worse than for anyone else except perhaps those unfortunate mystics hunted down in the Laurenzer Forst who were now detained inside the stinking and dreadful Löch. It could, therefore, be argued things were not so bad after all. There was always Brauer's where the travails of the day might be shared in a warm refuge from the daily grind.

For dogs, too, there was no escape from providence and cruelty lurking behind every encounter but for one dog sweet fortune was the day young Kläuschen adopted him. Axel Marx's hound, Ulf, sleeping before a roaring fire only had to stir and blink an eye to be offered a succulent scrap to gobble.

Durer leaned on his elbows. Beck was there; unaccountably on time for once, biting on his thumbnail. They were listening to Pirkheimer recounting how a clerk from the Council sent out to investigate a far-fetched story about the old abandoned bull sculpture came back with a more preposterous yarn of its transformation by witchcraft into a living being that wore shoes for one of nut-brown leather made for a large foot with a corn-coloured cord fastening and deer antler button was found next to it.

"Like Müller wears," Durer remarked casually, to illustrate the story.

"Müller?" Pirkheimer asked.

"Yes. You're not very observant, Willy. That's why I'm the artist and you are the intellect behind our civic life."

Pirkheimer looked at Beck. "You see what it is to be an artist, Otto? The artist notices everything - captures every minuscule detail we lesser mortals are oblivious to. Are you certain, Albi?"

Albrecht Durer nodded. He did not have to think about it for he knew absolutely Müller's entire wardrobe, including his footwear which consisted of a pair of down-at-heel black leather boots and shoes matching the description given by Pirkheimer.

"Of course, the only living entity in the beast was the man that was somehow forced into it." He shuddered. "Then the mystery of Müller's disappearance is solved. Poor fellow. Whatever his sins he did not deserve such an ending."

"I don't know," Beck piped up, "he was uncommonly cruel. If he did not deserve such an equally brutal dispatch from life then who does? The question is who freed Nuremberg from its man-monster?"

Contemplating that question as hard as they might none of the three could offer an answer so contented themselves with sharing a supper of fried carp with garlic and leeks washed down by Ana's blackest beer.

Ulf's furious barking disturbed the comfortable domesticity of Brauer's. With unaccustomed alacrity the hound leapt to his feet and bounded for the door.

Standing in the doorway was Axel Marx. Except for the racket coming from his dog the little man's appearance was met with stunned silence in the inn. Marx opened his mouth as if to speak then collapsed face down on the floor. Ulf licked

281

his master's face and hands and soon everyone was gathered around, staring down at the little cobbler and firing off questions that he was in no fit state to answer.

A way was cleared for Klara who knelt down beside Axel Marx cradling his head and spooning a little beer past his parched lips. His eyelids flickered and with more beer trickling down his throat Axel coughed and sat up. Ulf skipped about him. Axel got hold of the hound's ears and tugged at them till they nearly came away in his hands. His first words were, "Ulf, my Ulf."

Hans, the giant Abtrittanbieter, picked up the diminutive man and gently sat him down on a stool. Axel thanked him and smiled at the sea of faces surrounding him. He complained about his leg which he told them gave him great pain and was rubbing it when Klara brought him a dish piled high with his favourite boiled hock, soured cabbage and sprigs of tarragon which he shared with Ulf. Then a krug of Ana's best beer was placed in front of him, which he did not offer to the hound.

Once recovered Axel Marx told how after leaving Brauer's on the afternoon of the first Tuesday after Michaelmas he was making his way home along the river bank when overcome with exhaustion and the grass being damp he stepped onto a moored skiff to sleep off his fatigue. Ulf, who was afraid of water, wandered away. The next thing Axel knew the vessel was being carried downstream, moving fast on a river swollen by recent rains. A night passed and the whole of the next day before the current brought him close to shore where a fisherman near Eltmann out in the river in his own boat threw a rope to him and pulled him to land, or else he would have carried on out to sea.

"Those boys are forever playing mischief with our boats," cried a fisherman over his beer, "they think it amusing to loosen ropes and push our skiffs out into the river." Every head nodded for they had seen it happen before but not with such dramatic consequences.

Axel Marx explained that he spent two nights recovering from his adventure at the Eltmann fisherman's cottage before starting the long walk back to Nuremberg. It took him many days to cover the distance for his legs gave him so much pain he was forever having to sit down to rest them and the whole time he was gone he had so very little to eat he became weaker and weaker. Everyone in Brauer's agreed he was but half the man who left them more than a week since and if it was not Axel who was taken, mutilated and burnt from the midden, who was it?

Behind his hand Otto Beck whispered to Durer and Pirkheimer that Axel could afford to shed fat and was the better for no longer resembling one of Wedigo's porkers. Durer met Pirkheimer's eye.

"Say that again, Otto," Durer asked.

"I only meant ..." Beck began.

He was interrupted by Durer. "He did have a likeness to a large old cutter - certainly an old boar without the tusks. What say you, Willy?"

"I think you may be right. Remove head and limbs, throw it into a fire to scorch and disfigure and it could well have been mistaken for, forgive me for saying so, Axel; a shameful waste of pork, however."

The fisherman whose skiff was lost when Axel Marx went sailing down the river was the least contented of fellows in the city when Axel's tale was told, although relieved that the little man was safe. His luck turned when the good folk of Nuremberg paid for a new boat for him and the incident was quickly forgotten.

***

There was great sympathy in the town for Herr Wolgemut following news he had been deserted by his wife and consternation that responsibility for the theft of one of Albrecht Durer's pictures might have its source in that household, with some blaming their rivalry over who was Franconia's greatest painter. People quickly forgot that Herr Wolgemut was also said to have had a picture stolen. The

283

confinement of several mystics in the city's dungeons on suspicion of murdering the swineherd, Wedigo, and their possible involvement in other acts of brutality went some way to consoling jittery townsfolk who prayed their misfortunes were man-made and not God's judgment of them.

Chapter 30

One week on from the disappearance of Herr Müller few in Nuremberg were mourning his loss. The grain merchant's evil ways had touched too many families for pity although many acknowledged his brute of a father had been even worse.

As far as was known to the world Frau Müller ran away from her callous husband, abandoning her only child but truth is not always what is spoken. Frau Müller was herself a spiteful creature who taunted and berated her husband and took no care of her child - the child she did not succeed in murdering unlike those other babies she bore and whose innocent breaths were extinguished when her talon-like fingers squeezed and twisted their thin soft necks. One babe alone survived, a boy, rescued by his father the husband she attempted to poison more than once and the man who refused to expose his wife to torture in the city dungeon but instead locked her into one of the attic rooms in the granary. It was there she remained fed if not loved by him until one day he carelessly forgot to bolt her garret door and she crept out and taking up his dagger plunged it into his heart. After that her son became her gaoler, unsuspected by any one of their neighbours.

It was always Frau Müller's intention to kill the son who lived to spite her. She cared nought for children and it troubled her that he evaded her clutches for so long a time. Each day she waited for his return from the inn; drunk like his father. She did not possess much in that cell of hers but she did have infinite patience. One day her drunken son forgot to turn the key in the lock after taking her a dish of porridge. That was the day Herr Wolf sneaked up the long and steep stairs, blades of memories slicing the choking dusty air, to confront Herr Müller over the torment he suffered because of a bargain long-ago struck between Müller's father and Wolf's mother for his education. So preoccupied was he Wolf never noticed Frau Müller until she floated past him, grass-blade thin and repugnant, shrieking, her unkempt hair and ragged garments aflame. But by then she had struck him with her talons and Adolf Wolf only had time to be astonished before he, too, followed in the wake of the crazed woman.

She had not thought to burn down the granary. Her shawl fell from her shoulders as enchanted she watched the fire she built in the grate flicker into life and thrilled as it blazed when she threw on bedding and shoes and stools and bowls and cushions. Wolf's foot on the stairs she fancied belonged to her son and in Frau Müller's eagerness to get at him she grabbed her shawl, winding it around her; not noticing it to be alight. She rushed toward the one she believed was her son then soared like an angel, she thought, for the briefest of moments.

On their funeral pyre of yellow grain, Frau Müller and Adolf Wolf, smouldered for a whole day until the heat intensified and timbers and sacks and furniture and curtains and objects of every sort were consumed. By midnight the whole building was ablaze. It was as if all of Nuremberg's corruption was being cleansed by the inferno in number fourteen granary. Happily, the granary's yellow striped cat had the wits to escape out of a broken window; deftly landing on the steep roof he stealthily slid and clambered down until with admirable agility leapt onto an adjoining building and from there to the ground.

Chapter 31

"You have a face like three rainy days, Herr Durer," Ana prodded Albrecht Durer's ribs then clapped his shoulder, "I was sorry to hear about young Günter running off. You must be worried sick about him but we have to put our trust in the Lord that no ill-fortune befalls him."

"I pray that is so and he's not another victim of the Devil's hand," Durer said.

Ana looked at him, thoughtfully. "I can picture him now, dressed up in that blue jacket you're wearing today – it very nearly reached his ankles. I expect it was the colour that attracted him."

Durer leaned his head to the side. "Of course, he loved to wear this old thing; it's nearly worn out and the pockets hold nothing for long." He poked a finger through holes in both to prove the point.

"Günter was fond of toying with your curiosities wasn't he, Albi?" Pirkheimer asked.

Durer smiled at the memory.

"And his friendship with Joachim took him into Herr Wolgemut's print shop."

Durer looked at him, "What are you saying, Willy?"

"Who better placed than him to have taken your jasper talisman and dropped it at Wolgemut's?" Pirkheimer tapped a fat finger against Durer's sleeve.

Albrecht Durer thought for a moment. "Now you are saying Günter is our thief?"

Pirkheimer swallowed a mouthful of beer. "Isn't it possible?"

Albrecht Durer leaned back; his eyes shut tight in contemplation. "But why would he?" he mused.

"I only meant you are forever complaining that he picks up your things, to amuse himself – but there is another possibility, that he might have carried away your hare painting, too."

"But why, Willy? He's not a bad young lad," Durer insisted.

"A young fellow might not think through the consequences of his rash actions. Or perhaps he hoped to settle a score. You've been lauding Joachim so much lately and chosen him for Adam instead of Günter. What other reasons might he need?" Pirkheimer replied.

"He has been a bit grumpy recently, now I think about it," Durer squinted at Pirkheimer whose attention had strayed to Ana's young bar maid. "I still believe it more likely Joachim is the one. He's had ample opportunities to strike, so frequent is he in my workshop. When I think about it he was in my shop the day Günter discovered my *Field Hare* gone. And he's had all the time in the world to take any of Herr Wolgemut's own works. I think you are too quick to suspect Günter." Durer ran his fingers through his hair, deep in thought. "As for my jasper dog, I know Joachim picks up my trifles, as does the scamp Günter's been teaching to make brushes, for neither child before had seen anything so fascinating as the treasures I've collected on my travels. If they had a plaything it was merely roughly carved out of a twig by their fathers or a piece of spent candle wax moulded into a doll so I've never begrudged them amusing themselves with any of my things."

The young woman had disappeared into the kitchen so Pirkheimer turned his attention back to Durer.

"We know nothing for certain, my dear Albi, and you should not mention any of this to Herr Wolgemut for he might be inclined to turn out Joachim who's not completed his training. It would be wrong to jeopardise the boy's prospects on a whim." Pirkheimer examined his hands. "Then there are the boots?"

"Boots?" Durer asked.

"Joachim has come into possession of a fine pair of fern-green kid boots; I'm surprised you of all people haven't noticed, Albi."

Durer dredged his memory. "Ah, yes I do recall seeing him in a pair. This looks bad for Joachim - and me - for how could I use him as my Adam if what we fear turns out to be true?"

"Who more appropriate in the circumstances?" Pirkheimer chuckled.

Durer shook his head, "I see the direction this takes us but I cannot reconcile myself to the idea, Willy. He might have purchased them with what he won for the apprentice prize?"

"Then we come back to Günter," Pirkheimer mused. "You cannot deny, Albi, he's often shown himself to be jealous of Joachim – but the two might be in league with each other."

Durer considered this notion. "Both are good boys," he declared emphatically.

"Then we have to consider who else might benefit from taking your picture and a lady that has occurred to me is Frau Wolgemut," Pirkheimer said.

Durer looked sceptical. "Or Schmeichler?" he suggested.

"Schmeichler had no access to your apartments whereas Günter and Joachim and ... what precisely was your relationship with Gudrun Wolgemut, Albi?"

"Nothing too earnest," Durer replied.

Pirkheimer snorted and slapped his thigh. "Then let us toss a coin to determine who is the culprit between the two boys, shall we?" Pirkheimer picked a pfennig out of his purse.

"Be serious, Willy," Durer scolded.

"You have your *Field Hare* back; does it matter who the thief was? For a man who ought to be happy you are the essence of melancholy, Albi,"

"Yet you, yourself, said I was suspected of having had a hand in the theft of Herr Wolgemut's picture so what right have I to be joyful?"

"That is true but soon all of this will be forgotten."

Ana appeared at Pirkheimer's elbow. "I have a lovely dish of roast hare for you today, gentlemen, with a tasty cinnamon sauce. Aha, I can tell from your faces that does not sit well with either of you. If you prefer there is fish which is a piece of fried beaver tail with baked onions and bread. Would you be less despairing with a portion of that inside you?"

A generous platter of beaver was duly served along with bread and golden-skinned onions by Ana who then stooped down to retrieve a piece of paper from the floor. She handed it to Durer.

"Has this fallen out of your coat pocket, Herr Durer?"

Unfolding it Albrecht Durer screwed up his face. "It contains nothing more than an illiterate scribble," he insisted and turned it around trying to make sense of the badly formed letters.

"What is it, Albi? Has your Agnes informed you she will not be returning?"

Albrecht Durer handed over the note to Pirkheimer who sounded out what was written on it.

"Well, well, it appears young Günter seeks your forgiveness, Albi - admits he took your picture and tried to pin the blame on Joachim. At least that's what it says here."

Durer reached out and took the note back from Pirkheimer and after attempting to read it through again agreed with his interpretation of the uneducated scrawl.

Pirkheimer bit into a piece of beaver. It burned his tongue and fanning his open mouth with his hand he asked Albrecht Durer if he would try to trace him. "The lad is wicked to do such a thing and try make Joachim appear the villain. That explains his sudden disappearance."

Albrecht Durer told him he would not pursue the boy for he felt no animosity towards him but blamed himself for making Günther feel inferior to Joachim. He prayed Günter would come to no harm and that one day he would return to Nuremberg when they might again become friends. Folding the note he absent-mindedly slipped it back into his pocket before remembering the hole so tucked it into his leather pouch for safe-keeping and as a reminder to be more attentive to his young apprentices in future. He swept aside a black fly that landed on his lump of loaf.

Otto Beck's arrival was followed by Ana Brauer's delivery of a helping of roast hare and cinnamon for him. She drew their attention to Kläuschen, his short legs swinging from the great chair that for years was a second home to Herr Müller and which no-one else would now occupy but the child. Axle Marx pulled up a stool alongside the boy and Ulf settled down between them. Leatherman Herman banged his dagger's hilt on a table and launched into a rendition of *In the Tavern;* soon had Beck whistling in accompaniment. Others joined in and with every verse, and there were many of them, the volume of singing grew louder. The only glum faces in Brauer's belonged to a huddle of barrowmen occasionally looking over their shoulders as though expecting the Löchwirt or even the Devil to tap them on the back and with a curl of a finger urge them to follow him. Each one wished to get hold of Müller's chair and burn that too.

Serving her noisy patrons with beer, Anne Brauer, joined in the singing. Klara swaying in time to the music kept a close eye on her cinnamon sauce bubbling away over the fire. Kläuschen clapped his hands and swinging his legs to the rhythm he made up his own words to the songs. Ulf retreated under Axel Marx's stool, his paws covering his ears.

"There are times to be sad and times to be happy. Come my three handsome fellows - eat and drink up," Ana urged Durer, Pirkheimer and Beck, filling up their bierkrugs with her rich dark beer then with a quick hand flattened a black fly newly landed on the edge of the table.

Albrecht Durer signalled Pirkheimer and Beck to move in close. Frowning, he said, "Nothing makes me more angry than to hear anyone say you are handsome, Willy, for then I should have to be ugly; that would make me really mad."

They all laughed and clinked their krugs together, toasting each other.

"My, the hare smells good. That's something a picture can't create. Not even one of yours, Albi." Beck smacked his lips. "But what do you know, I've left my purse at home."

Pirkheimer and Durer rolled their eyes.

"Your nose is recovering well, Otto," Durer winked at him.

Willy Pirkheimer was poised to help himself to more beaver tail when he paused.

"Albi, re-assure me first, you haven't painted a beaver, have you?"

Post Script

The fortunes of the gentle folk of Nuremberg were mixed following the year 1504; some for good and some for ill.

Axel Marx quickly recovered from his ordeal on the river and his cobblers business kept him occupied when he was not in Brauer's tucking into Klara's hot delicacies and Ana's finest beer. Ulf was a lucky dog for he found himself with two homes and two masters who competed to feed him the greatest amount of scraps.

Ana Brauer and Klara lived on for several more years serving their customers the best beer in Nuremberg and the most delicious helpings of pork knuckles, hare and beaver in the whole of Franconia (always best accompanied by Klara's cinnamon sauce). As for Kläuschen he spent a lot of time playing with Ulf and learning from Ana and Klara how to brew and cook and keep patrons contented for they told him there would be a time when he would take over running the inn. And so he did.

The Italian merchants never did return to Nuremberg but were said to have set up their own shop in Venice with the goldgulden they took back from their trip in 1504.

Young Günter was another who kept clear of the city and he found work as a quill dresser and pen cutter in Frankfurt. There he was able to buy cheap print copies of Albrecht Durer's pictures. His favourite was Durer's *Adam and Eve* for he never lost his infatuation with Els and as for Joachim, he regretted that envy broke up their friendship and drove him away from Nuremberg and he had to admit that Joachim made a magnificent-looking Adam.

Herr Wolgemut's workshop continued to produce some of the finest woodcuts ever created which sustained their popularity as book illustrations. Michael Wolgemut never again spoke of his runaway wife Gudrun to anyone but Schmeichler.

Schmeichler remained faithful to Herr Wolgemut until his master's death then spent his remaining years in the tumbledown house once occupied by the cripple, Josef. What happened to Josef's old bear no-one can remember. As for Schmeichler he continued to suffer from chronic earache throughout his life.

Joachim completed his apprenticeship at Wolgemut's workshop before travelling to the Netherlands where he earned a reasonable living as a painter and printmaker until his death at the age of twenty-five. His early demise was said to have been the consequence of poisoning by lead due to his fondness for introducing red tints into his pictures; the shade created by roasting white lead till it altered colour, although others suspected alcoholic poisoning was the more likely cause.

Prince Ernest's travels took him over several seas and across many high peaks in search of his mystical hares. He was never again seen in Franconia nor in the whole of Germany and, in truth, that was a relief to all.

His Chamberlain and Steward both died fighting over their Prince's riches which they stole from him one night while he danced under father moon and sister stars; all alone and dressed in a tunic made out of hare pelts.

Els found her way to Heidelberg where she became a very capable reader and took advantage of the city's extensive library. Such was her desire to learn she dressed herself as a boy that she might study at the university and was among a group of theologian students invited to discuss his *95 Theses* with Martin Luther on the eve of him nailing a copy of them to the door of a church in Wittenberg. She returned Willy Pirkheimer's copy of de Cusa's treatise, *De Docta Ignorantia*, to him with a note of thanks, a map showing all the places she had journeyed to in the world and a list of places she hoped to see before she died. Between pages of the volume Pirkheimer found a bookmark - Albrecht Durer's *Adam and Eve* with a little cross inked above the head of Eva.

Maria Kohl found herself in Ammendorf where she was reunited with her brother, Thomas Hut. Following the death of their parents the siblings had taken different paths in life. Hut's appearance in Nuremberg had less to do with being reunited with his sister than confronting the wickedness of the city she described in her letters to him. When they met again briefly in Ammendorf Maria tried to dissuade Thomas from the life he had chosen with all its attendant dangers but he would not be persuaded. They continued to meet periodically until Thomas Hut was killed in the summer of 1525, fighting on the side of peasants in their uprising against the aristocracy.

Before this and soon after she left Nuremberg Maria found herself employment in a house close to the Franciscan monastery where locksmith and clockmaker Peter Henlein sought refuge. Their friendship continued until a day in 1509 when she and Henlein returned to Nuremberg. There, she again used her clever fingers to work their magic on tiny escapements in a clockmaker's workshop and not long after their return to the city Henlein's Nuremberg eggs, spring-driven portable clocks that could be carried on the person in little boxes, caused a sensation when they were manufactured. Though Peter Henlein never said as much in public he was grateful to Maria for her assistance in guiding him over how best to refine his timepieces and while Maria would have wished the pocket-watch had been acknowledged as principally her invention she was content to share her life with Henlein who had grown placid in nature since slaying the unfortunate Glaser and entering the Franciscan monastery as penance.

As for Otto Beck he never again came so close to realising fame as a clockmaker after the departure of Maria from his life and Henlein's little pierced brass boxes adorned gentlemen's dress instead of any he might have crafted had she stayed with him. In fact, by the time Beck succeeded with his prototype of a handgun Collado's interest in his weapons had waned and he took to employing a type of arcabuz manufactured in his own country which was gaining popularity for its effectiveness and reliability. A different Spanish soldier of fortune came to buy Beck's weapons but he did so only once for the journey was too exhausting for him. It was from the Spanish gentleman Beck learned that Collado had sailed to the island of Hispaniola in the Caribbean to teach its Taino people a harsh lesson in Christian values.

Willy Pirkheimer continued to enlarge his extensive library and when he was not serving the good people of Nuremberg as a magistrate and Councillor he would be in his library translating scholarly texts so that others might not have to and by his excellent efforts he fulfilled his ambition of improving school education for all children in Germany.

Of all Nuremberg's citizens it was, perhaps, Willy Pirkheimer who listened most carefully to the words spoken by Thomas Hut and soon found himself attracted to the philosophies of Martin Luther which inspired him to write a satire ridiculing the church that nearly led to his excommunication by the Pope, along with Luther, but in time Willy's support for the reformer fell away. His relationship with Albrecht Durer lasted to the painter's death and in his eulogy to Germany's finest artist Willy described him as *my best friend*.

Durer went back to Italy, staying there for two years honing his craft and never tired of experimenting in pursuit of perfection for his art - all paid for by his best friend, Willy Pirkheimer.

Under the tutelage of Willy Pirkheimer, Albrecht Durer continued his education and he created two very beautiful charts of the stars - the very first map of the constellations in the northern and southern hemispheres in the whole of the western world. He worked at his pictures and travelled until overtaken by infirmity and he even overcame his aversion to commissions for such was the clamour from the most powerful personages in Europe to own his masterful pictures. And yes, he completed the pair of oil portraits for the Schopper House. He even found time to write books - one, as might be expected, on human proportion and another on mathematics which as the first German text of its kind captured the interest of those great mathematicians and astronomers, Galileo and Kepler.

Albi took in his mother, Barbara, when illness made it impossible for her to stay in her own home and they all lived together in relative harmony, although an uneasy existence continued between Papagei and Katz who fought over most things, mainly food, but Katz drew the line at eating apples, holy or otherwise.

As for his own spiritual welfare, Durer, as with his dearest companion, Willy Pirkheimer, listened with curiosity to sermons preached by the very many theologians who passed through Nuremberg and for a time he, too, was attracted to the reforming ideas of Martin Luther. But only for a time.

In 1504, Albi's Agnes returned from Frankfurt weighed down with guilders and pretty brocades and her husband continued to paint and sketch her when she was not abroad marketing his work. They had to buy a larger trunk to contain all his many prints destined for markets and fairs in Germany and abroad so enthusiastic were the people to decorate their houses with them and preserve them as bookmarks.

In the end, Wolgemut gave his blessing for Joachim to pose for his former pupil. Albrecht Durer completed his *Adam and Eve* engraving and it became one of the most popular illustrations ever printed in all of Germany. An oil version also featured Els, his Eva, in all her youthful beauty alongside the mischievous Joachim, his pretty Adam. When Albi Durer completed his *Adam and Eve* engraving he remembered to sign it with his full name because an artist cannot be too careful when there are picture thieves about.

The End

www.ingramcontent.com/pod-product-compliance
Lightning Source LLC
Chambersburg PA
CBHW030609220526
45463CB00004B/1232